Distributed and Parallel Systems

In Focus:
Desktop Grid Computing

Distributed and Parallel Systems
In Focus:
Desktop Grid Computing

Edited by

Péter Kacsuk
Róbert Lovas
Zsolt Németh
MTA SZTAKI, Hungary

 Springer

Editors:
Péter Kacsuk
MTA SZTAKI
Computer & Automation Research Institute
P.O.Box 63
Budapest, H-1518 Hungary

Róbert Lovas
MTA SZTAKI
Computer & Automation Research Institute
P.O.Box 63
Budapest, H-1518 Hungary

Zsolt Németh
MTA SZTAKI
Computer & Automation Research Institute
P.O.Box 63
Budapest, H-1518 Hungary

ISBN 978-1-4419-4639-3   e-ISBN-13: 978-0-387-79448-8

Printed on acid-free paper.

Printed on acid-free paper.

springer.com

Contents

Preface

The seventh Distributed and Parallel Systems conference (DAPSYS) is organized by MTA SZTAKI Computer and Automation Research Institute in Debrecen. The series of DAPSYS events started as a small regional meeting early in the nineties, and since then it evolved a lot and became an acknowledged international scientific event. The scope of the event has changed as well during the years following the new trends in technology. The first event was dedicated to transputers whereas in recent years, it is tagged with cluster and grid computing.

This year the whole conference was devoted to grid computing. Since desktop grid systems were underrepresented at other conferences that deal with grid computing we decided to give a special emphasis on desktop grids. According to this, David Anderson was invited to give a keynote talk on BOINC systems, a large session was organized with talks on various aspects of desktop grid systems and finally, the EDGeS User and Industry Forum had also got a special session where talks and discussions addressed the problem of how to integrate service grids and desktop grids.

The papers presented in this volume give a good overview of recent advances in various aspects of grid computing. The proceedings is composed of five parts according to the major topics of the conference - albeit they cover a much broader range in this field. Part I is devoted to various aspects of desktop grid computing. Several papers discuss how to integrate desktop grids with existing service grids like the EGEE grid. One of the most important aspects of grid computing is how to port applications to the grid. Part II shows several case studies in the field of medical grid applications, climate modelling and digital library management. Grid resource management and scheduling is still an important issue in large production grid systems. Part III shows several new research directions in this field. Grid programming environments and particularly organization of grid workflow systems represent a major issue for the grid users. Part IV shows two systems (Kepler and P-GRADE) how to handle security issues and database resources in such workflow systems. Part V contains papers dealing with other important aspects of grid computing like QoS capabilities of grids, check-pointing in grids, batch query systems and finally a reputation-policy based trust model for grid resource selection.

There were three invited talks at the conference delivered by David Anderson, Denis Caromel and Márk Jelasity. David Anderson was talking on the future of volunteer desktop grid computing that was now aimed towards the exa-scale performance target. Denis Caromel gave presentation on the ProActive Parallel Suite, a GRID Java library for parallel, distributed, and concurrent computing, also featuring mobility and security in a uniform framework. ProActive aims at simplifying the programming of applications that are distributed on Local Area Network (LAN), on cluster of workstations, or on the grid. ProActive promotes a strong NoC approach, Network On Ship, to cope seamlessly with both distributed and shared-memory multi-core machines. Mark Jelasity explained how to combine P2P protocols into more complex, but still self-organizing and decentralized, protocols and frameworks. He also illustrated this compositional approach via an example application: heuristic function optimization, that was a common Grid application for solving very hard combinatorial or real valued optimization problems.

We would like to thank the members of the Program Committee and the additional reviewers for their work in refereeing the submitted papers and ensuring the high quality of DAPSYS 2008. Special thanks to those who helped us beyond their duties. We are grateful to Susan Lagerstrom-Fife and her assistant, Sharon Palleschi at Springer for their endless patience and valuable support in producing this volume. The conference could have never been realized without the devoted work of the local organizers: János Végh, Piroska Biró and Kornél Kovács. The proceedings was compiled in endless hours of checking every details by the tireless Eva Feuer. Special thanks to the webmasters Károly Göschl and Attila Csaba Marosi and Philippe Rigaux for providing the MyReview system.

Péter Kacsuk   Róbert Lovas   Zsolt Németh

Program Committee and Additional Reviewers

Conference Chair:

Péter Kacsuk (MTA SZTAKI, Hungary)

PC Chairs:

Róbert Lovas and Zsolt Németh (MTA SZTAKI, Hungary)

Members:

David P. Anderson (Univ. of California, Berkeley, USA)
Artur Andrzejak (ZIB, Germany)
Marian Bubak (AGH Krakow, Poland and Amsterdam University, The Netherlands)
Rajkumar Buyya (Univ. of Melbourne, Australia)
Beniamino Di Martino (Second Univ. of Naples, Italy)
Thomas Fahringer (Univ. of Innsbruck, Austria)
Gilles Fedak (LRI, France)
Ladislav Hluchy (II SAS, Slovakia)
Márk Jelasity (Univ. Szeged, Hungary)
Hai Jin (Huazhong Univ. of Science and Technology, China)
Zoltán Juhász (Univ. of Pannonia, Hungary)
Károly Kondorosi (Budapest Univ. of Technology and Economics, Hungary)
Dieter Kranzlmüller (Joh. Kepler Univ. Linz, Austria)
Domenico Laforenza (ISTI-CNR, Italy)
Erwin Laure (CERN, Switzerland)
Charles Loomis (LAL/CNRS, France)
Marta Mattoso (Federal Univ. of Rio de Janeiro, Brasil)
Ludek Matyska (Masaryk University, Czech Rep.)
Miguel Cárdenas Montes (CETA-CIEMAT, Spain)
Johan Montagnat (CNRS, France)
Norbert Podhorszki (Oak Ridge National Lab, USA)
Thierry Priol (INRIA, France)
Stefan Podlipnig (Univ. of Innsbruck, Austria)
Rizos Sakellariou (Univ. Manchester, UK)
Cevat Sener (Middle East Technical University, Turkey)
Luis Silva (Univ. of Coimbra, Portugal)
Wolfgang Schreiner (RISC Linz, Austria)
Domenico Talia (Univ. Calabria, Italy)
Ian Taylor (Cardiff University, UK)
Gábor Terstyánszky (Univ. of Westminster, UK)
Ramin Yahyapour (Univ. Dortmund, Germany)

Additional reviewers

Viet Tran
Salvatore Venticinque
Song Wu
Attila Csaba Marosi
Zoltán Farkas
Jan Astalos
Giuseppe Pirro
Max Berger
Fabricio Silva
Kassian Plankensteiner
Ada Lhola Casanovas León
Stefano Marrone
Carmela Comito
Viera Sipkova
Eugenio Cesario
József Kovács
Pingpeng Yuan
Deqing Zou
Simon Ostermann
Xuanhua Shi
Sergio Cruz
Attila Kertész
Ian Kelley
Gábor Gombás
Zoltán Balaton

I
DESKTOP GRIDS

DESKTOP RIBS

Enabling Java applications for BOINC with DC-API

Attila Csaba Marosi, Gábor Gombás, Zoltán Balaton and Péter Kacsuk

Abstract Desktop grids are an emerging trend converging volunteer computing and grid computing. Unfortunately existing applications usually have to be modified in order to run on desktop grid systems which makes them less attractive for application developers than traditional grid systems. DC-API is simple API that is specifically targeted for desktop grid systems with the goal to provide an API which hides the specifics of the underlying grid environment but require only minimal modifications to existing application source code. Native Java applications are not directly supported by BOINC. In this paper we describe DC-API, and show how the lack of Java support in BOINC is overcome with DC-API by providing an API for native Java applications on the BOINC platform.

1 Introduction

Desktop grids are an emerging trend in grid computing. Contrary to traditional grid systems, in desktop grids the grid system operators provide the applications and the users of the desktop grid system provide the resources to run the applications. Thus a major advantage of desktop grid systems is that they are able to utilize a huge amount of resources that were not available for traditional grid computing previously.

Users of scientific applications are usually concerned only about the amount of computing power they can get and not about the details how a grid system provides this computing power. Therefore, they want to develop a single application that in turn can run on any infrastructure that provides the most appropriate resources at a given time. Unfortunately existing applications have to be modified in order to run

Attila Csaba Marosi, Gábor Gombás, Zoltán Balaton, Péter Kacsuk

MTA SZTAKI Computer and Automation Research Institute Hungarian Academy of Sciences
H-1528 Budapest, P.O.Box 63, Hungary
e-mail: {atisu, gombasg, balaton, kacsuk}@sztaki.hu

on desktop grid systems and this makes desktop grids less attractive for application developers than traditional grid systems.

There are existing efforts like the GAT [4], SAGA [7] or DRMAA [11] for creating a unified API for grid applications. However, these are modeled after how traditional grid middlewares and batch schedulers work but this model is not adequate for desktop grids like BOINC [5]. The above mentioned APIs are overly complex for such a restricted environment that BOINC provides and they also fail to cover areas like logical file name resolution, checkpoint control, redundant execution and result validation that are required in a BOINC environment. Also the volatility of desktop grid environments where clients may come and go at any time, there is no guarantee that a client that started a computation will indeed finish it, presents a problem for interface designs based on traditional job submission principles.

DC-API is a simple API that is specifically targeted for desktop grid systems. Its goal is to provide an API that requires only minimal modification to existing application source code, yet is able to deliver most of the power of a desktop grid system. However, the DC-API is opaque in the sense that it can be implemented for traditional grid systems as well therefore, applications using the DC-API could be easily deployed on traditional grid infrastructures as well, without the need to modify the source code of the application.

In this paper we describe how DC-API hides the specific details of a grid environment and it's API by an example that enables to run native Java applications on the BOINC platform. Traditionally BOINC and it's API only supports applications written in Fortran, C or C++.

The paper is organized as follows. The next section discusses related work. Section 3 describes DC-API. In section 4 we present the approach used for running Java applications on the BOINC platform. The last section details future work and concludes the paper.

2 Related work

The Grid Application Toolkit (GAT, [4]) was developed by the European Grid-Lab [3] project to bridge the gap between existing grid middleware and application-level needs. The GAT allows an application to make use of different computing environments ranging from handheld devices to supercomputers. An important property of the GAT is the support of dynamic and self-adaptive applications. In order to provide maximum flexibility, the GAT consists of two parts: the engine and the adaptors. The engine provides the high-level API seen by the applications while the adaptors provide the glue code between the engine and the grid middleware.

The Simple API for Grid Applications (SAGA, [7][8]) is an ongoing effort of the OGF with similar goals as the GAT had. In fact, many people who contributed to the GAT are also contributors to SAGA. SAGA aims to provide a simple, stable, and uniform programming interface that integrates the most common grid programming abstractions. The key areas of SAGA are security, data management, job management and inter-process communication.

Both the GAT and SAGA seems hard to adapt to a desktop grid environment. First, the programming model of the desktop grid allows only master-worker applications where the functionality available for the master is completely distinct from the functionality available for the client (for example, it is impossible for the client to create a new job/workunit). Second, there are some areas like explicit data management or inter-process communication that the desktop grid does not support at all. Also all the API complexity that is required to model a traditional grid system is useless in the restricted environment the desktop grid provides. Therefore, an application using a generic grid API would be much more complex than one using the native desktop grid (BOINC) API which goes right against the idea of having a uniform API in the first place. Finally, both GAT and SAGA misses functionality specific to desktop grid systems like support for redundant computing, result validation, client-side logical name resolution or checkpointing support.

The Distributed Resource Management Application API (DRMAA, [11]) is a recommendation proposed by the Open Grid Forum [10]. Contrary to the GAT and SAGA that aim to cover most services provided by the grid middleware, the scope of DRMAA is limited to job submission, job monitoring and control, and retrieval of the finished job status. The DRMAA aims to provide a uniform API for accessing Distributed Resource Management Systems (DRMS). Also the DRMAA lacks support for redundant computing and result validation that is essential on a real desktop grid environment. The DRMAA contains no support for the desktop grid specific functionality required on the client side like logical file name resolving or checkpointing.

The Berkeley Open Infrastructure for Network Computing (BOINC, [5]), originated from the SETI@home project, is an effort to create an open infrastructure to serve as a base for all large-scale scientific projects that are attractive for public interest and having computational needs so that they can use millions of personal computers for processing their data. Today, most of the DG projects, including SZTAKI Desktop Grid (SZDG, [9]), utilize BOINC because it is a well-established free and open source platform that has already proven its feasibility and scalability and it provides a stable base for experiments and extensions. BOINC provides the basic facilities for a DG in which a central server provides the applications and their input data, where clients join voluntarily, offering to download and run an application with a set of input data. When the application has finished, the client uploads the results to the server. BOINC manages the application executables (doing the actual work) taking into account multiple platforms as well as, keeping a record of and scheduling the processing of workunits, optionally with redundancy (to detect erroneous computation either, due to software or hardware failures or clients being controlled by a malicious entity). Additionally, BOINC has support for user credits, teams and the web-based discussion forums, relevant in large scale public projects that are based on individuals donating their CPU time. These individuals must have a motivation for doing this. Apart from the project having a clearly stated, supportable and visionary goal, credits provide a kind of "reward" for the received CPU time, which leads to a competition between the users thus, generating more performance.

3 DC-API

The SZTAKI Desktop Grid is based on BOINC thus, applications using the BOINC API can run on it. However, a simpler and easier-to-use API, the Distributed Computing Application Programming Interface (DC-API), is provided. The DC-API is the preferred way for creating applications for SZTAKI Desktop Grid. It aims to be simple and easy to use. Just a few functions are enough to implement a working application, but there are additional interfaces in case the application wants greater control or wants to use more sophisticated features of the grid infrastructure.

DC-API backends exist to use the Condor job manager and BOINC as well as a backend for the Grid Underground middleware used by the Hungarian ClusterGrid Initiative [6]. A simple fork-based implementation that runs all workunits on the local host is also available. The ability of running the workunits locally makes application debugging easier. Since switching the application from using such a local implementation to e.g. BOINC needs only a recompilation without any changes to the source code, the complete application can be tested on the developer's machine before deploying it to a complex grid infrastructure.

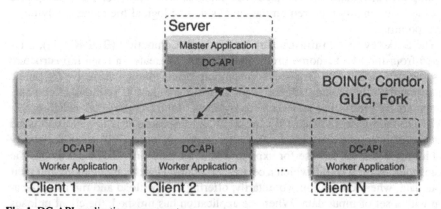

Fig. 1 DC-API application components

To accommodate the restrictions of different grid environments and to facilitate converting existing sequential code written by scientists not comfortable with parallel programming, the DC-API supports a limited parallel programming model only. This implies the following restrictions compared to general parallel programming:

- Master/ Worker concept: there is a designated master process running somewhere on the grid infrastructure. The master process can submit worker processes called workunits.

- Every workunit is a sequential application.
- There is support for limited messaging between the master and the running workunits. However, this it is not suitable for parallel programming, it is meant to be used for sending status and control messages only.
- No direct communication between workunits.

Following the Master/ Worker model, DC-API applications consist of two major components (see Figure 1): a master and one or more client applications. The master is responsible for dividing the global input data into smaller chunks and distributing them in the form of workunits. Interpreting the output generated by the workunits and combining them to a global output is also the job of the master. The master usually runs as a daemon, but it is also possible to write it so it runs periodically (e.g. from *cron*), processes the outstanding events, and exits. Client applications are simple sequential programs that take their input, perform some computation on it and produce some output.

A typical master application written using DC-API does the following steps:

1. Initialises the DC-API master library by calling the DC_initMaster function.
2. Calls the DC_setResultCB function and optionally some of the DC_setSubresultCb, DC_setMessageCb, DC_setSuspendCb and DC_setValidateCb functions, depending on the advanced features (messaging, subresults, etc.) it wants to use.
3. In its main loop, calls the DC_createWU function to create new workunits when needed and after specifying the necessary input and output files (DC_addWUInput, DC_addWUOutput) it can hand them over to the grid infrastructure for processing by calling the DC_submitWU function. If the total number of workunits is small (depending on the grid infrastructure), then the master may also create all the workunits in advance. If the number of workunits is large, the master may use the DC_getWUNumber function to determine the current number of workunits processed by the grid infrastructure, and create new workunits only if it falls below a certain threshold.
4. Also in its main loop the master calls the DC_processMasterEvents function that checks for outstanding events and invokes the appropriate callbacks. Alternatively, the master may use the DC_waitMasterEvent and DC_waitWUEvent functions instead of DC_processMasterEvents if it prefers to receive event structures instead of using callbacks.

A typical client application performs the following steps:

1. Initializes the DC-API client library by calling the DC_initClient function.
2. Identifies the location of its input/output files by calling the DC_resolveFileName function. Note that the client application may not assume that it can read/ create/ write any files other than the names returned by DC_resolveFileName.
3. During the computation, the client should periodically call the DC_checkClientEvent function and process the received events.
4. If possible, the client should call the DC_fractionDone function with the fraction of the work completed. On some grid infrastructures (e.g. BOINC) this will

allow the client's supervisor process to show the progress of the application to the user. Ideally the value passed to this function should be proportional to the time elapsed so far compared to the total time that will be needed to complete the computation.

5. The client should call the DC_finishClient function at the end of the computation. As a result, all output files will be sent to the master and the master will be notified about the completion of the work unit.

4 Java support for BOINC

Running Java applications on the BOINC platform represents two problems. First, BOINC API does not support Java, thus running an application written in Java would either require compiling it to native code or to use a wrapper designed for legacy (non-BOINC) applications. Second, Java requires a runtime environment on its own (Java Runtime Environment, JRE), which may not be already deployed on any client node or the already deployed version may not be suitable for the application. DC-API solves the lack of Java support in BOINC API by providing a Java binding of its API for Java applications via the Java Native Interface (JNI, [1]). JNI allows Java code to call and be called by native applications and libraries written in other programming languages, such as C or C++. The Java runtime deployment problem is solved either by bundling the JRE zipped with the application (license issues apply), or if the application is run in a Local Desktop Grid, then it can be assumed that the appropriate runtime is already deployed. Here we present the scenario when the Java runtime is assumed to be already deployed (see Figure 2). In this case Client 1 receives the following files as part of the application bundle:

- DC-API Java bindings and libraries
- A launcher application
- Java application .jar file(s) (WorkerApplication.jar)

A typical execution does the following steps:

1. The launcher is executed, but it does not contact the client. From the point of view of the BOINC client it's an invisible application, it does not use any BOINC API or DC-API functions.
2. If the runtime is to be deployed with the application, then the launcher checks if it is already there (the application might be resuming from a checkpoint). If not found, then it has to be either installed, or uncompressed in the working directory.
3. The launcher starts the Java application using the Java runtime. After that the launcher will wait for it's termination. This step is necessary because the BOINC client determines the outcome of the task based on the exit status of the application, in this case on the exit status of the launcher.
4. The Java application behaves like a normal DC-API client application, it has access to the full set of DC-API client functions via the interface provided with JNI. Typically the following steps are executed:

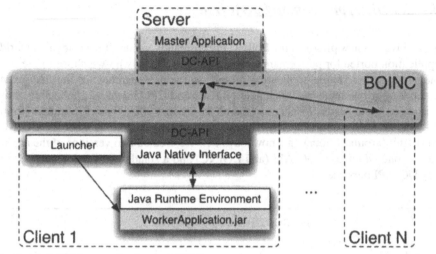

Fig. 2 A DC-API Java application on BOINC

   a. The application initializes the DC-API client library via the `DCClient.i-nit` method.

   b. Resolves the location of it's input and output files by calling the `DCClient.resolveFileName` method.

   c. During computation it calls periodically the `DCClient.checkEvent` method and processes the received events. One of the events is `Event.is-CheckpointRequest`, upon this event the application should checkpoint itself.

   d. Whenever possible, the application should call the `DCClient.fraction-Done` method with the percentage of the work completed. This will report the BOINC client, thus the user, the completion ratio of the current task.

   e. The `DCClient.finish` method should be called at the end of the computation with zero value (or anytime if error occurs with non-zero value). This will finish the execution.

5. After the application has finished, the launcher picks up it's exit status and exits with the same value. The output files are sent back to the master, and it is also notified about the completion of the task.

Beside BOINC, the DC-API backend also supports Condor, the Grid Underground middleware and a simple fork-based implementation, thus the DC-API - Java interface is available on any of these platforms. Currently only DC-API client side functions are available via this Java interface, there is no support for using them on the master side yet. There is no restriction to use the same programming language both on client and master side, master applications should use the C/ C++ DC-API now.

4.1 Sample appication and performance

Since Java is a new platform for BOINC unfortunately we don't have any real world application ported for performance evaluation yet. That's why we chose to use implement a rather simple application on our own which searches for the first given number of prime numbers. It is a deterministic and CPU intensive application, thus fits perfectly our needs. We chose to search for the first 100000 prime numbers (from 2 to 1299709) since this has a moderate, but similar run-time as a normal BOINC work unit (around 1 hour) on a nowadays PC. We created two versions of the application, one which uses DC-API (and BOINC) and a standalone version stripped of any DC-API dependencies.

```
DCClient cli = new DCClient();
long x=2, c=0;
Event e;
cli.init();
readCheckpoint();
while (true) {
    if (c == count)
        break;
    c = isPrime(x);
    if (x % 1000 == 0) {
        e = cli.checkEvent();
        if (e == Event.isCheckpointRequest)
            doCheckpoint(x, c);
    }
    x++;
}
cli.finish(0);
```

Fig. 3 Structure of the DC-API enabled Java application

The DC-API enabled one (see Figure 3) initializes the DC-API library, reads the checkpoint file if any exists and continues the work. It checks periodically for any event and checkpoints itself on Event.isCheckpointRequest. When finished it calls DCClient.finish(0) which will terminate the application.

The standalone version reads the checkpoint file, does periodic work, checkpoints during the work and quits when finished. Since there is no event to signal the checkpoint request, we used the default interval of BOINC, which is 300 seconds, for checkpointing period. The invoked checkpoint function is only chekpoints when at least 300 seconds passed since the last invocation.

We deployed these applications on an Intel Pentium 4 2.53GHz / 1GB RAM / Debian Linux 4.0 32bit node. We pre-installed the Java runtime (SE 6 update 6), thus the measurements made do not consider the overhead of downloading it with the application and uncompressing it later at the start of each run. We chose not to directly measure the overhead of the JNI calls, since they just act as forwarders to the DC-API library, rather to compare the overhead of the whole infrastructure (JNI + DC-API + BOINC) against the standalone version.

Type	Slowest run	Fastest run	Average time
JNI + DC-API + BOINC	4409.86 sec	4407.99 sec	4408.82 sec
Standalone	4371.76 sec	4369.60 sec	4370.71 sec

Fig. 4 Run-time (real, in seconds) of the sample DC-API enabled and standalone application

We ran each application 15 times, the standalone one was executed from shell, and the DC-API enabled one via BOINC. Measurements (see Figure 4) were made using the Linux *time* command, the DC-API enabled application was wrapped in a shell script (acting as the launcher application) which invoked the *time* command with the application.

We can see that the JNI + DC-API + BOINC infrastructure has only minimal ($\sim 1\%$) overhead compared to the standalone run.

5 Conclusion

There are existing grid APIs which could be partially implemented on desktop grid systems if the goal was to support applications that are primarily running on traditional grid systems but sometimes also has to support desktop grids. Many features of traditional grid systems are not supported on desktop grids therefore, any application that relies on them would not run on a desktop grid. On the other hand numerous desktop-grid specific functionality are missing from these grid APIs therefore, a full-blown desktop grid application would still need to use desktop grid specific APIs.

In this paper we presented DC-API, a simple uniform API for (desktop) grids. We've shown how it enables to run native Java applications on the BOINC platform, which directly does not support them. Future work will be lifting the limitation of the client side only Java support, and finding a solution for a better JRE deployment method consistent with the Java license.

The DC-API + Java package is currently available [2] upon request for Microsoft Windows and Linux platforms.

Acknowledgements The research and development published in this paper is supported by the European Commission under contract number IST-2002-004265 (FP6 NoE, CoreGRID).

References

1. Java Native Interface. http://java.sun.com/javase/6/docs/technotes/guides/jni/index.html
2. Sztaki desktop grid http://www.desktopgrid.hu
3. Allen, G., Davis, K., Dolkas, K., Doulamis, N., Goodale, T., Kielmann, T., Merzky, A., Nabrzyski, J., Pukacki, J., Radke, T., Russell, M., Seidel, E., Shalf, J., Taylor, I.: Enabling applications on the grid – a GridLab overview. International Journal on High Performance Computing Applications 17(4), 449–466 (2003)
4. Allen, G., Davis, K., Goodale, T., Hutanu, A., Kaiser, H., Kielmann, T., Merzky, A., van Nieuwpoort, R., Reinefeld, A., Schintke, F., Schütt, T., Seidel, E., Ullmer, B.: The Grid Application Toolkit: Towards generic and easy application programming interfaces for the grid. Proceedings of the IEEE 93(3), 534–550 (2005)
5. Anderson, D.P.: Boinc: A system for public-resource computing and storage. In: R. Buyya (ed.) Fifth IEEE/ACM International Workshop on Grid Computing, pp. 4–10 (2004)
6. Hungarian ClusterGrid Infrastructure Project. http://www.clustergrid.niif.hu/
7. Goodale, T., Jha, S., Kaiser, H., Kielmann, T., Kleijer, P., von Laszewski, G., Lee, C., Merzky, A., Rajic, H., Shalf, J.: SAGA: A simple API for grid applications - high-level application programming on the grid. Computational Methods in Science and Technology 12(1), 7–20 (2005). Special issue "Grid Applications: New Challenges for Computational Methods"
8. Goodale, T., Jha, S., Kaiser, H., Kielmann, T., Kleijer, P., Merzky, A., Shalf, J., Smith, C.: A simple API for grid applications (SAGA). Draft GWD-R.90, Open Grid Forum (2007)
9. Kacsuk, P., Podhorszki, N., Kiss, T.: Scalable desktop grid system. High Performance Computing for Computational Science - VECPAR 2006 pp. 27–38 (2007)
10. The Open Grid Forum. http://www.ogf.org
11. Rajic, H., Brobst, R., Chan, W., Ferstl, F., Gardiner, J., Haas, A., Nitzberg, B., Rajic, H., Tollefsrud, J.: Distributed resource management application api specification 1.0. Proposed Recommendation GFD-R.022, Global Grid Forum (2004)

Bridging the Data Management Gap Between Service and Desktop Grids

Ian Kelley and Ian Taylor

Abstract Volunteer computing platforms have become a popular means of providing vast amounts of processing power to scientific applications through the use of personal home computers. To date, with little exception, these systems have focused solely on exploiting idle CPU cycles and have yet to take full advantage of other available resources such as powerful video card processors, hard disk storage capacities, and high-speed network connections. As part of the EDGeS project, we are working to expand this narrow scope to also utilize available network and storage capabilities. In this paper we outline the justifications for this approach and introduce how decentralized P2P networks are being built in the project to distribute scientific data currently on the Grid.

1 Introduction

For a number of years, volunteer computing environments have been extremely successful in leveraging the idle resources of personal computers. This has primarily been orchestrated through a donation system whereby private individuals allow their otherwise idle computers to be used by a third-party application for processing data. To date, major volunteer computing systems, such as the Berkeley Open Infrastructure for Network Computing (BOINC) [1][2], have focused solely on harnessing available CPU processing power, and have yet to take full advantage of the other available resource capabilities. With the sharp increases in consumer networking speeds and storage capacities over the past few years, utilizing idle network bandwidth to distribute data has become both a possible and attractive opportunity for volunteer computing.

Ian Kelley and Ian Taylor
School of Computer Science, Cardiff University, Cardiff, United Kingdom
e-mail: {I.R.Kelley,Ian.J.Taylor}@cs.cardiff.ac.uk

Enabling Desktop Grids for e-Science (EDGeS) [3][4] is an EU FP7 project that is setting up infrastructure and building software to enable the integration of Service Grids, or traditional Grid environments [5] generally composed of clusters and supercomputers, and Desktop Grid [1][6] systems, such as the popular volunteer computing project BOINC. When moving jobs between these two environments, and specifically when transferring a job from a Service Grid to a Desktop Grid, there is a need for some form of data management scheme to serve the files to participating Desktop Grid worker nodes.

One way to offload the central network needs that are created in this process and limit exposure to foreign hosts is to use a brokered data distribution mechanism. These brokers would act as a buffer between the two systems, receiving data from local hosts and managing the wider distribution challenges. Using peer-to-peer (P2P) techniques to implement such a system could be seen as a viable alternative to centralized data distribution. Not only would this reduce the Service Grid resources needed to integrate with a Desktop Grid, it could also mitigate the potential risk involved in transferring jobs to the Desktop Grid. By providing an intermediary layer, one is able to limit the number of peers to which a Service Grid node must distribute data. This can be further refined by applying project-based security criteria to govern the membership composition of the data brokers. For the Desktop Grid network, a P2P data distribution system would also allow current projects to take full advantage of client-side network and storage capabilities, enabling the exploration of new types of data-intensive application scenarios, ones that are currently overly prohibitive given their large data transfer needs.

There are many ways the aforementioned functionality could be implemented, ranging from BitTorrent-style networks [7][8], where there is a central tracker and all participants share relatively equal loads, to more customizable networks that allow for clients and service providers to be grouped. Custom-built solutions would have the advantage of facilitating different network topologies and data distribution algorithms. This allows for tailoring the network for the needs of an individual application, albeit with the disadvantage of increased development effort and code maintenance. In the case of BOINC, each of these approaches has its own distinct advantages and disadvantages, as explored in [9], especially when one takes into consideration the target user-community and their needs. Through the course of the paper we will show the data distribution work being undertaken in the EDGeS project as it advances towards interoperability between Service Grids and Desktop Grids. In particular, we will explore some of the requirements and varying scenarios that can appear in typical BOINC projects, outline the relative benefits of applying these new techniques, and give an overview of the data distribution software we are building for EDGeS.

The paper is organized as follows: section 2 gives background on the tools and related technologies involved; section 3 discusses EDGeS' data needs; section 4 gives an introduction of BOINC-specific requirements; section 5 overviews select design issues when applying P2P technologies to volunteer computing; section 6 proposes our decentralized data center approach; and section 7 concludes.

2 Background and related work

BOINC is currently the most widespread and successful volunteer computing Desktop Grid application ever, with over 50 distinct projects[1] and almost three million total computers from over 200 countries registered to date[2]. For data distribution, BOINC projects generally use a single centralized server or a set of mirrors. This centralized architecture, although very effective, incurs additional costs and can be a potential bottleneck when tasks share input files or the central server has limited bandwidth. Increasing the number of mirrors to accommodate increased loads puts extra administrative burden on the project organiser and can prove very time consuming to manage.

Popular and proven P2P technologies [10][11][12] such as BitTorrent, or commercial solutions like Amazon's S3[3] or Google's GFS [13], could be fairly effectively applied to provide for the data needs of BOINC, at least as they relate strictly to distribution. However, in the case of commercial products, there is a direct monetary cost involved, and for P2P systems like BitTorrent, the facility to secure or limit who is able to receive, cache, or propagate different pieces of information is generally limited or nonexistent. For example, BitTorrent, like many other P2P systems, has focused on ensuring conventional file-sharing features, such as efficient transfers, equal sharing and file integrity.

Desktop Grid environments have different requirements to general file-sharing P2P communities because security can become more of a complex issue than solely guaranteeing data validity (see section 5.1). In Desktop Grids, it can be a requisite that only certain amounts of data are shared with an individual peer. Communities can also be reluctant to introduce a system that would have peers directly sharing with one another, as it might have the potential (or perceived potential) to have security implications for clients as ports are opened for outside connectivity. It is therefore important not only for data integrity and reliability to be ensured, but also to have available safeguards that can limit peer nodes' exposure to malicious attacks. It is these types of requirements that has prompted our work to create a custom P2P network for data distribution that provides both client and server safeguards and stricter controls for project administrators as to what network participants receive and distribute data.

3 EDGeS' data needs

In the EDGeS project a job can be transferred from a Service Grid to a Desktop Grid. When this occurs, there is a need for some mechanism that either moves the

---

[1] There are over 50 known BOINC projects. At the time of this writing, the BOINC website has a list of 25 in which they have been in direct contact with: http://boinc.berkeley.edu/projects.php

[2] http://boincstats.com

[3] http://aws.amazon.com/s3

job's input files directly to the Desktop Grid workers, or exposes them on the Service Grid host for Desktop Grid peers to directly access and download.

At first glance, perhaps the easiest solution to enable access to the needed files would be to simply expose the data directly from the Service Grid file system. Such an approach would closely mimic the current functionality found in most Desktop Grid projects, where data is distributed to all participants from a central machine or through a set of known and static mirrors. This solution, although seemingly attractive in its simplicity, has many limiting drawbacks. For example, the Service Grid machine where the data is hosted might not be able to effectively serve the numerous peers making requests due to bandwidth limitations. Where previously the data was likely to be stored locally, allowing many processors access to it on a shared file system, now each peer which wishes to perform work must download an individual copy of the data to be analyzed. This can very quickly lead to a large drain on network bandwidth, especially in the case of larger files that need to be distributed to multiple workers.

In addition to raw resource usage concerns, there might also be security infrastructure and policies that would prevent access to local files from foreign and untrusted hosts. Anonymous access is generally not an issue for most BOINC projects, as they are able to have dedicated and network isolated data servers. This could, however, quickly become problematic, both technically and politically, if one tried to somehow bootstrap a BOINC data server onto a cluster or supercomputer to enable access to users' files. The situation is further complicated by the often complex software dependencies in existing Grid systems that make deploying yet another Grid service either not possible or at the very least unwelcome.

EDGeS requires a system that can adapt to varying input file sizes and replication factors without unduly stressing or exposing the Service Grid layer. This requirement will become increasing relevant as the EDGeS project moves beyond its test servers, which we can manage and configure, and begins connecting a wide range of EGEE [14] resources to different Desktop Grid systems. In this scenario, each of these federated Service Grid nodes will have different security infrastructures, internal policies, and network connectivity traits that would essentially render useless any system that required them to install additional software or adapt security policy. By pushing data to a P2P environment and offloading data distribution, Service Grid nodes could transfer the data distribution responsibilities, making the integration of Service and Desktop Grids more accessible.

4 BOINC requirements

As briefly mentioned in section 2, there are several dozen BOINC projects in operation. Every one of these projects shares a common thread with one another; each has a highly parallel problem able to be split into thousands of independent tasks that can be asynchronously processed. It is these properties that allow BOINC projects to exploit a Desktop Grid environment and utilize the numerous volunteer computing resources that are made available in the process. What isn't apparent, however, is that each of these projects can have vastly different levels of data intensity. This can manifest itself in the form of varying data input and output file sizes, changing replication facts, and different throughput requirements.

Given the dissimilar requirements for BOINC projects, there are many considerations one must take when thinking of applying a P2P system to the BOINC middleware. Even if a list of all the possible data distribution-related aspects were complied, various communities and application groups would have different priority rankings as to which are the most important for their individual circumstances (e.g., security vs. usability). The list we present here does not delve into the details of different project's data requirements, rather, it represents a few of the cross-cutting issues that are generally present in any BOINC-based project. Additional example areas to explore, which are not covered here, include topics such as data access speed, encryption, support for large data sets, and fuzzy query matching when searching for data. However, for the interests of simplicity and because the previously mentioned areas are currently being investigated, we have limited the scope explored here to the four issues listed below, which we believe to be key areas one must address when considering a P2P system that will be useful to the BOINC community as a whole.

Firewall and Router Configuration — Depending on an individual project's configuration, firewall and router issues could be problematic, with a general tradeoff between "punching holes" in clients' firewalls to be able to exploit their bandwidth and the security concerns and extra software development or configuration this demands. In volunteer computing projects it is especially important to provide a high level of security to participants. If NATs are bypassed, they need to be done in a secure and transparent (to the end-user) manner.

Malicious Users — The issue of which nodes are able to propagate data on the network, and therefore which ones will have the ability to inflict damage, will largely depend upon the individual policies of each hosting project. In the most restrictive case, only trusted and verified participants would be certified to propagate data. In looser security configurations, which allow for the exploitation of a larger pool of resources, security would have to be more flexible. Regardless of the decision, data signing can help to prevent any analysis of corrupted data. This makes network flooding the major concern, however, this can be limited relatively easily by implementing a ranking system to report misbehaving data providers.

Exploiting Network Topology — The ability to exploit network topology such as LANs and WAN proximity is a useful way to further limit the amount of necessary bandwidth to serve project files. The trade-off is generally that the looser the system becomes in its ability to adopt and utilize network proximity (such as providing caching nodes on LANs) the more exposed the network is to abuse and potential misconfiguration.

Integration with BOINC — It is important for any software that wishes to provide an added value to the larger BOINC community to have little or no impact on current operating procedures. Requiring external libraries or other similar dependencies could prove to be problematic and limit widespread uptake. The BOINC client is currently written in C++ and any successful add-on would most likely have to adapt to this requirement.

A more in-depth discussion of the above concerns and how they relate to the data distribution software being designed in EDGeS, along with a comparison to BitTorrent is discussed in [9].

5 Design considerations

Beyond the issues above, there are a number of general factors that become important when designing and deploying a data serving network across large-scale volunteer networks such as those in the BOINC community. For example, the size of the network can vary dramatically between the extremely popular BOINC projects and their less successful counterparts. Aside from sheer network size, different projects' will have varying data input and output file sizes, with some projects having a peer transfer over a gigabyte per month while others require only a fraction of this amount. For each project within BOINC, these factors are slightly different, and the optimal network setup for one project might not be very efficient for another. These differences make designing an optimal network for BOINC as a whole a challenging task. Yet as shown in [15], the application of a P2P network layer would allow many additional and unused network and storage resources to be leveraged by BOINC projects without sacrificing necessary processing power.

In section 6, we introduce the data distribution software we are in the beginning phases of developing. However, before talking of the implementation and design specifics, it is useful to further expand upon the requirements listed in section 4 and discuss some of the cross-cutting security issues shared between BOINC projects. This will help to set the stage for the proposed architecture.

5.1 Security aspects

When building a P2P network for volunteer computing, there are a number of security requirements beyond the traditional notion of simply ensuring file integrity. Due to the volatile and insecure nature of BOINC networks, a product of their open participation policies, there can be reason to enforce limitations on which entities are allowed to distribute and cache data. When opening the data distribution channels to public participation, security can become a concern. In this context, the area of security can be roughly split into the following two distinct realms: *user security* and *data security*.

User security refers to the ability to protect the "volunteers" in the network from any harm that could possibility be inflicted on their machine by another network participant. This is a very important issue when one is within the realm of volunteer computing, as the resources are typically donated home computers that likely contain volunteers' important personal information and documents. In the case of a security breech in which these volunteer resources were compromised by some malicious entity, the potentially fallout could be enormous. Fear of a harsh backlash has been one of the limiting factors to the incorporation of standard P2P technologies into the BOINC middleware. Even in the event where no actual security breech takes place, *requiring* peers to share data with one another via P2P protocols, such as BitTorrent, which enforces sharing, could have the down-side of alienating potential volunteers. This could result from any number of factors, ranging from a volunteer's unwillingness to donate network resources (perhaps due to bandwidth requirements from other computers on the same network or a metered data connection) to misconceived public perception that associates peer-to-peer technological implementations with some of the more controversial uses of the technology.

It is necessary to be cognizant of the fact that the BOINC community relies upon volunteers to function, and any "peer-to-peer" data distribution scheme that is implemented must allow for users to opt-out if they do not wish to share their bandwidth or storage capacity. Even in the instance where users have opted to share data, a generally high level of consideration has to be given to ensure that their computers are adequately protected from attacks. In current BOINC environments this is solved by having a centralized, and presumably non-hostile, authority that distributes both executables and data. Although even in this scenario, there are still chances that the servers could be compromised, or that the executables distributed have inherent security flaws, this is generally a very minimal risk and would be a consequence of actions of the application stakeholders, not third-party unknown distributers. It is these considerations and requirements that make applying P2P protocols such as BitTorrent, which enforce tit-for-tat sharing, problematic.

Data security can be a complex matter. First, there is the issue of file integrity, which we will not go into in detail here, mainly because there are many well-known and suitable techniques to validate the authenticity of files, such as hashing and signing. More interesting and novel is investigating security schemes for which to select and distribute data-sets to peers. When looking at this issue in more detail, it can further be broken down into two broad subject areas: *authentication* and *authorization*.

Authentication is the verification process by which an entity identifies itself to others and gives evidence to its validity. Public key infrastructure (PKI) [16] is a proven tool that can be fairly effectively applied for performing peer identity authentication. In the simplest case, this can be done by having a central authority (i.e., the BOINC manager) sign and issue either full or proxy certificates to those it deems trustworthy enough to distribute data on its behalf. When another peer on the network contacts this "trusted" entity, it can use the public key from the centralized BOINC manager to verify the authenticity of the trusted peer. This process can likewise be performed in reverse, provided clients are also issued certificates, as a means for the data distributers to validate the identity of the clients and verify they have the proper credentials to retrieve data. The process of using certificates for mutual authentication can be a fairly effective solution that would provide individual peers with certainty that the host they are retrieving data from has been delegated the proper authority and visa versa. More interesting use-cases that provide for interaction between multiple virtual organizations (VOs) and hierarchal delegation (e.g., certificate-chaining and cross-certification agreements) can be derived from this simple arrangement, but are beyond the scope of this paper [17][18].

Authorization is a much more interesting question than authorization. This is primarily because there are standardized techniques for authentication that can be widely applied to many different applications with little or no modification. Authorization conversely is application-specific, differing with each individual application's unique needs and authority structures. Although there are tools to help define authorization policies and enforce them [19], the policies themselves will be different with each application.

At the most basic level of authorizing select peers to cache and distribute data as they see fit, authorization is very simple and should not prove problematic. For example, it is possible to issue special certificates to the data cachers (as mentioned in the authentication section) that allows them to validate as data distributors. However, when more dynamic and customizable queries are needed, such as finer-grained control over what data can be propagated by individual data cachers, the issue of authorization becomes more complex. When this occurs, the issue requires more due diligence, and any scheme that goes beyond a simple yes/no query must be customized specifically to the target environment, in this case, not only BOINC, but potentially each target community.

6 Proposed architecture: *ADICS*

The peer-to-peer Architecture for Data-Intensive Cycle Sharing (ADICS) [20] is an effort to build a P2P software layer that can be used by scientific applications, specifically those engaged in volunteer computing, to distribute, manage, and maintain their data. Therefore, the core infrastructure of ADICS is being built with the needs of a scientific user and application in mind. As a software development package being supported by the EDGeS project, ADICS is taking very close consideration of the issues raised in section 3. It should be noted, however, that the core infrastructure is being architected to be fairly application agnostic and should therefore be applicable to other applications that want to distribute data in a peer-to-peer environment.

Based upon the previously mentioned security and user requirements, the network we have chosen to implement at this time is an architecture that has three distinct entities: *workers*, *data centers*, and *data providers*. In this 3-tiered, bridged architecture, the *data provider* pushes files to the *data center* overlay network, which self-organizes using P2P techniques to propagate data amongst itself. This data center layer then serves pull requests for data from the *workers*. Figure 1 gives a generalized overview of how the different components in ADICS relate to one another after the initial discovery phase. During discovery, a worker node would send a request to known access points in the data center overlay network and retrieve an updated list of connection points from which it can harvest data. If this process fails, likely due to a stale list of hosts, the worker node is able to contact the static data provider to request a new data center reference. Subsequent requests for data are made to the data center layer, and the worker is then able to contact one or more centers for downloading.

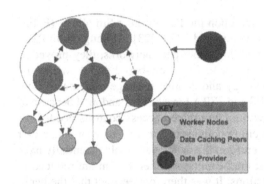

Fig. 1 ADICS schematic of the organization of the distributed entities that shows a data provider serving data to the caching layer, which is, in turn, distributed to the worker nodes.

The reasoning behind this is to allow for only a subset of peers that match certain performance and security thresholds to share data with the rest of the network. By implementing an opt-in and (for the moment centrally) validated system for data sharing, many of the security considerations (see sections 4 and 5) such as router configuration, automatically opening ports, and rouge hosts providing data can be marginalized. In this scenario, the *data center* subset of peers on the network act as "true peers" in the sense that that both send and receive on an equal standing with their data center neighbors, however, they act solely as servers to the *workers*. One benefit of this approach is that, *workers* continue to operate relatively unchanged from their previous BOINC working conditions, with the relatively minor addition of a distributed data lookup.

Secure data centers are the name we have given members of the super-peer overlay that are engaged in data sharing. The *secure* aspects becomes apparent when constraints are later put upon the registration phase, thereby restricting the set of peers that are allowed to propagate data. Policy decisions as to which participants, if any, are allowed to host and redistribute data would be made by each individual BOINC project, with ADICS providing the base infrastructure to aide the process as well as a default implementation. Once the general tools are in place, more complex scenarios can be explored that go beyond simply restricting data center membership. For example, constraints could be introduced to govern the relative sensitivity of data and retention policies. Adding these new types of functionality would allow for more advanced use-cases, albeit with the additional costs of software and network complexity.

Based upon the preliminary results of [21] and the arguments presented here, it is our belief that decentralized data centers can prove to be both valid and useful solutions to distributing data in Desktop Grid environments. There is, however, a tradeoff between functionality and complexity that needs to be adequately addressed and balanced if such technologies are to be adopted by production environments such as BOINC.

6.1 Prototype development

Initial development in ADICS was based upon the Peer-to-Peer Simplified (P2PS) middleware [22], a generic P2P infrastructure and JXTA [23]. Although both P2PS and JXTA provide generic tools for building super-peer networks, they proved to be limiting either in their ability to scale or to form role-based groups where the developer can explicitly form the topology and control message relaying without major modifications. Specifically, P2PS and JXTA have been abandoned because of two main reasons. First, neither allow the fine-grained access controls needed for the data layer. Second, there are no caching policies in either system for data rather than metadata (adverts or queries). Therefore, the data layer would essentially have to be built from scratch, meaning that the benefits of either system are reduced to providing their respective P2P abstractions. It was therefore decided that the benefits of using these systems were far outweighed by the drawbacks of the additional dependencies they placed upon the end-user, and their increased complexity.

The current focus is on implementing a specific system that fits into the current BOINC messaging layer, yet is generic enough to be applied in a number of different ways. To this end, we are developing a prototype that will help to define the entities and evolve the design of the network and its messages. This will allow us to validate the selected topology and show that it is useful to solve the security and data propagation issues introduced earlier in this paper.

Figure 2 gives a general overview of the different network interactions that a worker has in the current prototype. In order to enable the prototype to function independently of BOINC and speed development, we have implemented a very basic work generation entity (the Network Manager) that generates work units to fulfill client requests and begin the data retrieval cycle. It should be noted that in the prototype available at the time of this writing, the data center layer is fed by the central repository, and does not self-propagate data amongst itself.

- **(1)** A worker requests a *WorkUnit* from a known Network Manager server.
  (1b) The worker receives the response and extracts a list of *DataQueries*, which contain information on how to identify the job's data dependencies. Currently this is a unique ID, however, it could also be a more sophisticated query.
- **(2)** The worker contacts a Data Lookup Service, and provides it with one or more *DataQueries*. Currently this service is known and centralized, however, there are plans to decentralize it and provide it as a service on the Data Center layer.
  (2b) The Data Lookup Service attempts to match each *DataQuery* to a real file

mapping and, if successful, returns a *DataPointer* for each *DataQuery*. The *DataPointer* contains a list of Data Centers that are believed to have he file, as well as any associated metadata about the file that is available.

- **(3)** For each *DataPointer*, the worker extracts the location of one or more Data Centers that are believed to host the file. The worker then directly connects to one or more (currently one) Data Center for retrieval.

(3b) The Data Center retrieves the file from its local disk space and sends it to the worker.

In its current implementation, the prototype is very similar in nature to how early Napster worked, with a central metadata server keeping track of where data is located. The Data Lookup Service is also reminiscent of a BitTorrent tracker, which performs essentially the same functions on behalf of a single file.

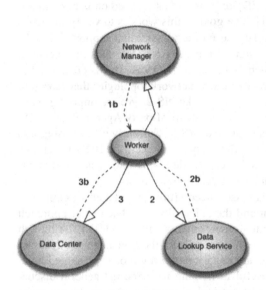

Fig. 2 Diagram showing the basic flow of messages from the worker to the various other network entities.

One of the main differences between these previous systems and the described here data center scheme is the potential for the addition of security criteria which restricts the data service layer to a subset of the available peers. The next step in ADICS development is to decentralize the data lookup facility through implement self-organizing traits on the data center layer, and to add security constraints on the propagation and lookup of data. At the time of this writing, this is currently a work-in-progress.

One of the clear issues raised in section 4 was that of integration with the existing BOINC software stack. ADICS is currently being designed and built in Java, which naturally creates a client dependency on a JRE. As mentioned in section 4, this can pose a problem when trying to later integrate ADICS into the BOINC client layer. Two possible solutions to this problem are: *(1)* add a JRE to the required software to run BOINC, which could severely limit adoption of ADICS; and, *(2)* create a C++ implementation of ADICS for *workers* that provides download capabilities. This would allow for the core discovery and data propagation layer to be left in Java. By doing so, we would limit the JRE requirement to nodes that wish to operate as data centers. Current design and plans for ADICS are pursuing option *1*, in order to build a working system as quickly as possible. The necessity of option *2* will be reassessed later based upon feedback from the BOINC user-community.

It should be noted that the software discussed here is currently under heavy development and is expected to evolve as new challenges are encountered. As part of the EDGeS project deliverables, the first public prototype of ADICS will be released in December 2008. This prototype will have functionality that allows for the propagation, caching, and sharing of data, using the decentralized data center architecture outlined here.

6.2 Research theories verified through simulation

Much work in the few months since EDGeS started has focused on using simulation tools, such as NS-2 [24] and [21]. The goal of this work is to verify the ideas presented here and define the general structure of a network that supports EDGeS' needs and attempts to model the transfer of typical sized data files and network loads for current BOINC projects, such as Einstein@HOME. This is currently being achieved through the construction of reusable network topologies that represent standard home Internet connections in systems like NS-2. We are applying these topologies to the ADICS prototype code though the third-party AgentJ libaries [25] that allows for the attachment of Java entities to NS-2. Currently we are using this to represent the behaviour of the central data repository (i.e., the BOINC server), the data caching layer, and the connected peers, while taking into consideration parameters such as the network links and the underlying protocols.

Previous simulation work [21] was also successfully undertaken to explore a more general cycle-sharing paradigm and the suitability of a data center approach for caching job input files in distributed environments such as BOINC. Although the work presented in that paper was more generalized, the fundamental "dynamic caching" and data distribution aspects are consistent with the ones presented here. These prior simulations were very useful in helping to shape the general discussion and move towards the more specific network simulations that are taking place now. We are continuing to refine those simulations to mimic real-life use-cases, in addition to the NS-2 models previously mentioned.

7 Conclusion

In this paper we have discussed some of the data issues that arise in the EDGeS project as Service Grid jobs are migrated to a Desktop Grid environment. One low-cost way to provide the needed bandwidth and data storage to support this scenario is to exploit client-side network capacities in a P2P-type system for distributed data sharing and propagation. The brokered approach outlined here, ADICS, can provide a happy medium between a "true" P2P system implementation that treats participants relatively equally and the current static mirroring being used by BOINC projects. ADICS has three main entities: data providers that push data onto the network; data centers (or cachers) that conform to some security requirement that allows them to propagate data on the data providers' behalf; and, data consumers (or workers) that execute jobs and request input files from the data center layer. The architecture outlined here is currently being pursued within the EDGeS project. It is hoped this paper will further the discussion on the applicability of P2P technologies in the scientific community and encourage others to explore it as a valid and useful approach for data distribution.

Acknowledgements This work was supported by the CoreGRID Network of Excellence, the Center for Computation & Technology at Louisiana State University, EPSRC grant EP/C006291/1, and the EU FP7 EDGeS grant RI 211727.

References

1. "BOINC - Berkeley Open Infrastructure for Network Computing." [Online]. Available: http://boinc.berkeley.edu/
2. D. P. Anderson, "BOINC: A System for Public-Resource Computing and Storage," in *5th IEEE/ACM International Workshop on Grid Computing*, Pittsburgh, USA, November 2004, pp. 365–372.
3. "Enabling Desktop Grids for e-Science." [Online]. Available: http://www.edges-grid.eu
4. Z. Balaton, Z. Farkas, G. Gombas, P. Kacsuk, R. Lovas, A. C. Marosi, A. Emmen, G. Terstyanszky, T. Kiss, I. Kelley, I. Taylor, O. Lodygensky, M. Cardenas-Montes, G. Fedak, and F. Araujo, "EDGeS: The Common Boundary Between Service and Desktop Grids," in *To be published in a special volume of the CoreGRID Springer series.*, 2008.
5. I. Foster and C. Kesselman, "Globus: A Metacomputing Infrastructure Toolkit," *Int. Journal of Supercomputing Applications*, vol. 11, no. 2, pp. 115–128, 1997.
6. F. Cappello *et al.*, "Computing on Large-Scale Distributed Systems: XtremWeb Architecture, Programming Models, Security, Tests and Convergence with Grid," *Future Generation Computer Systems*, vol. 21, no. 3, pp. 417–437, 2005.
7. B. Cohen, "Incentives Build Robustness in BitTorrent," in *Workshop on Economics of Peer-to-Peer Systems (P2PEcon'03)*, Berkeley, CA, June 2003.
8. "Bittorrent." [Online]. Available: http://www.bittorrent.com/
9. F. Costa, I. Kelley, L. Silva, and I. Taylor, "Peer-To-Peer Techniques for Data Distribution in Desktop Grid Computing Platforms," in *To be published in a special volume of the CoreGRID Springer series.*, 2008.
10. J. Kubiatowicz, D. Bindel, Y. Chen, S. Czerwinski, P. Eaton, D. Geels, R. Gummadi, S. Rhea, H. Weatherspoon, W. Weimer, C. Wells, and B. Zhao, "OceanStore: an architecture for global-scale persistent storage," *SIGPLAN Not.*, vol. 35, no. 11, pp. 190–201, 2000.
11. S. S. Vazhkudai, X. Ma, V. W. Freeh, J. W. Strickland, N. Tammineedi, and S. L. Scott, "FreeLoader: Scavenging Desktop Storage Resources for Scientific Data," in *SC '05: Proceedings of the 2005 ACM/IEEE conference on Supercomputing.* Washington, DC, USA: IEEE Computer Society, 2005, p. 56.
12. I. Clarke, S. G. Miller, O. Sandberg, B. Wiley, and T. W. Hong, "Protecting Free Expression Online with Freenet," *IEEE Internet Computing*, pp. 40–49, January, February 2002.
13. S. Ghemawat, H. Gobioff, and S.-T. Leung, "The Google file system," *SIGOPS Oper. Syst. Rev.*, vol. 37, no. 5, pp. 29–43, 2003.
14. "EGEE: Enabling Grids for E-science in Europe." [Online]. Available: http://public.eu-egee.org

15. D. P. Anderson and G. Fedak, "The computational and storage potential of volunteer computing," in *CCGRID '06: Proceedings of the Sixth IEEE International Symposium on Cluster Computing and the Grid.* Washington, DC, USA: IEEE Computer Society, 2006, pp. 73–80.

16. "IETF Public Key Infrastructure Working Group." [Online]. Available: http://www.ietf.org/html.charters/pkix-charter.html

17. K. Berket, A. Essiari, and A. Muratas, "PKI-based security for peer-to-peer information sharing," *Peer-to-Peer Computing, 2004. Proceedings. Proceedings. Fourth International Conference on*, pp. 45–52, 25-27 Aug. 2004.

18. J. E. Altman, "PKI Security for JXTA Overlay Networks," IAM Consulting, Inc., Tech. Rep., 2003.

19. T. Barton, J. Basney, T. Freeman, T. Scavo, F. Siebenlist, V. Welch, R. Ananthakrishnan, B. Baker, M. Goode, and K. Keahey, "Identity Federation and Attribute-based Authorization through the Globus Toolkit, Shibboleth, GridShib, and MyProxy," in *NIST PKI Workshop*, April 2006.

20. "Peer-to-Peer Architecture for Data-Intensive Cycle Sharing (ADICS)." [Online]. Available: http://www.p2p-adics.org

21. P. Cozza, I. Kelley, C. Mastroianni, D. Talia, and I. Taylor, "Cache-enabled super-peer overlays for multiple job submission on grids," in *Grid Middleware and Services: Challenges and Solutions*, D. Talia, R. Yahyapour, and W. Ziegler, Eds. Springer, 2008, to appear.

22. I. Wang, "P2PS (Peer-to-Peer Simplified)," in *Proceedings of 13th Annual Mardi Gras Conference - Frontiers of Grid Applications and Technologies.* Louisiana State University, February 2005, pp. 54–59.

23. "Project JXTA." [Online]. Available: http://www.jxta.org/

24. "The Ns2 Simulator." [Online]. Available: http://www.isi.edu/nsnam/ns/

25. I. Taylor, I. Downard, B. Adamson, and J. Macker, "AgentJ: Enabling Java NS-2 Simulations for Large Scale Distributed Multimedia Applications," in *Second International Conference on Distributed Frameworks for Multimedia DFMA 2006*, Penang, Malaysia, 14th to 17th May 2006.

Utilizing the EGEE Infrastructure for Desktop Grids*

Zoltán Farkas, Péter Kacsuk and Manuel Rubio del Solar

Abstract Today basically two grid concepts rule the world: service grids and desktop grids. Service grids offer an infrastructure for grid users, thus require notable management to keep the service running. On the other hand, desktop grids aim to utilize free CPU cycles of cheap desktop PCs, are easy to set up, but the availability towards users is limited compared to the service grid. The aim of the EDGeS project is to create an integrated infrastructure that gathers the advantages of the two grid concepts. A building block of this infrastructure is bridging between the different grid types. In the paper we focus on bridging from desktop grids towards service grids, i.e. making desktop grids able to utilize free service grid resources.

1 Introduction

In the past years, two main grid concepts have evolved: service and desktop grids. The main differences between the two concepts are the infrastructure topology and elements, and the users' role. In case of service grids [1], the infrastructure consists of a set of services that must be maintained in order to keep them running: resource brokers, information system services, storage areas, computational resources with

Zoltán Farkas
MTA SZTAKI, H-1518 Budapest, P.O. Box 63, e-mail: zfarkas@sztaki.hu

Péter Kacsuk
MTA SZTAKI, H-1518 Budapest, P.O. Box 63, e-mail: kacsuk@sztaki.hu

Manuel Rubio del Solar
CETA-CIEMAT, Paseo Ruiz de Mendoza 8, 10200 Trujillo, Spain, e-mail: manuel.rubio@ciemat.es

* The EDGeS (Enabling Desktop Grids for e-Science) project receives Community funding from the European Commission within Research Infrastructures initiative of FP7 (grant agreement Number 211727). The work presented here was partly funded by FP6 CoreGrid Network of Excellence (contract number IST-2002-004265).

a frontend node (gatekeeper) and a set of worker nodes that actually process work. Grid users are entities that have proper rights to use these services, this is achieved by using certificates. Basically any kind of application can be executed on service grids, that can also be executed on a traditional PC. Grid users make use of services to run their applications, and it is the services' task to perform the job execution. Well-known examples for service grids are Condor [2], Globus [3] [4], LCG-2/gLite (EGEE) [5], ARC [6] or Unicore [7]. On the other hand, desktop grids are very easy to set up: a central service contains the set of jobs to run, and desktop PC owners from all over the world can connect to offer their PC's free CPU cycles for processing the jobs by installing a very simple client application. So, in case of desktop grids, the expression 'user' is a synonym of 'service provider' or 'computing resource owner'. The access to the desktop grid server is limited, so only dedicated entities have the possibility to add jobs for processing. Typical application scenarios for desktop grids are parameter study or master-worker applications. Examples for desktop grids are BOINC [8], XtremWeb [9] or Condor[2].

At the beginning of 2008, a new FP-7 founded project, EDGeS [10] has been started that (besides others) aims to join the advantages of the two grid concepts by creating an integrated infrastructure that supports both service and desktop grids. An initial task of this work is to create a bridge that can be used to transfer applications between representatives of the two main grid concepts, i.e. make desktop grids capable of running service grid jobs and vice versa. In this paper, we focus on running desktop grid jobs within service grids, specifically, running BOINC jobs within EGEE. In section 2 we present a few different solutions. Next, in section 3 we present our work. Afterwards, section 4 presents our observations about the solution's performance. Finally, in section 5 we discuss about possible extensions, and conclude our work.

2 Existing solutions

In this section we present three approaches that solve interoperability between desktop and service grids, and compare them. The three approaches solve the following issues: running BOINC applications on Condor, running XtremWeb applications on Condor, and running BOINC applications on EGEE.

2.1 Running BOINC applications on Condor

The solution developed by MTA SZTAKI [11] enables exploiting of Condor resources by BOINC. The idea behind the solution is to modify the BOINC client application so it doesn't start the real application for the job (or workunit, in BOINC

---

[2] We rate Condor as a desktop grid, too, because it offers the exploitation of desktop grid machines

terms), but executes a wrapper application that creates a Condor job by extracting the workunit information and submits, watches and gets the results of the job interfacing with Condor. In order to provide this functionality, the modified BOINC client has to be run on a Condor submit machine, and is set up to report fake information about itself: instead of reporting the CPU number of the Condor submit machine, the user has to set the number of Condor execution machines in the local Condor pool, and this number is reported to the BOINC server as the number of CPUs on the machine. With this trick, the BOINC server sends enough workunits to flood the local Condor pool with BOINC jobs.

2.2 Running XtremWeb applications on Condor

XtremWeb is an open source platform for building desktop grids. In XtremWeb, the Coordinator is responsible for storing jobs to be processed, and communicate with Clients and Workers. Clients can be used to send work to the Coordinator, and Workers are entities that actually process the created jobs. In [12] authors showed that XtremWeb Workers can be submitted to Condor pools, so they fetch work from the Coordinator and process the downloaded work on Condor worker nodes. Every submitted Worker processes one unit of work. The solution assumes that the Workers running on Condor worker nodes have internet connection to the XtremWeb Coordinator.

2.3 Running BOINC applications on EGEE

The LHC@Home project [13] uses a similar solution to the one mentioned in subsection 2.2, but focuses on running BOINC applications on EGEE. The idea is to submit BOINC clients to EGEE: the submitted job (the BOINC client) is assigned to a worker node by the resource broker. Once the job is started on the allocated node, the BOINC client connects to the BOINC server in order to fetch work, and processes it. Once the workunit has been processed, its result is uploaded back to the server machine. Just like the XtremWeb to Condor solution, this method also assumes that worker nodes have the possibility to open outbound internet connections.

2.4 Summary of existing solutions

Table 1 shows a comparison of already existing solutions mentioned in subsections 2.1, 2.2 and 2.3.

Property	BOINC to Condor	XtremWeb to Condor, BOINC to EGEE
Firewall issues	No	Yes
Middleware overhead	Some	Almost none
Watch jobs	Yes	No
Implementation	Some	Almost none
Supported DG	Basically any	Depends on submitted worker
Modify client	Yes	No

Table 1 Existing solutions

In table 1 firewall issues means how the solution operates regarding internet connections. The BOINC to Condor solution assumes there is no outbound connection from the worker nodes, but the other two solutions do. By Middleware overhead we mean the amount of communication required with the middleware (Condor or EGEE). The BOINC to Condor solution has to keep track of all submitted jobs, on the other hand the XtremWeb to Condor and BOINC to EGEE solutions only submit workers, and from that point on the worker takes care of processing workunits. The watch job property is a subset of middleware overhead, indicates whether the solution has to keep track of submitted jobs or not. Implementation indicates how much effort should be done in order to make the solution work. The supported desktop grid in the BOINC to Condor solution depends on the method workunits are mapped to service grid jobs (so basically supports any kind of desktop and service grid), the other two solutions depend on the submitted workers. The BOINC to Condor solution requires the modification of the official BOINC client, on the other hand the XtremWeb to Condor and BOINC to EGEE solutions don't.

3 Bridging from desktop grids to service grids

According to the summary of the already existing solutions in table 1, we propose using a solution similar to the BOINC to Condor solution, as this method provides a generic way to connect a desktop grid to a service grid, and assumes the connected service grid is a black box, i.e. communicates only through a well-defined interface the service grid provides.

As the first step of the EDGeS project, we have implemented a prototype of the BOINC to EGEE bridge based on the BOINC to Condor solution. The implemented prototype enables running workunits fetched from BOINC servers on an EGEE VO in a coordinated way. Based on the BOINC to Condor solution, we had to implement the following functionalities: create JDL submit files out of workunit informations, use the EGEE WMProxy API to submit created JDL files, observe the execution of submitted EGEE jobs, and finally download the results of finished jobs.

The outlines of the developed BOINC to EGEE bridge can be seen on figure 1. Following the Condor cluster integration solution, the bridge receives workunits from the BOINC server using a modified CoreClient. The CoreClient starts a Job-

Wrapper process for every workunit slot. This process is responsible for arranging the previously mentioned functionalities (JDL file creation, submission, watching execution, result download). Next, we will describe the different operations in detail.

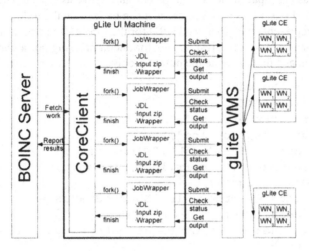

Fig. 1 Overview of the BOINC to EGEE bridge prototype

For every submission we generate a universally unique identifier (UUID)[16]. This UUID is used as a prefix for every file related to the management of a workunit. Using this method, we can resolve filename conflicts of generated files.

3.1 JDL file creation

Job submission in EGEE is performed using JDL files[14], so in order to talk to the resource broker, we have to create such a file. The starting point, the modified CoreClient application created a very simple jobwrapper description file, that contains the most important informations for running the downloaded workunit: the name of the executable files and their location on the filesystem, the name of the input files and their location on the filesystem, the name of the created output files and their proposed location on the filesystem, and finally the *main* executable and its command line arguments. The extra location on the filesystem attribute is crucial, as BOINC stores references to the files in the workunit's directory, not the real file contents (e.g. an input file called in.txt in the workunit's directory has the contents ../../projects/abc_abc/in.txt_<ID>, where <ID> is a unique identifier).

Using this jobwrapper description file's contents, the JobWrapper creates a compressed archive containing every executable, input file, and the description file. It also creates a wrapper script, that is able to uncompress the archive, execute the application using the provided description file, and create a final compressed archive containing the produced output files. Using these files, the JobWrapper creates a JDL file, that uses the wrapper script as the executable, the wrapper script and the input archive as the InputSandbox, and the output archive as the OutputSandbox.

The produced JDL file is very simple, as it can be seen on the following example, where <ID> represents the generated UUID for the job, <ID>.tgz is the input file archive, the script <ID>.sh is responsible for uncompressing this archive, start the real executable, and finally create the output archive <ID>.out.tgz:

```
JobType = "Normal";
Executable = "<ID>.sh";
StdError = "stderr.log";
StdOutput = "stdout.log";
InputSandbox = {"<ID>.sh","<ID>.tgz"};
OutputSandbox = {"stderr.log", "stdout.log",
    "<ID>.out.tgz"};
Requirements = (other.GlueCEStateStatus==
    "Production");
Rank = (-other.GlueCEStateEstimatedResponseTime);
RetryCount = 10;
ShallowRetryCount = 10;
```

Now every information is gathered to run the job on an EGEE worker node.

3.2 Job execution

For the management of a job's life cycle we're using the EGEE WMProxy C++ API[15]. Job execution involves the following steps:

1. proxy delegation: this function requires a delegation identifier. We're using the generated UUID, as the delegation identifier.
2. job registration using the created JDL file: this methods awaits two arguments. The delegation identifier and the JDL file. Using the already existing informations, we can register the job. However, this function call doesn't start the job yet.
3. input sandbox upload: the job registration returns a JobIdApi structure that contains the registered job's EGEE identifier. Using this identifier we have to query the proposed locations (URIs) of InputSandbox files on the WMS server. According to our experiments two URIs are returned: a GridFTP[17] one, and an HTTPS one. In the bridge, we're using the GridFTP URI to upload the wrapper script and the input archive using the GridFTP C API.
4. job starting: once the input sandbox has been uploaded, we can trigger the job start function using the jobStart function and the EGEE identifier.

5. job progress watch: the submitted job's status is periodically (every 5 minutes) polled from the logging and bookkeeping service. We report every status information, but assume the job has been finished only when it enters some terminal status: aborted or finished with success.
6. job results download: this functionality is very similar to the input sandbox upload. We query the job's output sandbox URIs from the WMS server, and fetch every produced output file (an output archive, in our case) using the GridFTP C API.
7. purging the job: this is the final step of a job's life cycle. Once every result has been obtained, we have to call the `jobPurge` function using the job's identifier. This function call frees every allocated space related to the job on the WMS server.

4 Performance measurements

There are some aspects of performance question when considering the implemented bridge. First, it is an important question what the performance requirements of the bridge implementation are. Second, we would like to see if the bridge is really able to perform as machine with n processors. Finally, it is a question how heavy the implementation uses the EGEE services. All the tests have been performed processing workunits of SZTAKI Desktop Grid (SZDG)[18] on the SEE-GRID[19] and VOCE[20] virtual organizations of EGEE.

We can state, that the performance requirements of the bridge implementation are very low. According to our measurements, managing the life cycle of a single workunit requires at most one second of CPU time on a 1,8 GHz AMD Opteron 2210 processor.

Regarding the computing performance of the bridge, we have set up the following test scenario: a machine with two processors processing SZDG workunits on both CPUs, and a bridge installation capable of processing 20 workunits in parallel. Ideally the performance of the bridge is expected to have about 10 times the performance of the desktop machine. Initially the average credit granted to the two 'machines' was identical, however the bridge has processed far more workunits than the desktop machine. We explain this with the redundant computing of BOINC: although the bridge processes a lot of workunits, the same workunits are also sent to normal machines where these workunits are placed in queues, thus a canonical result will be created later. After a few days, the performance of the bridge started to grow, and after a week's operation, the average granted credit rates have become the following: about 100 credits for the desktop machine, and about 800 credits for the bridge, i.e. on longer terms the bridge has 8 times the performance of the desktop machine, which is lower than the expected 10 times speed-up. The lower performance can be explained with the overhead of EGEE and with the lower performance of worker nodes in the selected VOs. The reliability of the final bridge prototype is above 99%, only 6 out of about 750 workunits have finished with failures.

On EGEE hand, we have faced some major problems during the development of the bridge. First, in order to make the bridge stable almost every function using EGEE services has to be executed in a loop, trying to call the function at most 3 times for cases where an error might occur during the service calls. This extra functionality has done a lot to achieve the bridge stability mentioned at the end of the previous paragraph. Second, after some time the WMS refused to accept the jobs. After a discussion with the VO administrators, we received the explanation that the WMS has to be restarted periodically in order to make it stable. The restart period wasn't sufficient for the job submission rate the bridge created, so the restart period had to be set shorter (to 6 hours instead of 24 hours).

5 Future work and conclusions

Based on the experiences in section 4, we propose extending the bridge with a job queue. Entities in the job queue are already submitted jobs or jobs waiting for submission. In order to lower the usage of EGEE services, the bridge should periodically check if there are jobs that haven't been submitted, and submit the unsent jobs as parametric or collection jobs. Using this way the bridge won't overload the WMS server, thus the reliability of the bridge and the infrastructure used can be gained. Besides this, the CPU usage of the bridge can be lowered even more.

In the paper we have presented an approach for running desktop grid workunits on EGEE infrastructures. First, we have presented and compared existing solutions. Next we have shown the outlines of the prototype, as the starting point we choose the BOINC and Condor cluster integration created by SZTAKI. Here we have also presented in detail every step that has to be taken in order to run a workunit on EGEE. Finally, we have measured the performance of the created bridge and examined it in some aspects. According to our experiments, the performance of the bridge is close to our expectations, and the reliability of the solution is very good.

References

1. I. Foster, C. Kesselman: The Grid 2, 2nd Edition, ISBN: 978-1-55860-933-4, Morgan Kaufmann, 2003.
2. T. T. D. Thain and M. Livny. Condor and the grid. chapter 11. John-Wiley & Sons, Ltd., 2003.
3. I. Foster, C. Kesselman: The Globus Project: A Status Report, Proc. IPPS/SPDP '98 Heterogeneous Computing Workshop, pp. 4-18, 1998.
4. I. Foster: Globus Toolkit Version 4: Software for Service-Oriented Systems, IFIP International Conference on Network and Parallel Computing, Springer-Verlag LNCS 3779, pp 2-13, 2006.
5. The gLite webpage,
   http://glite.web.cern.ch/glite/
6. M.Ellert et al.: Advanced Resource Connector middleware for lightweight computational Grids, Future Generation Computer Systems 23 219-240, 2007.
7. A. Streit, D. Erwin, Th. Lippert, D. Mallmann, R. Menday, M. Rambadt, M. Riedel, M. Romberg, B. Schuller, and Ph. Wieder L. Grandinetti (Edt.): UNICORE - From Project Re-

sults to Production Grids, Grid Computing: The New Frontiers of High Performance Process-ing, Advances in Parallel Computing 14, Elsevier, 2005, pages 357-376

8. D. P. Anderson. Boinc: A system for public-resource computing and storage. In R. Buyya, editor, Fifth IEEE/ACM International Workshop on Grid Computing, pages 4-10, 2004.

9. F. Cappello, S. Djilali, G. Fedak, T. Herault, F. Magniette, V. Neri and O. Lodygensky: Com-puting on Large Scale Distributed Systems: XtremWeb Architecture, Programming Models, Security, Tests and Convergence with Grid FGCS Future Generation Computer Science, 2004.

10. The EDGeS project webpage,
    http://www.edges-grid.eu

11. Z. Balaton, G. Gombas, P. Kacsuk, A. Kornafeld, J. Kovacs, A. C. Marosi, G. Vida, N. Pod-horszki, T. Kiss: SZTAKI Desktop Grid: a Modular and Scalable Way of Building Large Computing Grids, Parallel and Distributed Processing Symposium, 2007. IPDPS 2007. IEEE International

12. O. Lodygensky, G. Fedak, V. Neri, F. Cappello, D. Thain and Miron Livny: XtremWeb and Condor : Sharing Resources between Internet Connected Condor Pools in Proceedings of the Workshop on Global and Peer-to-Peer Computing on Large Scale Distributed Systems colocated with IEEE/ACM CCGRID2003, Tokyo Japan, May 2003.

13. The LHC@home webpage,
    http://lhcathome.cern.ch/lhcathome/

14. Job Description Language (JDL) Attributes Specification,
    http://edms.cern.ch/document/590869/1

15. Workload Manager Proxy API C++,
    http://trinity.datamat.it/projects/EGEE/wiki/apidoc/3.1/htmlcpp/index.html

16. DCE 1.1: Remote Procedure Call, Open Group Technical Standard, Document Number C706 August 1997 737 pages, http://www.opengroup.org/publications/catalog/c706.htm

17. GridFTP Protocol Specification (Global Grid Forum Recommendation GFD.20). W. Allcock, editor. March 2003.

18. SZTAKI Desktop Grid webpage,
    http://szdg.lpds.sztaki.hu/szdg/

19. The SEE-GRID VO webpage,
    http://www.see-grid.eu/

20. The VOCE VO webpage,
    http://egee.cesnet.cz/en/voce/

Integrating Condor Desktop Clusters with Grid

Konstantinos Georgakopoulos and Konstantinos Margaritis

Abstract Grid infrastructures today are expanding slowly because adding computing resources is sometimes an expensive and bureaucratic procedure. In contrast, desktop grid technologies like Condor and B.O.I.N.C provide an easy and inexpensive way of creating large distributed systems that provide their idle computing time for job execution. We successfully tested the interconnection of a Condor pool with an EGEE site and we are in the process of expanding this infrastructure inside the University. We will also investigate the possible security, reliability and connection issues as we envision the expansion of this infrastructure to other remote computing resources like school computer labs.

Keywords: Desktop Grids, Condor, EGEE, Interconnection, B.O.I.N.C

1 Introduction

The majority of today's production grid infrastructures use a organization and computing model that is based highly on hierarchy, security, dedication of resources (both computing and human) and continuous availability of systems involved. Furthermore, the expansion of the current infrastructure is slow because computing resources that are accepted as part of the grid are mainly expensive dedicated clusters that meet some very specific criteria.

Other grid-like models, like the ones of Condor [10] and B.O.I.N.C [1], try to harness the idle computing time of non-dedicated resources like personal desktop computers and computer labs of academic organizations or even schools. These models can provide an inexpensive mass computing power that would otherwise be wasted. With the constant evolution of these technologies countries can now capitalize on the use of their national computing infrastructures by adding them to the grid.

In the following sections we outline the basics of a typical Grid infrastructure and also the fundamental components of the Condor system. We then present the

Konstantinos Georgakopoulos and Konstantinos Margaritis

Department Of Applied Informatics, University Of Macedonia, Egnatias 156, Thessaloniki, Greece, e-mail: kgeorga@uom.gr, kmarg@uom.gr technical specifications of the Grid-to-Condor interconnection followed by references to similar attempts like the Live WN project [5, 8] and the Lattice project [7, 9]. Our testbed for this research was a Condor pool we set up and the gLite Pre-Production site we administer as part of the EGEE [4] project. We finally present our future plans in expanding this infrastructure and give some conclusions regarding this research.

2 General characteristics of Grid systems

A typical Grid infrastructure comprises of some basic components each of them has a very specific function to execute. Taking as an example a typical gLite infrastructure these basic components are [3]:

A **Computing Element (CE)** which is basically a collection of computing resources at each site. A Computing Element includes a **Grid Gate (GG)** which is the interface of the cluster to the outside world and a number of **Worker Nodes (WN)** where the jobs actually run. The CE contains a number of queues to differentiate some property of the job (e.g VO, job length, RAM required etc.).

A **Workload Management System (WMS)** which is responsible for accepting jobs from users and then assign them to the most appropriate CE for execution. The process of choosing an appropriate CE for the job is based on user requirements, locality of files and Computing Element load.

A **User Interface (UI)** which is the system where users log in, create a GSI proxy certificate for authentication and submit their jobs to the WMS. Jobs are created using a language known as **Job Description Language (JDL)**.

When a user submits a job to a WMS the job is transferred to the WMS and the match making process occurs. The job is then submitted to the appropriate CE along with a wrapper script and the input files of the job are transferred to the WMS for retrieval by the CE. When the job completes the output files are transferred from the CE to the WMS for retrieval by the user.

3 The Condor system

Condor is a high throughput system which has a similar architecture with the Grid but it is focused on the efficient use of all available resources. Furthermore, Condor has the ability of exploiting the idle time of non-dedicated computing resources and also to manage resources that are added or removed dynamically. A typical Condor cluster, or "pool", has some basic components [10]:

A **Submit Node** which is the system where users log in and submit their jobs. Condor provides its own job description language for job submission.

A number of **Execute Nodes** where the jobs finally run. The execute nodes publish their characteristics to the pool so the user's job requirements will be met through a match making process that will take place.

A **Central Manager** which is the system responsible for accepting jobs and finding the appropriate execute node for the job to run. The mechanism used by Condor for matchmaking is known as ClassAds.

Another interesting key point is that new Execute Nodes can be added on the fly because Condor, by default, manages the addition of new resources with an access list based policy. Condor also doesn't require dedication of resources. The provider of Execute Nodes (e.g a university) can configure the nodes to provide computing cycles only when the processor is idle or, for example, when the average system load is below some specific threshold.

4 Bridging Condor with gLite

The idea of expanding a Grid infrastructure using Condor is based on the fact that LCG and gLite middleware can support Condor as a batch system although this is not widely used. The process of connecting a Grid site with a Condor pool is not a straight-forward process and the existing documentation is very limited and incomplete. We based our initial steps on the documentation found on the related CERN wiki [7] although further testing and configuration tweaking was necessary to make the connection actually work. To test this interconnection we used our gLite pre-production grid site we administer as part of the EGEE project.

4.1 Initial Setup

We began by setting up an autonomous Condor pool with four systems (a central manager/submit node and three execute nodes). We then created a testing application that would be used for submitting a large number of distributed jobs. The application was essentially a brute force attack on a MD5 string which was appropriately parameterized so it could be divided into autonomous sub-jobs. We tested the pool using this application and we were focused mainly on the reliability that Condor provides for running jobs. For example we simulated conditions when an Execute Node was suddenly removed from the pool (e.g by removing the network cable) and examined how Condor rescheduled the job to another node. We also tested Condor's checkpointing features with similar experiments. The results showed that Condor handles very well this type of situations and jobs will not be lost under any conditions.

4.2 Creating the Bridge

After testing the Condor pool we proceeded by configuring the LCG CE of our pre-production site to use Condor as a batch system. This change was made in the main configuration file of LCG (site-info.def) in which we also created two condor queues for the appropriate VO's (dteam and ops). These queues act as a gateway and when the job is submitted to the CE it will be forwarded to the Central Manager for final execution. We also changed configuration files mainly in the information system so that the Condor queues are published correctly. One final change was in the middleware component which is responsible for translating a JDL job to a Condor job before submitting it.

For this bridge to work the LCG CE had to be configured as a Submit Node for the Condor pool. So it was necessary to install the Condor software on the CE and make the appropriate changes to the pool policy so that the CE could submit jobs to the Central Manager.

After completing this interconnection the job flow follows the following steps:
- The user logs in to the User Interface of a Grid site and creates a proxy certificate for authentication. He then submits a job in the JDL format to the CE.
- The job is transferred to the WMS and it is forwarded to CE along with a wrapper script.
- The CE translates the job from the JDL format to the Condor job language and forwards it to the Central Manager via the Condor queues and the appropriate Condor job submission command.
- The job arrives at the Central Manager where the matchmaking process occurs and the job is sent to the appropriate Execute Node.
- The Execute Node communicates with the WMS for file retrieval and then executes the job via the wrapper script produced by the WMS.

4.3 Final notes

We tested this infrastructure in the same way we originally tested the standalone Condor pool. Condor provides the same reliability features for jobs even when they are submitted through the Grid. One thing that must be pointed out is that job checkpointing doesn't seem to work for jobs submitted through the Grid and this is caused by the wrapper script provided by the WMS. Changing this script so it complies with the Condor requirements can be a possible solution to this problem.

Regarding security, Condor provides various ways of securing the pool regarding who is allowed to submit jobs the pool and also provides many mechanisms for user authentication. It also supports authentication via the x509 certificates that are used in the GSI infrastructure of the Grid. The proxy certificate that is created by the user on the UI gets forwarded to Execute Node so that proper authentication can be made with the WMS. Condor can also provide encryption in every daemon-to-daemon communication so that certificates won't be intercepted by malicious users.

One important note is that by expanding the Grid with volunteered resources we provide access to the job and the job data to users that are potentially malicious. Traditionally Grid resources are trusted because they reside inside a computer room and are controlled by system administrators. Volunteered resources are not controlled by anyone except the user that provides them. It is clear that this issue must be addressed either in the form of screening the resources added or by some form of job protection on the Execute Node.

5 Related projects

The field of desktop grids is relatively new and new projects emerge that attempt to provide a bridge to volunteer resources for the Grid.

The Live Worker Node project [5, 8] has created a live cd/dvd linux distribution that can transform any computer to a worker node for the Grid. The project was created by a number of researchers at the National Technological University of Athens and it is still being developed and tested. The project is fully compatible with the existing EGEE infrastructure but still requires a central Computing Element for nodes to attach. Furthermore the number of nodes that can attach to the CE is fixed and cannot exceed a predefined number.

The Lattice project [7, 9] was started at the University of Maryland and has created some GRAM components that can bridge a Globus/Grid infrastructure with a B.O.I.N.C infrastructure. Via the GRAM components, jobs that are submitted to Globus are translated to B.O.I.N.C work units and are executed on a B.O.I.N.C project. This is a very interesting attempt and is still under development but lacks further documentation for actually installing and using these components.

A very promising attempt is starting with the EDGeS project [2] which will create a bridge for the EGEE resources to desktop grids created with B.O.I.N.C. The project will initially create the bridge so that B.O.I.N.C jobs can be forwarded to EGEE resources and later on will create the bridge components so that Grid jobs can be submitted to a B.O.I.N.C infrastructure.

6 Conclusions

Desktop grids can provide a solution so that countries can better exploit their already existing computing infrastructures rather then purchasing new expensive hardware every time the Grid infrastructure needs upgrading based on the current trends. Furthermore, by involving large user and academic communities we can create new social bonds and bring the science closer to the public.

Condor provides a reliable solution for creating large infrastructures of distributed computers that can potentially be added to the Grid. Our attempt is to further investigate the possibility of creating Condor pools with scattered resources and resolve the potential issues that arise from this expansion. Key points are security, reliability and ease of deployment in order to present a viable proof of concept.

We can envision a future for the grid where all of these emerging technologies (gLite, Condor, B.O.I.N.C, etc) will be incorporated into a single infrastructure. Since the initial basic issues in the development of the Grid (establishing a stable infrastructure, developing the middleware) are now resolved for the most part a new social and technical challenge arises: Can the grid community embrace and exploit these alternative solutions? It is possible that a new model for the Grid is needed, one that will be less bureaucratic and more efficient.

References

1. Anderson, D. P., 2004. B.O.I.N.C. A system for public resource computing and storage. *In proceedings of the 5th IEEE/ACM International Workshop on Grid Computing, 2004, Pittsburgh, U.S.A*
2. Balaton, Z., Farkas, Z., Kacsuk, P., Kelley, I., Taylor, I. and Kiss, T., 2008. EDGeS: The Common Boundary Between Service and Desktop Grids. *In Proceedings of the CoreGrid Integration Workshop, 2-4 April 2008, Crete, Greece*
3. Burke, S., Campana, S., Lorenzo, M.P., Nater, C., Santinelli, R., Sciaba, A.: Glite 3.1 User Guide (2008). https://edms.cern.ch/document/722398/ . Cited 07 Mar 2008
4. EGEE II project homepage. Enabling Grids for E-sciencE. http://www.eu-egee.org/. Cited 10 Dec 2007
5. Gorgatos, F., Kouretis, G., 2007. LiveWN: CPU scavenging in the Grid Era. *In: Proceedings of the 3rd EELA Conference, 3-5 December 2007, Catania, Italy*
6. Installation Instructions for Condor on the LCG CE https://twiki.cern.ch/twiki/bin/view/EGEE/InstallationInstructionsForCondorOnTheLcg-CE . Cited 15 Oct 2007
7. Lattice project homepage. http://lattice.umiacs.umd.edu/ . Cited 15 Oct 2007
8. Live Worker Node project homepage. Add Computational Resources to the Grid. http://gridathome.sourceforge.net/index.php?page=news. Cited 20 Oct 2007
9. Myers, D. S., A. L. Bazinet and M. P. Cummings. 2008. Expanding the reach of Grid computing: combining Globus- and BOINC-based systems. Pages 71-85. In E.-G. and A. Zomaya (Eds.) *Grids for Bioinformatics and Computational Biology, Wiley Book Series on Parallel and Distributed Computing.* John Wiley & Sons, New York.
10. Tannenbaum, T., Wright, D., Miller, K. and Livny, M., "Condor - A Distributed Job Scheduler", in Thomas Sterling, editor, *Beowulf Cluster Computing with Linux*, The MIT Press, 2002. ISBN: 0-262-69274-0

Prediction of the Jobs Execution on the Community Grid with Added Network Latency

Jakub Jurkiewicz, Krzysztof Nowiński, Piotr Bała

Abstract In this paper we investigate behaviour of the grid system built of large number of relatively unreliable processing units (CPUs). In order to simulate realistic grid different mean times before failure (MTBF) are assumed for different nodes. In addition, a simplified network model is included. We present results of simulations on a model of such grid system and analyse its efficiency in terms of total execution time of simple jobs.

1 Introduction

The majority of grid models, such as Network Weather Service [9] or GridSim [4] and task schedulers for grids, are based on the assumption of limited number of reliable computing nodes connected with high bandwidth network and focus on large task scheduling in non-trivial workflows. Community grids based e.g. on SETI@HOME [10] or BOINC [2] packaged are characterised by:

1. relative abundance of computing nodes
2. unreliability of nodes causing usually complete loss of current computation results
3. limitation of network performance varying with the current network traffic regardless of the grid.

Jakub Jurkiewicz
Interdisciplinary Center for Mathematical and Computational Modelling (ICM), University of Warsaw (UW), Pawińskiego 5a, 02-106 Warsaw, Poland, e-mail: kura@icm.edu.pl
Faculty of Mathematics, Informatics and Mechanics, University of Warsaw

Krzysztof Nowiński
ICM UW, e-mail: know@icm.edu.pl

Piotr Bała
ICM UW, e-mail: bala@icm.edu.pl
Faculty of Mathematics and Computer Science, Nicolaus Copernicus University, Toruń, Poland

These limitations reduce usually job model to a series of trivially parallel tasks scheduled to the computing nodes. The paper proposes a model of a community grid developed for the purpose of experimenting with various task scheduling strategies, taking into the above listed peculiarities of such grids.

2 Computational grid model

In this paper we focus on the grid built from a large number of unreliable units connected to the supervisor server responsible for dividing job into individual tasks, sending them to individual processing units and merging the results.

All computational units (nodes) are nearly identical, in respect of computational speed and capacity. The nodes are vulnerable to failures. For purposes of our model we assume a two peak distribution of MTBFs of nodes with peaks at $2/3$ and $4/3$ of global average MTBF. We assume a fixed probability of failure for each node leading to exponential distribution of uptimes of this node (see [7]).

Network is built from seven rings of limited bandwidth, connected by (practically) infinite speed ring. Every node communicates only with the server. The network is simultaneously used by other users (independent from the grid). Grid data transfers have lower priority than other transfers, leading to a simple model of varying latency and bandwidth of the network links. We assume that connection between a computational unit and a ring is the fastest ADSL (8 Mb/s). Server is connected directly to the ring. Simulations are made for three types of rings: high speed rings constant of 10 Gb/s, ATM ring of 150 Mb/s with constant usage of 12 Mb/s, and ATM ring with usage taken from time series built on the real data basis with average 12 Mb/s.

Network and time series
Recent works [6] [1] showed that properly built time series can effectively predict network traffic. However, most of the simulations were made for short term predictions and small steps between measures. In our simulations we use tasks that need at least 80 seconds for transfer before and after computations. Latency is usually 10-20 ms for wide area networks - thus it can be neglected. We assume that the network bandwidth is constant for 360 seconds and we take this as network step resolution for our simulation. When we tested a real network, we found that SARIMA model [3] $(1,0,1) \times (0,1,1)_{240} \times (0,1,1)_{1680}$ fits best to the real data. Seasons' lengths of 240 and 1680 represent daily and weekly cycles. We use for every ring,as history, real data of point-to-point Internet traffic and during simulation we generate data substituting, in algorithm for time series prediction with white noise generated from normal distribution.

Task scheduling
In the model described here the job consists of independent tasks executed on different nodes. Traditional approach to the scheduling assumes that number of tasks

is significantly larger than number of available nodes and a queue scheduler focuses on the choosing of tasks to be executed.

Because in large grid infrastructures the number of nodes could be significantly larger than the number of tasks, the scheduling should focus on picking up the best processing elements for the execution. In the case of unreliable nodes a bad scheduler can assign tasks to the processing elements which will always go down before task is finished and will take infinitely long time to complete. If tasks are scheduled randomly we can expect that only part of them will be lost and the job will be finished in a reasonable time.

Below we will consider various scheduling strategies: random, higher MTBF first, backup scheduling.

- **Random strategy** - the simplest possible method is to schedule a job to a node randomly drawn from free nodes pool. It is important to simulate this baseline for comparison. Any scheduler worse than the random one shouldn't be used.
- **High MTBF first** - because computers uptimes are taken from exponential distribution it is reasonable to approximate uptime left by MTBF. This leads to a scheduler assigning a job to a free node with the highest MTBF.
- **Backup scheduling** - means assigning a task to more than one node at a time. It is the best strategy for the scheduling in system with infinite network speed, as in Fig. 1. However, the simulation showed that such strategy is useless for systems with limited network.

Network aware scheduler

Network aware scheduler is created from a scheduler by adding a rule prohibiting task from execution on a node, when: $S_{hr} < n_{tot} \times S_{ep}$ and $D \times n_{tot}/S_{hr} < t_{je} + D/S_{ep}$, where D is a sum of sizes of data that need to be transferred before and after every task, S_{hr} is current bandwidth of ring to which the hub is connected, t_{je} is time of task execution (without transfers) and S_{ep} is bandwidth of ring node connection, n_{tot} is number of nodes processing tasks (including transfer).

Since this simplified network awareness algorithm did not increase the grid performance, we added additional condition prohibiting scheduling job to node if estimated total completion time T is smaller than MTBF: $T = t_{je} + t_{tr} < MTBF$, where t_{tr} is time needed for transfer of data. If we assume that data needed to transfer is identical for all nodes, then:

$$\frac{n_{tr}}{n_{tot}} = \frac{t_{tr}}{t_{tr} + \overline{t_{je}}} \tag{1}$$

$$t_{tr} = D \times \frac{n_{tr}}{S_{hr}} \tag{2}$$

where $\overline{t_{je}}$ is average computation time and n_{tr} is number of nodes that are making transfer of data. These equations are true only provided that hub ring is at least in 100% used. After substituting t_{tr} in (1), calculating n_{tr} and then substituting in (2), we arrive at:

$$t_{je} + \frac{D}{S_{hr}} \times (n_{tot} - \frac{\overline{t_{je}} \times S_{hr}}{D}) = t_{je} + t_{tr} < MTBF \tag{3}$$

3 Simulations

Simulation parameters

The schedulers have been tested on computations that are one week long. We assume that during 5 hours on Monday morning there are no submission events and, therefore, we can treat such time as a catch-up fine for our queue system.

We tested schedulers on a system consisting of different number of computers (from 100 to 700) and one server. Using historical data from ICM cluster, we generated job submission for one week period. Each simulation contained 713 jobs, each job consisted of 64 equal tasks involving computations lasting from 900 to 2700 second. Every task needs to send 80 MB of data to node before computations and send back 80 MB after they are finished. We have tested average MTBF of 2700 seconds. Every simulation was repeated four times to minimise random variations.

Measures

We used two measures number of unfinished jobs at the end of simulation, and average time (applied only for finished jobs), that takes from submitting a job to the system to getting the results.

Simulation results

Results of simulation for the system with infinite speed network are presented in Fig. 1 and Fig. 2.

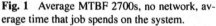

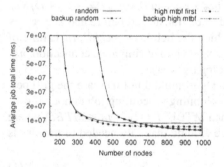
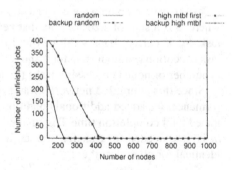

Fig. 1 Average MTBF 2700s, no network, average time that job spends on the system.

Fig. 2 Number of unfinished jobs for average MTBF 2700s, no network.

Results show that double schedulers, trying to finish the job as soon as possible are better in case of a big number of computational nodes, and they are worse on small grids. Moreover, as expected, choosing computer with higher MTBF first is good strategy.

When network efficiency is taken into account the results change significantly - see Fig. 3 and Fig. 4. Backup scheduler is not shown because it leads to unacceptable results.

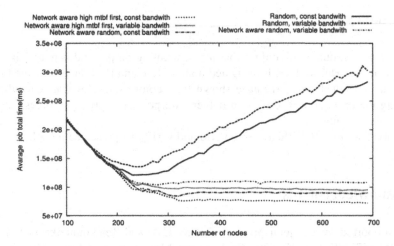

Fig. 3 Average MTBF 2700s, average time that job spends on the system.

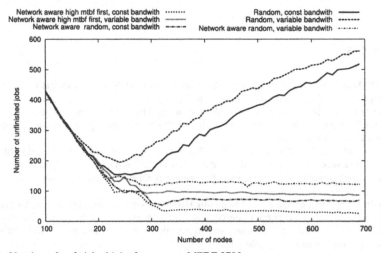

Fig. 4 Number of unfinished jobs for average MTBF 2700s.

The results are as follows:

- network aware scheduler combined with high mtbf first is the best strategy,
- schedulers that don't care about network become worse with a raising number of computing nodes,
- usually job submissions are correlated with available network bandwidth - therefore network with constant bandwidth shouldn't be used for simulation purposes, because it overestimates grid performance.

4 Summary

The presented simulations confirm that job scheduling on the grid is not trivial. In the presented model we have investigated node failure and its influence on the total execution time of the job. We have shown that, contrary to classical scheduling, retarding the execution of jobs, even if there are potentially free resources, could lead to better results.

In future we plan to build a desktop grid and verify the presented model.

5 Acknowledgements

Work supported by the joint project of ICM UW and Telekomunikacja Polska S.A 22/06/6727/K/2006/YCZ268 Grid System Monitoring and Control Tools under grant FSO 023/2006.

References

1. Basu S, Mukherjee A, Kilvansky S (1996). Time series models for Internet traffic, Technical Report GIT-CC-95-27, Georgia Institute of Technology.
2. Berkeley Open Infrastructure for Network Computing. http://boinc.berkeley.edu/.
3. Box GEP, Jenkins, GM, (1976). Time series analysis: Forecasting and control, , 2nd ed., Holden Day, San Francisco.
4. Buyya R, Murshed M (2002). GridSim: A Toolkit for the Modeling and Simulation of Distributed Resource Management and Scheduling for Grid Computing. In: The Journal of Concurrency and Computation: Practice and Experience (CCPE), Volume 14, Issue 13-15, Wiley Press.
5. SungJin Choi, MaengSoon Baik, ChongSun Hwang, JoonMin Gil, HeonChang Yu (2004). Volunteer availability based fault tolerant scheduling mechanism in desktop grid computing environment. In: Network Computing and Applications, 2004. Proceedings. Third IEEE International Symposium..., (pp. 366– 371)
6. Groschwitz N, Polyzos G (1994). A time series model of long-term traffic on the NSFNET backbone. In: Proceedings of the IEEE International Conference on Communications, ICC' 94.
7. Nurmi D, Brevik J, Wolski R (2003). Modeling machine availability in enterprise and wide-area distributed computing environments. Technical Report CS2003-28, U.C. Santa Barbara Computer Science Department.
8. Press WH, Teukolsky SA, Vetterling WT, Flannery BP. (1992). Numerical Recipes in C: The Art of Scientific Computing , 2nd edition, Cambridge Univ. Press, N.Y.
9. Wolski R, Spring N, Hayes J (1999). The Network Weather Service: A Distributed Resource Performance Forecasting Service for Metacomputing. In: Journal of Future Generation Computing Systems, Volume 15, Numbers 5-6, (pp. 757–768).
10. Seti@HOME project website. http://setiathome.berkeley.edu/

II
GRID APPLICATIONS

The Porting of a Medical Grid Application from Globus 4 to the gLite Middleware

Károly Bósa and Wolfgang Schreiner

Abstract In this paper, we compare two implementations of a grid-based software system on the grid middleware Globus Toolkit 4 and gLite, respectively. This system called "Grid-Enabled SEE++" is a grid-based simulation software that supports the diagnosis and treatment of certain eye motility disorders (strabismus). First, we developed a parallel version of the software with the help of Globus 4. Since we met with some limitations of Globus 4, we also designed and developed a version of SEE++ based on gLite. We focus on the differences between the initial Globus version and the gLite version of our software system and report on some comparative benchmark results.

Key words: "Grid-Enabled SEE++", Grid Applications, Grid Middleware, Globus, gLite

1 Introduction

Nowadays various types of grid middleware (Unicore, Globus, LCG, gLite, etc.) are in use by several research projects. These systems have many similar features, but there are almost no reports in literature which compare them next to each other in similar circumstances. We had the opportunity to make such a comparison, since we developed two versions of a grid application on the basis of the popular grid middleware systems Globus Toolkit 4 [9] and gLite [8], respectively.

Károly Bósa
Research Institute for Symbolic Computation (RISC),
e-mail: Karoly.Bosa@risc.uni-linz.ac.at

Wolfgang Schreiner
Research Institute for Symbolic Computation (RISC),
e-mail: Wolfgang.Schreiner@risc.uni-linz.ac.at

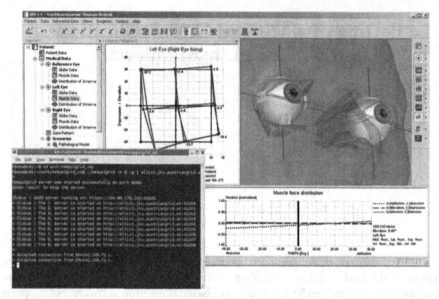

Fig. 1 The Output of the "SEE++ to Grid Bridge" and the GUI of SEE++ Software System

The core software called "Grid-Enabled SEE++" is a grid version of the SEE++ software system [6, 12, 16] for the biomechanical 3D simulation of the human eye and its muscles (see Figure 1). The software deals with the support of diagnosis and treatment of *strabismus*, which is the common name of the misalignment of the eyes where eyes point in different directions such that a person may see double images. The goal of "Grid-Enabled SEE++" is to adapt and to extend SEE++ in several steps and to develop an efficient grid-based tool for "Evidence Based Medicine" which supports the surgeons in choosing optimal surgery techniques for the treatments of different syndromes of strabismus.

The doctors intend to work with the software in an interactive manner (changing the eye model parameters by a manual trial and error method), hence the adequate response times are essential for the usability of SEE++. It is also possible to semi-automatize the determination of the patient pathology on the grid (a non-linear optimization problem) by the procedure called *pathology fitting* [3].

In [3, 4], we combined the SEE++ software with the Globus middleware applying both the *pre-Web Service* (pre-WS) and the *Web Service* (WS) frameworks and developed a parallel version of the simulation. By this, we speeded up this simulation by a factor of 14–17.

Furthermore, we reported the prototype implementation of a medical database component for "Grid-Enabled SEE++" [13], which is going to be used for storing patient medical data with eye model parameters. These stored pathological cases will be utilized as initial estimations by the new grid-based pathology fitting algorithm presented in [3].

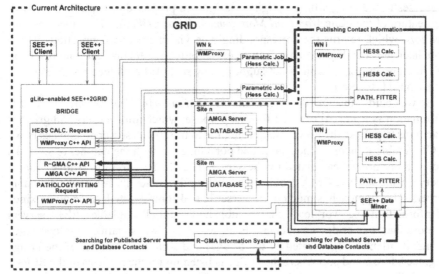

Fig. 2 The Design of the gLite Compatible SEE++

Since we met with some limitation of the Globus Toolkit 4 [4], we also elaborated an initial design of a SEE++ version compatible with the gLite grid middleware [5] in the frame of *"Enabling Grids for E-sciencE 2" (EGEE2)* project [7].

The topic of this paper is to present a refined architecture adapted to the recently implemented gLite-based SEE++ and to report a comparison between this new version of our software system and its other version based on Globus 4. The new design is described in Section 2. In Section 3, we focus on the new features of the gLite compatible SEE++. Finally, we present in Section 4 an experimental comparison with benchmark results between the Globus and the gLite-based versions.

2 The New Architecture based on gLite

As in the case of the Globus-based version, the initial component of the gLite-based version is the "SEE++ to Grid Bridge", via which the unchanged SEE++ client can get access to the infrastructure of the grid (see the box in Figure 2 bordered by the dashed line). Before the bridge accepts the computational requests from the SEE++ clients, it starts some grid-enabled SEE++ servers in the grid. These processes behave as some kind of "executer" programs for the computation tasks such that the remarkable latencies of the job submissions for the computational requests can be avoided. The "SEE++ to Grid Bridge" is able to split calculation requests of clients into subtasks [3] and to distribute them among the servers (data parallelism).

Nevertheless, we found the same problem as in the Globus version of our software, namely how to send back the contact information of the started server/executer processes to the bridge. In the original design, we proposed to exploit an interesting feature of the gLite *Workload Management System (WMS)* [17] called *interactive jobs* which returns the corresponding data via interactive connections. However later we found that such a feature exists only as a theoretical option for job submissions in gLite, but it is not supported by real grid architectures (EGEE [7], int.EU.grid [10], etc.).

So we decided to apply the *"Relational Grid Monitoring Architecture" (R-GMA)* information system [14] of gLite for this purpose, which allows users and grid applications to publish their own data. From time to time, each server announces into a R-GMA table its address (hostname and port) together with the number of subtasks received but not yet calculated by the server. The "SEE++ to Grid Bridge" runs a query on the table R-GMA regularly as well and updates its list of the available servers. This approach is much more versatile and sophisticated, since many kinds of information (e.g. workload) can be published about all available SEE++ servers to more than one bridge component. Each server is always started with two arguments: its identifier (generated by the bridge) and a unique identifier of the bridge (e.g. the address and port where the bridge is listening for the requests of the SEE++ clients). These two pieces of data are used as a primary key in the R-GMA system, when a server publishes its own contact and workload information.

Every "SEE++ to Grid Bridge" can be tuned such that it either uses only those servers that were started by itself or it always chooses for each calculation request some servers from the pool of all servers available on the grid; this choice is made with the help of R-GMA on the basis of the published workload information. A server terminates, if it does not receive any computational request for a predefined time interval (typically one hour).

The approach to apply executer jobs works only if the *worker nodes (WNs)* on where these jobs are executed are not located within private subnetworks. To enforce this constraint, we applied the following *Requirement* condition in the JDL [11] file of the job submission:

```
Requirements = other.GlueHostNetworkAdapterOutboundIP==True;
```

This constraint guarantees that the SEE++ servers are started only on those WNs, that are able to interact through the Internet. We also applied a *Rank* criterion, that helps to choose WNs from those which fulfill the Requirement:

```
Rank = (other.GlueCEStateWaitingJobs == 0 ?
               -other.GlueCEStateEstimatedResponseTime :
               -other.GlueCEStateWaitingJobs);
```

According to this criterion, those WNs are preferred which either are idle (there is not any scheduled job in the state "WAITING") and have minimal communication latencies or (if there are not enough idle WNs) which have the minimal number of waiting jobs.

The further parts of the design regarding a distributed medical database based on the database access service of gLite called *AMGA* [2] and the grid-based pathology fitting algorithm (depicted on Figure 2) remain as they have already been proposed in [4].

SEE++ Versions / Features	Globus–Based SEE++ Version	gLite–Based SEE++ Version
Computations are performed	by server jobs	by server jobs
SEE++ clients interact with the server jobs	via a bridge component	via a bridge component
The communication protocol between the software components	SOAP	SOAP
Server jobs are submitted on the grid	one by one as single jobs	as a special collection of jobs (parametric job)
Server jobs return their contact information	by a "forked" and terminated instance of each job	via R–GMA tables
Resource discovery	not implemented	automatic (part of the job submission framework)
Proxy renewal for long–running jobs	not implemented	automatic (part of the job submission framework)
"File stage on"	no (Servers must be preinstalled on the corresponding grid nodes)	yes (the executables of the servers are sent to the WNs by the job submission framework)
Platform dependency	on every UNIX/Linux based platform where Globus runs	only on x86 platforms with Scientific Linux (dependency of the existing gLite versions)

Fig. 3 A Comparison between the Two Versions of "Grid-Enabled SEE++"

3 New Features of the gLite-Based Version

In Figure 3, we summarized and compared the essential features of the versions of our "Grid-Enabled SEE++" software system based on Globus Toolkit and gLite respectively.

An advantage of the application of gLite is the implicit and automatic support for resource discovery, which is part of the job submission framework i.e. hidden from the API and UI levels. In Globus, if the developers would like to provide their software with this property, they have to implement it on their own by using of a non-trivial API (which we did not apply in our Globus-based SEE++).

One of the essential distinctions between the Globus and gLite-based SEE++ is how the server contact information is returned to the bridge component. In Globus, we applied some kind of "hack" for overcoming this problem. According to this, a server started on a grid node forks itself after it has allocated a port number and terminates [3]. Unfortunately, this technique may induce some problems in the local resource management systems (e.g. PBS). Namely, such a local scheduler may assume the resource is free and may assign some other jobs to it or it may kill the forked process (in order to clean up). Although we could handle these situations in the case of some local batch queueing systems by applying some simple techniques described in [4], we could not find a general solution. By employing the new publishing method based on R-GMA, such a problem cannot arise at all (moreover there exists additional benefits as discussed in Section 2).

We employed user proxy certificates stored on a *MyProxy* [15] server, since the SEE++ servers have to be authenticated (by a valid proxy available on a MyProxy server) for accessing the R-GMA grid service from remote WNs. As a side effect of this requirement, our application is equipped with the automatic proxy renewal function: the long-running SEE++ servers are not killed on the WNs by the local resource management after the proxy of their user/submitter expires as long as the proxy credential can be renewed from a given MyProxy server.

The SEE++ server jobs are executed on the gLite architecture as *parametric jobs* via the *Workload Management Proxy (WMProxy)* [17]. A parametric job is a special type of job collections and it is defined as a set of jobs which are identical apart from the values of their parameters. On the one hand, this speeds up the job submission time compared to individual jobs and it saves a lot of processing time by reusing the same authentication for all the jobs in the collection; on the other hand, it is possible to monitor and control each of its jobs separately (via the parametric job handle). At the submission of a parametric job, the JDL file is usually supplemented some additional lines as follows:

```
[
...
JobType="Parametric";
...
Arguments = "_PARAM_ bridge-URL:port";
...
StdError = "stderr_PARAM_.log";
OutputSandbox = {"stderr_PARAM_.log"
...
Parameters = numberOfServerJobs;
ParameterStart = 0;
ParameterStep = 1;
...
]
```

The JDL file for a parametric job may contain a built-in variable called _PARAM_ and three additional specific attributes *Parameters*, *ParameterStart* and *ParameterStep*. These attributes represent respectively the maximum value (or in case of non-numeric parameter the set of values) of, the starting value of and at last but not least the step for the modification for the (numeric) values of the parametric variable _PARAM_. In our case, the variable _PARAM_, which has a different value for each single SEE++ server job is employed to determine the identifier of a SEE++ server (see the first argument in the line of JDL attribute *Arguments* above). Additionally, we also assign a log file with a unique name (generated with help of the parametric variable) to the standard error of each server job; these files will be collected if the executions of the server jobs are over (see the JDL attributes *StdError* and *OutputSandbox* above).

To avoid the pre-installation of the SEE++ servers on the grid, we exploit the "file stage on" feature of the WMProxy to transfer the executable and some other input files to the corresponding WNs in the job submission phase.

Summarizing this section, our gLite compatible SEE++ has some new features, which we achieved with investing relatively few efforts. To extend the Globus-based version with these properties is either not feasible or it requires much more time and human resources.

4 Experimental Comparison

The basis for this experimental comparison is the simulation of a typical medical examination called *Hess-Lancaster test*, whose parallel gridified implementation can represent a wide group of grid applications, see Section 4.1. In Section 4.2, we present the outcome of some benchmarks performed with this mentioned medical simulation.

4.1 A Medical Simulation as the Basis of the Comparison

In [3], we combined the SEE++ software with the Globus middleware [9] and developed a parallel version of the simulation of the Hess-Lancaster test. Now, we reimplemented this parallel simulation in gLite, too.

From the Hess-Lancaster test the reason for the pathological situation of a patient can be estimated. The outcome of such an examination consists of two *gaze patterns* of blue points and of red points respectively (see the diagram in the middle of the GUI of SEE++ on Figure 1). The blue points represent the image seen by one eye and the red points the image seen by the simulated other eye; in a pathological situation there is a deviation between the blue and the red points.

The default gaze pattern that is calculated from the patient's eye data by SEE++ comprises 9 points. Bigger gaze patterns with 21 and 45 points are possible and provide more precise results for the decision support in case of some pathologies, but their calculations are more time consuming. The size of the gaze pattern determines the size of the problem, too. The maximum number of grid jobs we used in a session was 45, because gaze patterns used in medical examinations can consist of at most

Number of SEE++ Server Jobs	1	3	9	25	30	45
Submission via Globus pre−WS architecture	0,85s	0,92s	0,98s	1,06s	1,09s	1,15s
Submission via Globus WS architecture	9,5s	10s	11s	15s	16s	20s
Submission via WMProxy (gLite) including Resource Discovery, File Staging (2Mb) and Publishing Contact Information via R−GMA	38s	46s	91s	142s	156s	224s

Fig. 4 Startup Times in Globus and in gLite Versions

45 gaze points (in the case of the application of 45 jobs, only one gaze point was computed by one server job in a session).

Our experiences with the simulation of the Hess-Lancaster test on different middlewares can help and facilitate the work of many grid application developer research groups, because its implementation represents the following very frequently applied programming strategies of nowadays grid applications:

Parameter Study   Since the calculations of each gaze points is completely independent from each other, there is no communication among the server processes. Hence our simulation is a typical example for the *parameter study*, where the same algorithm is executed on several grid node but with different arguments.

Interactivity   "Grid-Enabled SEE++" has other important characteristics that are a distributed simulation backend connected to an interactive real-time user interface (the doctors change the eye parameters by a manual trial and error method and in turn they wait for the results of the simulation). These characteristics are present in many classical grid monitoring applications and additionally there are numerous research efforts for establishing interactive grid architectures [10].

4.2 Benchmarks

In some benchmarks, we have compared the effectiveness of the two versions of "Grid-Enabled SEE++". Figure 4 and Figure 5 depict the average execution time of 5 computations in different situations where 1, 3, 9, 25, 30 or 45 processors were used on the grid (one server process was started on each processor).

The reported measurements were accomplished on different hardware architectures in case of Globus and gLite respectively. The reason for this fact that we do not have access to any grid testbed, where both required grid middlewares are deployed and available on the same computational resources. Moreover we intended to investigate the behaviors and the applicabilities of our SEE++ versions on some real grid

Number of Jobs/Servers	1	3	9	25	30	45
Hess Test with Globus Compatible SEE++	27.18s	18.81s	9.11s	2.17s	2.10s	1.89s
Hess Test with gLite Compatible SEE++	39.48s	28.05s	16.87s	4.63s	4.21s	3.03s

Fig. 5 Execution Times in Globus and gLite

architectures (as described in detail below) providing *"production services"* instead of within ideal circumstances on an artificial grid testbed.

The test cases based on Globus 4 were executed on the Austrian Grid site altix1.jku.austriangrid.at, which contains 64 Intel Itanium processors (1.4GHz) and resides at the Johannes Kepler University (JKU) in Linz. The "SEE++ to Grid Bridge" and SEE++ clients were always executed at the RISC institute located in Hagenberg which has a one Gigabit/sec connection to the JKU. In case of 25 or more processors, we used some processes on the grid site altix1.uibk.ac.at in Innsbruck that comprises 16 CPUs of the same type.

The test cases based on gLite were performed on some clusters of the architecture of the *Int.EU.Grid* Project [10]. The server jobs were randomly disseminated among some clusters in Germany (122 CPUs), Poland (32 CPUs), Slovakia (32 CPUs) and Spain (20 CPUs). All of these CPUs are based on Intel x86 and x86-64 architectures, but their speed characteristics is unknown.

As a first step, we have compared the costs of the submissions of our SEE++ server processes via Globus pre-WS and WS architectures and gLite WMProxy, see Figure 4. We found it quite challenging to start more than 20–25 jobs on the gLite architecture, because in these cases some jobs often got stuck in the submission procedure with the state "WAITING" for a long time (from 10 minutes to several hours). Therefore, the values related to gLite are the average values for 5 "successful" job submissions.

From the values listed in Figure 4, we can see obvious differences among the overheads of the job submissions in the different architectures. Globus (both the pre-WS and the WS architectures) seems much more efficient. Nevertheless, this comparison is not completely fair with respect to gLite, since Globus performs only simple job submissions to one or two dedicated sites, while in the startup phase gLite additionally discovers resources, transfers files to the WNs (with a total file size of approx. 2Mb) and finally publishes the server contact information via R-GMA.

In the second step, we have investigated the performance of our parallel grid-based simulation on Globus and gLite, see Figure 5 and Figure 6. We do not report different results for the tests run with Globus based on pre-WS and WS architectures, because apart from how the SEE++ servers are started on the grid, there is not difference the operation of the two Globus-based versions of our software. In these test cases, we speeded up the simulation by a factor of 12–14 in Globus and by a factor 9–13 in gLite.

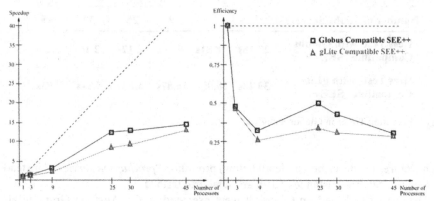

Fig. 6 Speedup and Efficiency Diagrams in Globus and gLite

Apparently the results achieved with Globus look better again, but as in the previous comparison the measured values do not reflect the whole picture: in the tests based on Globus we employed homogeneous hardware and there were fast connections between the bridge and the servers with relatively consistent quality. In the gLite tests the hardware environment was heterogeneous and the communication latencies were higher with large variations. Nevertheless, the average values in Figure 5 are closer to each other when we applied 25 or more jobs, because in the case of more jobs, the load can be more balanced among the various grid nodes. These facts imply that the differences between the values concerning to Globus and gLite on Figure 5 and Figure 6 are caused mostly by the disparity of the hardware architectures of the two testbeds rather than by the applied grid middleware.

5 Conclusions and Future Works

Our comparisons show that while the Globus Toolkit 4 is faster and more efficient, gLite is much more sophisticated and developer friendly. Therefore, it seems more appropriate as a basis of further development.

Another difference of the middlewares is the quantity of existing documentation. In case of Globus 4, the documents are often sketchy and the complete examples are mostly missing (especially in case of the WS C APIs). On the contrary, there is sufficient information and example source codes available in gLite.

Our next step will be the porting of our medical database to AMGA [2], which provides a unified access to them with the grid style certificate-based authentication and authorization. Since AMGA supports among other database systems MySQL as well, it would be possible to reuse the same medical databases in the Globus Toolkit 4 and the gLite environments. On the basis of these developments, we are going to continue the implementation of the grid-based pathology fitting. These achievements should make SEE++ an effective grid-based tool for giving effective decision support to the surgeons before eye surgeries.

Acknowledgements The work described in this paper is partially supported by the Austrian Grid Project [1], funded by the Austrian BMBWK (Federal Ministry for Education, Science and Culture) under contract GZ BMWF-10.220/0002-II/10/2007.

This work makes use of results produced by the Enabling Grids for E-sciencE project, a project co-funded by the European Commission (under contract number INFSO-RI-031688) through the Sixth Framework Programme. EGEE brings together 91 partners in 32 countries to provide a seamless Grid infrastructure available to the European research community 24 hours a day [7].

References

1. Austrian Grid home page. http://www.austriangrid.at
2. AMGA Project home page http://amga.web.cern.ch/amga/
3. Károly Bósa, Wolfgang Schreiner, Michael Buchberger, Thomas Kaltofen. *SEE-GRID, A Grid-Based Medical Decision Support System for Eye Muscle Surgery*, 1st Austrian Grid Symposium, December 1-2, 2005, Hagenberg, Austria. OCG Verlag, pp. 61-74.
4. Károly Bósa, Wolfgang Schreiner, Michael Buchberger, Thomas Kaltofen. *A Grid Software for Virtual Eye Surgery Based on Globus and gLite* ISPDC 2007, Hagenberg, Austria, July 5-8, 2007. IEEE Computer Society, pp. 151-158.
5. Károly Bósa, Wolfgang Schreiner, Michael Buchberger *The Porting of a Grid Software for Virtual Eye Surgery from Globus 4 to gLite*, Poster on the 3rd EGEE User Forum, Clermont-Ferrand, France, Februar 10-14, 2008.
6. Michael Buchberger, *Biomechanical Modelling of the Human Eye*, Ph.D. thesis, Johannes Kepler University, Linz, Austria, March 2004.
   http://www.see-kid.at/download/Dissertation_MB.pdf
7. EGEE-II home page, 2008. http://www.eu-egee.org
8. gLite 3.0.0 home page, 2008. http://www.glite.org
9. The Globus Tookit home page, 2008. http://www.globus.org/toolkit/
10. Int.EU.Grid Project home page, 2008. http://www.interactive-grid.eu/
11. *Job Description Language Attributes Specification*,
    https://edms.cern.ch/file/590869/1/EGEE-JRA1-TEC-590869-JDL-Attributes-v0-8.pdf
12. Thomas Kaltofen, *Design and Implementation of a Mathematical Pulley Model for Biomechanical EyeSurgery*, Diploma thesis, Upper Austria University of Applied Sciences, Hagenberg, June 2002.
    http://www.see-kid.at/download/Pulley_Model_Thesis.pdf
13. Daniel Mitterdorfer, *Grid-Capable Persistance Based on a Metamodel for Medical Decision Support*, Diploma thesis, Upper Austria University of Applied Sciences, Hagenberg, July 2005.
14. Relational Grid Monitoring Architecture (R-GMA) home page. http://www.r-gma.org/
15. MyProxy home page, 2008. http://grid.ncsa.uiuc.edu/myproxy/
16. SEE-KID home page, 2008. http://www.see-kid.at
17. Workload Manager Proxy (WMProxy) C++ API Manual, 2008.
    http://egee-jra1-wm.mi.infn.it/egee-jra1-wm/api_doc/api_docwmproxy_cpp/

Euro-Mediterranean Centre for Climate Change Data Grid

Sandro Fiore, Salvatore Vadacca, Alessandro Negro and Giovanni Aloisio

Abstract Earth Science is strongly becoming a data intensive and oriented activity. Petabytes of data, big collections, huge datasets are continuously produced, managed and stored as well as accessed, transferred and analyzed by several scientists and researchers at multiple sites.

From the data grid perspective, a key element to search, discover, manage and access huge amount of data stored within distributed storages is the related data and metadata framework.

This paper describes the Euro-Mediterranean Centre for Climate Change Data Grid dealing with both architectural and infrastructural issues concerning the adopted grid data and metadata handling systems.

1 Introduction

The next generation of climate modeling scientists and researchers will face a complex and critical challenge, such as dealing with increasingly complex simulation models and huge quantities of related datasets, which are already too massive for current storage, manipulation, archiving, navigation, and retrieval capabilities [14, 4]. From the data grid perspective, a key element to search, discover, manage and access huge amount of data stored within distributed storage devices is the metadata handling framework.

While from the data handling perspective several solutions are already available and are currently adopted, centralized solutions are usually proposed to face up to metadata management. In this paper we propose the CMCC Data Grid System, a distributed data grid solution (leveraging P2P and grid protocols/services) to the management of the climate data production of the recently established *Euro-*

S. Fiore, S. Vadacca, A. Negro and G. Aloisio
Euro-Mediterranean Centre for Climate Change, viale Augusto Imperatore 16, 73100 Lecce, Italy
e-mail: {sandro.fiore, salvatore.vadacca, alessandro.negro, giovanni.aloisio}@unile.it

Mediterranean Centre for Climate Change (CMCC) [10].

Taking into consideration the climate data growth rate, it is our considered opinion that centralized solutions for metadata management are not feasible (they do not scale as needed) and are not suitable to fully address availability, scalability, robustness and efficiency at such large scale. Despite the classical approaches, data-grid-enabled solutions greatly address scalability (users, data, queries, etc.), transparency (access, integration, management, presentation) and efficiency (performance) allowing the management of tens and hundreds of petabytes of distributed datasets. The CMCC Data Grid (proposed within this work) exploits the CMCC Grid Metadata Handling System, a framework that provides both access to and integration of climate metadata stored into different and widespread data sources. It provides a strong virtualization layer in grid to deal with both metadata search and discovery, and access, delivery and management of scientific datasets.

The outline of the paper is as follows. In Section 2, we talk about the CMCC initiative, whereas in Section 3 we describe the CMCC Data Grid, highlighting main requirements, metadata management, data grid architectural and infrastructural issues as well as the CMCC Data Distribution Center. In Section 4 we recall related work. Finally, we draw our conclusions in Section 5.

2 The CMCC Initiative

The Italian government, through the Ministry of the Environment and Protection (MATT), the Ministry of Education, University and Research (MIUR), and the Ministry of Economy and Finance (MEF) recently started an initiative aimed at establishing a national research centre devoted to climate research.

This Centre, namely the *Euro-Mediterranean Centre for Climate Change* (CMCC), aims at furthering knowledge in the field of climatic variability, including causes and consequences, through the development of high-resolution simulations and impact models. The Centre represents the most ambitious initiative undertaken in Italy, within the framework of the National Research Plan, and specifically the National Research Plan on Climate.

The realisation of the Centre has been assigned to a consortium of six Italian research Institutes led by the National Institute of Geophysics and Vulcanology (INGV) and composed by the Fondazione Eni Enrico Mattei (FEEM), the University of Salento (UNILE), the Italian Aerospace Research Center (CIRA), the University of Benevento (UNISANNIO), and the Consorzio Venezia Ricerche (CVR).

The CMCC aims at producing models, simulations, computational and data grid middleware, applied software and training of personnel of the highest qualifications, both in the specific field of climate modelling, and in the field of information technology. The centre develops, verifies and maintains documented models of climatic simulation. It also maintains through a data grid environment climate datasets for the study of climate variability and for the validation of simulation models. Finally, it provides a support to users with consultancy concerning the efficient use of systems, models and data of the Centre. Particular care is dedicated to promoting and spreading the activities and results of the CMCC.

One of the main challenges of the CMCC (which is strongly discussed within this work) is to build a data grid infrastructure able to effectively and notably help scientists in managing, sharing, publishing, accessing and analyzing their climate data.

3 CMCC Data Grid

In the following we highlight the key factors related to the CMCC Data Grid environment. After discussing the main requirements, we will emphasize metadata management issues, data grid architecture and infrastructure discussing the grid metadata handling system. Moreover, we will also introduce the CMCC Data Distribution Centre, which is the primary entry point (web gateway) to the CMCC.

3.1 CMCC Data Grid Requirements

In the following we highlight the main requirements that have led the data grid architecture design at CMCC, trying to clearly identify and summarize the related key issues.

Heterogeneity. The CMCC data environment is intrinsically heterogeneous both from the hardware and the software point of view. This leads to require data grid middleware able to deal with diverse platforms, storage systems, metadata management systems, etc.

Security. The CMCC security requirement includes: a unified security paradigm, single sign-on, mutual authentication between the involved actors, data encryption, global and local authorization. Moreover, data grid services (both for data and metadata) must provide a wide set of data access policies to supply users with a fine grained control aiming at well defining *who* can access *what/where* and under *what* conditions.

Transparency. The CMCC data grid must provide a high level of transparency concerning the access to data and metadata. This goal can be achieved both with data grid services able to uniformly cope with different back-end data systems (from the middleware point of view) and with intuitive clients and charming high level interfaces such as graphical user interface and/or grid portals (from an end-user point of view).

Scalability, autonomy and fault tolerance. Such a climate data grid environment must provide a high level of scalability and autonomy. The candidate approach for the management of data and metadata must be fully decentralized due to: (i) the nature of the CMCC infrastructure (distributed), (ii) the huge amount of data that will be produced and managed (petabytes of data), (iii) the number of involved actors (which can potentially increase in the next years). Such a decentralized approach leads to a high level of autonomy, fault tolerance and scalability.

Interoperability. The proposed CMCC environment must be highly interoperable from different points of view. Basically, interoperability will be achieved by standard adoption. Concerning the *middleware*, the adopted paradigm will be service oriented; more specifically, the deployed data grid services will be WS-I compliant, which means based on SOAP, XML and WSDL W3C standards. Moreover, OGF [30] specifications issued by the DAIS-WG [7] will be taken into account for the metadata services. Concerning the CMCC *metadata* schema, it will be inferred starting from ISO [18] standards for geographic metadata information as strongly required by the interdisciplinary CMCC metadata working group.

3.2 CMCC Metadata Management

Metadata management is a critical issue in such a distributed context, since it allows searching, discovering, describing, cataloguing, annotating datasets, making them effectively accessible and shareable by the scientific community. Concerning this topic, it is worth noting here that two elements are complementary and fundamental: *metadata schema definition* and *software metadata stack*. They jointly contribute (see Fig. 1) to really address metadata management.

Concerning the former (metadata schema definition, *physical layer*), since the start of the CMCC project it was established an internal working group to properly address and define the CMCC metadata schema. A preliminary outcome of this working group is the *CMCC Metadata Agreement v1.0*. It has been designed addressing and fulfilling CMCC user requirements as from the consolidated *ISO 19115* [19] (Geographic Information Metadata) and *ISO 19139* [20] (Geographic MetaData XML encoding, an XML Schema implementation derived from ISO19115) standards. The CMCC metadata agreement represents a tradeoff between the need to fully and richly describe climate datasets, scientific experiments, models, citations, etc. and to have a light metadata publishing process for data providers. Additional details about the CMCC Metadata Agreement are out of the scope of this paper and will be extensively discussed in a future work.

On the other side, concerning the latter (software metadata stack), the data grid group at CMCC defined the entire stack from an architectural point of view. It involves the following four layers: *low-level APIs*, *low-level services*, *high-level services* and *applications*. In the following, we describe each of them in more detail.

Low-level APIs. At this level, we find core libraries to automatically extract metadata from the input/output files of scientific experiments. These are exploited by low-level data publication services to generate/extract metadata and provide automatic ingestion primitives. These libraries must be able to interact both with relational (RDBMS [31]) and hierarchical (XML) database engines.

Low-level-services. At this stage we find the basic services to deal with metadata

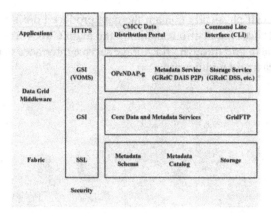

Fig. 1 Software metadata stack

(metadata extraction, search, validation, etc.). They represent the core services for advanced metadata facilities developed at higher levels.

CMCC grid metadata handling service. At this level we can find a complete set of metadata facilities (search and browsing of metadata, publishing, etc.), exposed as Web Services (the *CMCC grid metadata handling service* described in Section 3.5), secured by design and available for external use of client applications.

Applications. At this stage we can find an user-friendly and complete suite of client applications dealing with metadata search, discovery, browsing, annotation, etc. Some examples are the CMCC Metadata Command Line Interface and the CMCC Data Portal.

Additional infrastructural and implementation details about the CMCC grid metadata handling service and the application layer (CMCC Data Portal) can be respectively found in Sections 3.5 and 3.6.

3.3 CMCC Data Grid Architecture

The CMCC Data Grid Architecture (in the large) is depicted in Fig. 2. As we can argue, the proposed architecture is intrinsically distributed and by design provides both data and metadata handling facilities. It exploits the data grid paradigm to manage heterogeneous and geographically spread datasets, efficiently transfer files, carry out distributed search and discovery, provide transparent and ubiquitous web access to remote storage devices supplying the user with an integrated, secure, easy to access and robust environment for climate change data management.

In the following we detail the needed components for such a distributed environment, highlighting project requirements while considering 4 key aspects: *data*, *metadata*, *user interface* and *security*.

Data. Storage devices, disk caches, tape libraries, etc. should be considered at this level. They will physically contain the data produced during the scientific activity. Storage devices are distributed among the main CMCC centers and datasets will be accessible in grid through grid storage service interfaces that represent a key element of the data grid middleware.

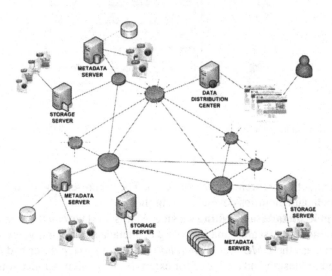

Fig. 2 Data Grid Architecture

Metadata. At this stage we need to consider the Database Management Systems (DBMSs), which will physically contain the climate metadata. The *CMCC grid metadata handling service* will provide access in grid to the stored metadata and will be able to cope with different data models (hierarchical and relational) as well as heterogeneous DBMSs (RDBMSs and XML-DB engines) at the same time. Since metadata (as well as data) will be physically distributed, the grid metadata handling system will exploit a P2P network to (i) interconnect all of the involved peers, (ii) enhance scalability and (iii) provide users with distributed search and discovery facilities.

User Interface. From the user perspective, the access to the metadata handling system can be carried out either by means of a command line interface or a web-based one (CMCC Data Distribution Center). The second choice (see Section 3.6) is better, since a data grid portal represents a user-friendly interface and it provides the highest level of pervasiveness and ubiquity. Different web-gateways could be installed on different sites to provide a higher level of availability and fault tolerance.

Security. Within the proposed data grid architecture, there will be two related components: a CMCC Certification Authority, to issue user, service and host certificates, and a CMCC authorization service (centralized), to enhance both scalability and flexibility concerning role-based authorization management.

3.4 CMCC Data Grid infrastructure

The CMCC Data Grid Infrastructure (see Fig. 3) is basically made up of the following layers: *fabric*, *data grid middleware* and *application*. Moreover, the *security framework* is part of the proposed infrastructure as well and it should be considered orthogonal to the previous ones.

In the following we will describe our actual infrastructural choices concerning physical storage devices and DBMSs, grid services, security framework, data grid portal, etc. bearing evidence of the move from the architecture design towards a real grid infrastructure and motivating how our technical choices can address and fulfill projects requirements.

Security framework. Concerning security, we decided to adopt the widely accepted and de-facto standard Globus Grid Security Infrastructure (GSI) [34] protocol. The full adoption of this security framework provides: mutual authentication based on X509v3 certificates (issued by the CMCC Certification Authority), authorization, data integrity and confidentiality, delegation, etc. Moreover, we provide role-based authorization by means of a VOMS [1] server, deployed in Lecce and acting as a centralized CMCC authorization service. VOMS allows role-based authorization management through groups and roles. It enhances scalability and flexibility concerning user data access policies management. Even if it is centralized, to provide fault tolerance the same service will be mirrored at two other sites (Bologna and Capua). Several groups and roles for CMCC users (i.e. scientists, administrators, etc.) have been defined to provide a direct mapping between classes of users and capabilities/privileges, both for the adopted data and metadata grid services.

Fabric. At this level we find the distributed storage and DBMS facilities to

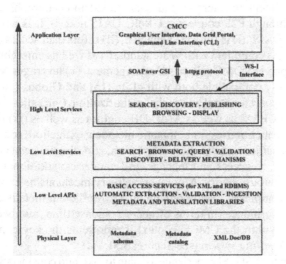

Fig. 3 CMCC Data Grid Infrastructure

manage both files and databases. Disk caches, storage systems and tape libraries (several petabytes of aggregate storage) allow users to store huge experimental climate datasets (potentially composed of millions of files). Concerning the metadata management, different CMCC centers chose diverse DBMS solutions to manage their own metadata. Right now, while in Lecce (main production site) there is an Oracle DBMS, Bologna and Capua run Postgresql.

Middleware. From a technological point of view, for the data grid part we adopted two different services developed within the Grid Relational Catalog Project (GRelC) [2]: GRelC Data Storage Service (GRelC DSS) [12] and GRelC Data Access [13, 11] and Integration Service (GRelC DAIS, which is the adopted *grid metadata handling service*). In the next phase we plan to extend the middleware adding data replication services.

- *GRelC DSS* virtualizes and grid enables heterogeneous physical storage resources. The aim of this data grid service is to efficiently, securely and transparently manage collections of data on the grid promoting flexible, secure and coordinated storage resource sharing, across virtual organizations, taking into account novel grid standards and specifications. The GRelC DSS is a WS-I compliant web service server. To address security and performance requirements, the GRelC DSS was conceived as a pre-threaded GSI and VOMS enabled web service server, supporting gridFTP and HTTPG (HTTP over GSI) for file transfer and written in C language. However, additional information can be found in [12].

- *GRelC DAIS* provides data access and integration facilities concerning metadata management (the GRelC Data Gather Service (DGS) [3] was the ancestor of this service and it provided only basic data integration capabilities). GRelC DAIS is a GSI and VOMS enabled web service server addressing extreme performance, interoperability and security. The GRelC DAIS provides advanced functionalities to transparently integrate heterogeneous, distributed and geographically spread grid data sources (through P2P connected GRelC DAIS nodes). It is worth noting here that the GRelC DAIS: (i) is fully GSI enabled, (ii) offers data access and integration capabilities, (iii) is compliant with W3C standards as well as emerging OGF specifications, (iv) supports VOMS role-based management, (v) leverages on grid/P2P protocols, (vi) is fully compatible both with gLite [15] and Globus [16] middlewares, (vii) provides support for local and global authorization, (viii) allows dynamic binding to relational DBMS as well as XML-DB engines as well as (ix) leverages a rich set of core metadata libraries for automatic metadata extraction, conversion, etc..

Basic functionalities include: query submission, grid-db management, user/VO/ACL management, etc. to access and manage grid-databases; additional functionalities concern asynchronous queries. Moreover, delivery mechanisms exploiting streaming, chunking, compression and prefetching allow efficient metadata delivery with high level of performance (in terms of query response time, number of concurrent accesses, etc.). Within the CMCC context it represents the key component of the *grid metadata handling system* (see Section 3.5).

Starting from the ESG [8] experience we plan to take into consideration OPeNDAP-g [23] servers in order to have GSI and gridFTP support to the classical OPeNDAP server [29]. As a final remark, in the next phase we plan to include SRM [33] and grid middleware for data replication between storage systems (based on the GRelC DAIS server) to produce replicated datasets at several sites increasing data availability.

Application. At this level we find the classical user interface based on a CLI approach and so providing a wide set of commands to interact with the entire CMCC data grid system. Analysis tools, as well as clients to carry out search, discovery and publish activities on metadata/data are also provided to climate scientists and providers.

Moreover, a data grid portal (CMCC Data Distribution Center, see Section 3.6) will ease the access to the entire CMCC production activity (i) providing high level interfaces, (ii) simplifying the metadata search and discovery phases as well as the climate metadata publishing. It provides a seamless and ubiquitous way to access to the entire CMCC data production.

3.5 CMCC Grid Metadata Handling System

The CMCC Metadata Handling System is a key element for the management of the distributed scientific activity. Each CMCC centre has production capabilities since it maintains supercomputers to run models, storage devices to holds datasets and DBMSs to manage metadata.

The proposed system is able to provide both access to and integration of metadata stored on different and geographically spread CMCC metadata sources leveraging on a P2P infrastructure/network of GRelC DAIS (*CMCC grid metadata handling service*). There is no single point of failure and no centralized management for this service due to the scalable architecture.

Within the CMCC Data Grid, the GRelC DAIS topology is a connected graph involving all of the sites. A GRelC DAIS is deployed at each site, providing *metadata access* and *management* functionalities for the local metadata DB. Moreover, it provides metadata integration and query forwarding capabilities for distributed searches.

The metadata DB consists of two parts: a *relational database* containing basic information about the available datasets (abstract, title, temporal and geographical extent, keywords, link to the XML document describing the entire dataset, etc.) and an *XML database* containing a collection of XML documents (one for each dataset, experiment or service) reporting all of the information about the related datasets. The XML schema of these documents is the aforementioned CMCC metadata agreement.

The metadata search, discovery and access is based on the following procedure:

- the CMCC user submits (using a valid proxy) the search query to a selected GRelC DAIS (called agent node);
- for each submitted query, the GRelC DAIS performs a double action: (i) forwards the query to the neighbors (this action is then recursively carried out by other GRelC DAISs) and (ii) submits the query to the local metadata DB (re-

lational part). The query path is called *direct-path* and it is inferred at runtime on a best effort basis. It is worth noting that, using a Universal Query Identifier (UQI), duplicate queries are discarded and cycles/loops are avoided, as they are identified by the distributed routing algorithm;

- the GReIC DAIS (through the *reverse-path*) recursively retrieves, collects and merges partial results coming from its neighbors. The global answer is then stored on the agent node;
- the user checks the status of the query on the agent node and retrieves the resultset as it becomes available. At this stage the query response describes a filtered list of climate datasets satisfying user requirements;
- after having identified the target dataset (and so the target GReIC DAIS), the user can access to its full XML metadata description by directly querying the XML database of the target GReIC DAIS. The complete (or a filtered version) XML metadata document is then retrieved on the client side (it then contains gridftp url to download experimental data through direct access to the grid storage services).

The entire process leverages on a two-step query: *integration* (concerning the relational databases) and *access* (regarding the XML ones).

It is important to remark that each GReIC DAIS is linked to at least two neighbors to provide high level of fault tolerance. Hops To Live (HTL) and Time To Live (TTL) support allows specifying time and space parameters/constraints for the distributed queries.

3.6 CMCC Data Distribution Center

The CMCC Data Distribution Center is the Data Grid Portal available at CMCC. It provides a ubiquitous and pervasive way to ease *data publishing*, climate *metadata search* and huge *datasets access* by the scientific community. Since it does not centralize any functionality concerning authorization or authentication for fault tolerance reasons it could be mirrored at several sites providing several web entry points to the CMCC system.

The grid portal security model includes the use of HTTPS protocol for secure communication with the client (based on X509v3 certificates which must be loaded into the browser) and secure cookies to establish and maintain user sessions. An user can create its own proxy directly from the browser without needing to run *grid-proxy-init* or *voms-proxy-init* commands on a separate shell. Security is guaranteed only by exploiting grid user certificates (providing as input the only users PEM passphrase). No login (username & password) information must be provided by the user and/or must be managed/stored on the portal side.

The CMCC DDC is now in a pre-production phase and it is currently used only by internal users (CMCC researchers and climate scientists). Right now it offers several functionalities, which can be classified as follows:

- *Login/logout to/from the grid* to authenticate the grid user and open/close an HTTPS session.
- GRelC DAIS Server List to manage the list of GRelC DAIS servers. Usually administrators introduce their own servers as well as end-users specify the agent nodes they usually query.
- *Search Engine* to perform search and discovery activities on the web portal by introducing one or more of the following search criteria: horizontal extent (which can be specified by interacting with a geographic map), vertical extent, temporal extent, keywords, topics, creation date, etc. By means of this page the user submits the first step of the query process on the distributed CMCC metadata DB (*relational part*). After that, she can choose one or more datasets retrieving and displaying the complete XML metadata description (from the browser). This way, the second step of the query process is carried out accessing to a specific document of the CMCC metadata DB (*XML part*). After that, through the web interface, the user can access to and download the data stored on the storage device. Requests concerning datasets stored in deep storage are served asynchronously.
- *Metadata Insert/Update* allows CMCC data providers to populate metadata within the CMCC metadata DB (both relational and XML part) through guided web pages. This functionality is intended both for new data and for update of existing ones.
- *Visualization Map* allows users to display monitoring information about the current GRelC DAIS network deployment, managed datasets, system administrators, site name, etc. It is intended for monitoring and administration purposes.

4 Related Work

In the last years, other projects addressed similar issues at an international level (Earth System Grid [8], C3-Grid [5], Nerc DataGrid [24]), with important differences (with respect to the proposed CMCC initiative) from the *middleware*, *metadata schema* and *metadata handling system* points of view.

The Earth System Grid (ESG) [4, 23] integrates supercomputers with large-scale data and analysis servers located at numerous national labs and research centers to provide a seamless and powerful environment that enables the next generation of climate research. The ESG project concentrates a lot of emphasis has been concentrated on the infrastructural part; it exploits *Globus middleware* and concerning the data grid part it leverages *GridFTP services*, *Storage Resource Manager*, *Replica Location Service* and *Opendap-G* servers. Concerning metadata management, ESG adopts a *centralized relational database* deployed at NCAR (directly queried by the portal) for descriptive or logical metadata which accurately describes a climate model experiment by means of a *Climate Model Metadata* [9] (CMM). Concerning location or physical metadata (for replica management), ESG adopts a hierarchical and distributed framework based on Replica Location Services [17].

The C3Grid [32, 21] project has been set up to enable an easier and more efficient resource management for the climate community, in order to improve the efficiency of scientific work both in terms of data storage and of computing. C3Grid strongly addresses data processing and data reuse through (i) portal integration of data processing workflows, (ii) grid workspace with data/job co-scheduling and (iii) metadata generation part of workflows. It offers an interoperable framework able to deal both with gLite and Globus based environments. Moreover, C3Grid provides an uniform discovery of German climate data related providers (DKRZ, WDC Climate, IFM-Geomar, PIK, GKSS) through: (i) *ISO 19115/19139 metadata* based profile, (ii) OAI-PMH [28] harvesting of metadata and GridSphere based Portal. Finally a *central metadata index* is used for metadata search from the C3Grid portal.

The NERC DataGrid [24] (NDG) is a UK e-Science project that provides discovery of, and virtualised access to, a wide variety of climate and earth-system science data. Climate Science Modelling Language information Model (CSML) [6] has been developed by the NDG project as a standards-based data model and XML markup for describing and constructing climate science datasets. It uses conceptual models from emerging standards in GIS to define a number of feature types, and adopts schemas of the Geography Markup Language (GML) where possible for encoding. In the NDG project a lot of emphasis has been devoted to metadata model [26], approach to discovery and use of data [27], data interoperability in the climate sciences [35], NDG security [22], rather than the data grid infrastructural part (from a grid middleware point of view), compared with the other projects we mentioned before. Initial delivery services did not conform to any standard, de facto or otherwise. Concerning distributed climate metadata search, NDG Discovery [25] is now based on Open Archives Initiative Protocol for Metadata Harvesting.

5 Conclusions and Future Work

The paper presented a complete overview of the CMCC Data Grid environment, a distributed system aiming at managing huge amount of climate data for the scientific community.

We discussed several issues, concerning the architectural design and the infrastructural implementation, highlighting metadata access, integration and management (CMCC grid metadata handling system), security (at different levels), grid portal (CMCC DDC). We also presented a complete list of functionalities provided by the CMCC DDC.

Future work will be related to the enhancement of the infrastructural part (caching capabilities of the P2P metadata handling system, new query responses, metadata replication issues), the addition of new components for climate datasets replication and the CMCC DDC extensions. Moreover, the CMCC metadata agreement will be further extended and completed taking into account new scientific requirements. Data publishing will be strongly supported through portal web pages too, in order to ease and speed up the related process.

Future work will be also related to the implementation and deployment of components able to transparently and securely process climate datasets (by means of dataflows) and exchange data (providing replicas) between the internal CMCC centres. This work will leverage existing grid technologies (as discussed within this work) and new ones in the next years, providing an enhanced collaborative environment to (i) describe data and workflow processes, (ii) manage and access to huge climate datasets, (iii) provide easy to access visualization and post-processing tools, (iv) manage replicated datasets, (v) increase the sharing of scientific results and new knowledge.

References

1. Alfieri, R., Cecchini, R., Ciaschini, V., Dell'Agnello, L., Frohner, A., Gianoli, A., Lorentey, K., Spataro, F.: VOMS, an Authorization System for Virtual Organizations. In Proceedings of the European Across Grids Conference, pp. 33-40 (2003)
2. Aloisio, G., Cafaro, M., Fiore, S., Mirto, M.: The Grid Relational Catalog Project. In: Advances in Parallel Computing, Grid Computing: The New Frontiers of High Performance Computing, L. Grandinetti (Ed), pp.129-155, Elsevier (2005)
3. Aloisio, G., Cafaro, M., Fiore, S., Mirto, M., Vadacca, S.: GRelC Data Gather Service: a Step Towards P2P Production Grids. In: Proceedings of 22nd ACM SAC 2007, Seoul, Korea, pp. 561-565 (2007)
4. Bernholdt, D., et al.: The Earth System Grid: Supporting the Next Generation of Climate Modeling Research. In: The Computing Research Repository (CoRR) (2007)
5. C3grid project - http://www.c3grid.de
6. Climate Science Modelling Language (CSML) - http://ndg.nerc.ac.uk/csml
7. Database Access and Integration Services WG (DAIS-WG) https://forge.gridforum.org/projects/dais-wg
8. Earth System Grid - http://www.earthsystemgrid.org
9. Earth System Grid II - Final report - http://datagrid.ucar.edu/esg/about/docs
10. Euro-Mediterranean Centre for Climate Change (CMCC) - http://www.cmcc.it
11. Fiore, S., Cafaro, M., Negro, A., Vadacca, S., Aloisio, G., Barbera, R., Giorgio, E.: GRelC DAS: a Grid-DB Access Service for gLite Based Production Grids. In: Proceedings of the 4th International Workshop on Emerging Technologies for Next-generation GRID (ETNGRID 2007) - June 18-20, 2007 - Paris (France) - pp. 261-266 (2007)
12. Fiore, S., Mirto, M., Cafaro, M., Aloisio, G.: GRelC Data Storage: Lightweight Disk Storage Management solution for bioinformatics "in silico" experiments. In: Proceedings of the 20th IEEE International Symposium on Computer-Based Medical Systems (IEEE CBMS 2007) - June 20-22, 2007 - Maribor (Slovenia) - pp. 495-502 (2007)
13. Fiore, S., Negro, A., Vadacca, S., Cafaro, S., Mirto, M., Aloisio, G.: Advanced Grid DataBase Management with the GRelC Data Access Service. In: Proceedings of the 5th International Symposium on Parallel and Distributed Processing and Applications (ISPA 07) - August 29-31, 2007 - Niagara Falls (Canada) - LNCS 4742, pp. 683-694 (2007)
14. Foster, I.: Service-Oriented Science. Science. Vol. 308, no. 5723, pp 814-817 (2005)
15. gLite: Lightweight Middleware for Grid Computing - http://glite .web.cern.ch/glite
16. The Globus Project - http://www.globus.org
17. Globus Replica Location Service - http://www.globus.org/rls
18. ISO - International Organization for Standardization - www.iso.org
19. ISO 19115:2003 Geographic information - Metadata - http://www.iso.org/iso/iso_catalogue/catalogue_tc/catalogue_detail.htm?csnumber=26020
20. ISO/TS 19139:2007 Geographic information - Metadata XML schema implementation - http://www.iso.org/iso/ iso_catalogue/catalogue_tc/catalogue_detail.htm?csnumber=32557

21. Kindermann, S.: Climate Data Analysis and Grid Infrastructures: Experiences and Perspectives. In Proceedings of the Grid-Enabling Legacy Applications and Supporting End Users Workshop (GELA) - June 20, 2006 - Paris (France): within the framework of the 15th IEEE International Symposium on High Performance Distributed Computing (2006)

22. Lawrence, B.N., Kershaw P., Blower, J.: Practical access control with NDG-security. Submitted and accepted, AHM 2007 (2007)

23. Middleton, D.E., et al.: Enabling worldwide access to climate simulation data: the earth system grid (ESG) In: Scientific Discovery Through Advanced Computing (SciDAC 2006) - June 25-29, 2006 - Denver, CO. Published in Journal of Physics: Conference Series 46, pp. 510-514 (2006)

24. Nerc Data Grid - http://ndg.badc.rl.ac.uk

25. Nerc Data Grid Discovey - http://ndg.nerc.ac.uk/discovery

26. O'Neill K., et al.: The Metadata Model of the NERC DataGrid. In: Proceedings of the UK e-Science All Hands Meeting, Cox, S.J.(Ed.) ISBN 1-904425-11-9 (2003)

27. O'Neill K., et al.: A specialised metadata approach to discovery and use of data in the NERC DataGrid. In: Proceedings of the UK e-Science All Hands Meeting, Cox, S.J.(Ed.) ISBN 1-904425-21-6 (2004)

28. Open Archives Initiative - Protocol for Metadata Harvesting v.2.0 - http://www.openarchives.org/OAI/openarchives protocol.html

29. OPeNDAP - http://www.opendap.org

30. Open Grid Forum - http://www.ogf.org

31. Ozsu, M.T., Valduriez, P.: Principles of Distributed Database Systems, 2nd edition. Prentice Hall(Ed.), Upper Saddle River, NJ, USA (1999)

32. Schindler, U., Brauer, B., Diepenbroek, M.: Data Information Service based on Open Archives Initiative Protocols and Apache Lucene. German e-Science Conference 2007, Baden-Baden (2007)

33. Shoshani, A., Sim, A., Gu, J.: Storage Resource Managers: Essential Components for the Grid. In Nabrzyski,J., Schopf, J.M., Weglarz, J.(Eds.): Grid Resource Management: State of the Art and Future Trends. Kluwer Academic Publishers. (2003)

34. Tuecke S.: Grid Security Infrastructure (GSI) Roadmap. Internet Draft (2001) - http://www.gridforum.org/security/ggf1_200103/drafts/draft-ggf -gsi-roadmap-02.pdf

35. Woolf, A., et al.: Standards-based data interoperability in the climate sciences. EGU 1st General Assembly (2004)

Towards a GRID-Based Digital Library Management System

Gheorghe Sebestyén-Pál, Doina Banciu, Tünde Bálint, Bogdan Moscaiuc, and Ágnes Sebestyén-Pál

Abstract: This paper describes an ontology-based approach for the design of a digital library management system dedicated for scientific and technical purposes ant it analyses the issues concerning the implementation of a digital content management system on a GRID infrastructure. The authors propose an implementation model that benefits from the services offered by a GRID middleware. As part of the solution two in-depth search techniques are presented.

1 Introduction

As the information quantity grows in an exponential rate, content administration, management and dissemination are becoming critical aspects of today's information society. The way in which content is managed influences the efficiency of activities in many fields. Digital content is one of the few "products" that can be manipulated, processed and commercialized purely with electronic means. The growing attention regarding ubiquitous computing and the huge amount of existing information sources is leading towards a world where sophisticated information management is becoming a crucial requirement.

The architecture of a future digital libraries (DL), as outlined in DELOS project [1], should be able to allow any users transparent access and modification of all the digital content anytime from anywhere in an efficient, effective and consistent way. The term digital library has a variety of potential meanings, ranging from a digitized collection of documents that one might find in a traditional library to collections of all kind of digital information along with the services that make the information useful to all possible users (e.g. Internet search engines, library systems).

A first necessary step in the process of designing a DL system is the specification of goal(s) and required features and functionalities. It is also important to establish the group of users or entities (e.g. an organization or company) to whom the DL is designated. This analysis revealed that a DL management system should offer powerful user functionalities (such as search,

Gheorghe Sebestyen-Pal, Tunde Balint, Agnes Sebestyen Pal
Technical University of Clu-Napoca, G. Baritiu no. 26-28, email:
gheorghe.sebestyen@cs.utcluj.ro

Doina Banciu
University of Bucharest, email: banciud@ici.ro

browse, annotation) and that it should guarantee quality of service as well (such as availability, scalability, performance). Moreover, it should be extensible, easy to install and maintain and it should assure inter-operability with other DL applications.

Current developments on Service-oriented Architectures [2], Peer-to-Peer and Grid computing promise more open and flexible architectures for DLs. With the help of these technologies researchers wish to solve the problems which arise due to increased heterogeneity of the content, services and metadata, as well as due to the omission of a central control instance.

In [3] the authors evaluate the feasibility of using a Grid infrastructure as support for a digital content management system. The outcome of this paper is that Grid computing can be used mainly for computer-intensive, in-depth search, on huge volumes of data.

This paper presents the main requirements and guidelines for the implementation of a digital content management system and offers an architectural solution for a generic digital library dedicated for scientific and technical purposes. As central part of this architecture is the concept of digital object, which allows association of physical documents (files), metadata and functionalities based on different criteria. This approach allows definition of multiple relations and offers different perspectives (views) on the existing repository of digital documents. An important aspect emphasized in the paper is the need for powerful in-depth search techniques that allows data retrieval and classification adapted to the needs of the users.

The rest of this paper is structured as follows: Section 2 present some related project; Section 3 introduces the main concepts used in a digital library; Section 4 presents the main requirements for a digital library system; Section 5 presents a proposed model for a digital library for scientific and technical purposes; Section 6 describes some solutions regarding information retrieval in a digital library; Section 7 describes some experimental results. Finally, Section 8 contains the concluding remarks.

2 Related Work

In the last decade, in order to achieve higher computing performance, greater data-storage facilities or an enhanced cooperative research infrastructure, an intense research activity was performed in the direction of GRID infrastructures. At the beginning, GRID computing facilities were developed mainly for scientific purposes. Nuclear and high energy physics, bio-chemistry and aero-spatial research are some examples of fields that require huge amount of storage resources and high performance computing facilities. CERN is one of the main promoters of GRID research; the experiments which will be made in the next years at CERN will generate a huge amount of data that must be stored in real-time on distributed databases. The EGEE [13] initiative is intend to develop the necessary GRID computing infrastructure that covers the storage and processing requirements for the high energy physics experiments.

As part of the EGEE initiative, the Diligent project is intended to define and implement digital libraries on GRID infrastructure. In the first stage the research team tried to identify the requirements imposed for a digital library in two very different areas: arts (paintings) and satellite imaging. Based on these requirements a GRID-based digital library architecture was specified and implemented [14]; now the final release of the library services is available.

The Delos Network of Excellence is a European research project intended to define and implement digital libraries on new computing and communication technologies. The main contribution of this project was the definition of goals and scope for the research in the field of digital libraries. The workshops and conferences organised through the project revealed new functional and architectural requirements for digital library systems; the concept of digital library evolved from a static digital document repository to a more dynamic knowledge exchange environment.

The goal of the BRICKS project [15] is to design a user and service-oriented space to share knowledge and resources in a multi-cultural heritage. The aim is to define a digital library architecture for a very broad and heterogeneous user community that involves cultural heritage and educational institutions, research community, industry, and citizens. BRICKS offer automatic indexing and annotation functionalities, access services, multimedia document generation facilities and a collaborative environment between distributed users. Its architecture is decentralised and service-oriented.

The aim of the OpenDlib project [16] was to develop a software toolkit that can be used to set up a digital library according to the requirements of a given user community. The system allows generation of new documents and harvesting of content from existing sources.

Other significant implementations of digital libraries are the Fedora and the DSpace open source software. Fedora is organised around the concept of digital objects, which are a collections of physical documents and their associated metadata. DSpace is a DL framework with basic store, access and search functionalities, useful to instantiate digital libraries for dedicated purposes.

Based on the experiences from the above presented projects the authors tried to identify and test those facilities of a digital library that can be mapped on a GRID infrastructure. The identified drawbacks are caused mainly by the way in which jobs are executed today in a GRID structure.

The main arguments regarding the fact why a digital library system could benefit from a Grid infrastructure are the following:

- the volume of documents stored in a digital library is huge and the data is distributed
- concurrent access to documents for a great number of users require replicated data and multiple search engines

- multimedia streaming for many users require dedicated servers and re-
  served communication bandwidth
- automatic data indexing and annotation require high performance
  computing facilities
- users should be organised in virtual organisations in order to access
  and control different parts of a digital library's repository
- complex data-processing procedures can be applied on the library's
  documents in an easier way with the job distribution facilities offered
  by a GRID infrastructure
- the reaction time for complex processing procedures may be reduced
  to an acceptable interval (e.g. acceptable for an interactive processing)
  in case of GRID computing

Taking into consideration that today digital libraries are dynamic repositories of
distributed knowledge intended to facilitate information exchange and cooperation
between remote users, their implementation requires an adequate computing and
communication infrastructure. GRID middleware services can cover many of the
facilities needed to implement the main services of a digital library. The following
sections present a possible approach and an architectural model for a digital library system.

3 Ontological Approach for DL Design

As cooperation and interoperability between distributed applications are important
requirements for modern ITC products, an ontological approach offers the necessary basis for platform and implementation independent data exchange.

In the case of digital libraries an ontology-based design offers more flexibility
in organizing the digital content and allows qualitatively improved information retrieval. Instead of key-words or metadata based search the user may navigate
through complex relations (links) between digital objects and contexts. The present paper is focused mainly on digital content used in technical and scientific
fields and therefore the concepts and relations upon which the digital library
model is built are specific for these fields. For instance terms like project, conference or scientific article are important concepts in the present model, but they may
be of less importance for digital libraries built in other fields.

Terminology proves to be a barrier in describing a digital library, because some
words have different connotations for people of varying backgrounds [4]. In order
to eliminate ambiguities it was considered useful to specify the meaning of some
concepts and terms.

The first concept is that of digital library, defined as a collection of digital content dedicated for a well defined purpose and to which a number of users (actors)
and specific functionalities are associated. Digital libraries may be dynamically
created, modified and deleted in accordance with a given goal or purpose. It serves
a given community of users organized in virtual organizations, providing the

means for content preservation, data access and cooperative work. For example a digital library may be created as support for a research project, for an academic course or for a scientific event (e.g. conference). This approach is significantly different form that of a digitized classical library mainly because of the library's goal and its accompanying content manipulation functionalities.

In accordance with the present model a digital library contains items called "digital objects". Information stored in a digital object is divided into "data" and information about the data, known as "properties" or "metadata". As outlined in [5] a digital object should have a machine and platform independent structure that allows it to be identified, accessed and protected, as appropriate. A digital object may incorporate not only informational elements, i.e., a digitized version of a paper, movie or sound recording, but also the unique identifier of the digital object and other metadata about the digital object.

Digital objects may be organized in "collections", in accordance with some given criteria. A digital collection is a set of document-type and/or multimedia information created by information professionals for a user community or a set of communities. A digital collection may contain multiple other collections, giving in this way the possibility for hierarchical constructions. A digital object may be part of a number of collections, even if it is preserved as a single item. For instance an article may be: part of a given author's paper list, a document of a conference and in the same time a result of a research project.

A community of users, associated with a given digital library is structured as a "virtual organization". The members of a virtual organization can belong to different real organizations distributed in all over the world, but they all share a common goal (e.g. work on a common research project). In achieving this goal they share their resources e.g. knowledge, experimental results, instruments, etc., for the duration of their collaboration. A virtual organization will be enabled to dynamically create and modify its own collection specifying a number of requirements on the information space (e.g. content domain, document type). In a virtual organization users may have different "roles". A role defines the data access rights for a group of users in a virtual organization. Such rights may be: read-only, creation, modification or deletion of digital objects, allocation of access rights to other users, etc.)

This paper presents the basic concepts characteristic for an ontology that models the domain of technical and scientific content. The elementary component of the digital library is the digital object consisting of a data and a metadata part. Many of the digital object types taken into consideration are borrowed from the Dublin Core resource type proposal [6]. The digital object types include concepts like article, book, manual, technical and financial documentation, technical and scientific report, master or PhD thesis, etc. Collections group digital objects together and define more complex digital content required for representing projects, academic courses or events like conferences or workshops.

The concept of virtual organization can be used to model different activities and interactions between users of the digital library. Figure 1 demonstrates a way to model projects. The research team responsible for developing the project forms the virtual organization. Each user involved in the project participates as a member of the organization. The members have access to the resources of the project based on the role defined in the organization. The digital content produced during the activities of a project form a collection of digital objects (reports, articles etc.). Such collections of objects can be presented at events (for example conferences).

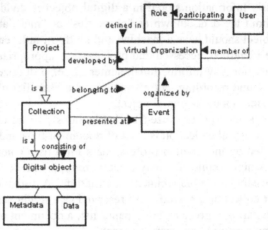

Fig. 1. Ontology for technical and scientific content

Another representative example for the use of digital libraries is the context defined by academic courses. The digital objects consist of lectures, course notes, books, laboratory works, slideshows posted by lecturers or professors. Students have a more limited access regarding the collection of the course material, generally only being allowed to read (and not modify) the digital content. Specific digital documents that can be considered useful in the given context are course websites, attendance charts, assignment lists, assessment information (grades), etc.

The ontology-based model of DLs presented above can be considered an efficient solution for representing and organizing digital content. On one hand the concepts and interactions involved are defined in a logical and accessible way ensuring that both the developers and the users of the system can easily understand the model. On the other hand the set of concepts included in the representation are selected and defined in such a way as to ensure the ease of interaction and communication with existing or standard models of libraries, supporting knowledge sharing tasks such as exchanging data among databases, integrating databases with other databases and providing network-based services for data processing.

4 Requirements for a DL System

There is a set of core digital library functionalities that every digital library should provide. This set includes: content submission, storage, indexing and efficient data access. Extra functionalities may be required such as: intelligent discovery of objects (documents, video, images, etc.), automatic metadata extraction, annotation and document classification.

In important issue that a DL management system must consider is information storage. The designer has to take into account beside the space requirements, the fact that information resources must be persistent and highly availability. Given that a digital object has many parts (metadata, preservation files, delivery files), another issue that arises is the interconnection of these parts. Possible solutions for data persistency are: replication, mirroring or migration, although all of these techniques have some drawbacks (like keeping consistency among replicas).

Traditional digital libraries keep content under control in their local repositories and offer access only for their registered users. But in a decentralized, distributed architecture, metadata and also the content have to be available for all parties regardless of their location. Decentralized architectures by definition avoid having central control, because these are candidate single point of failure and performance bottleneck. Therefore, metadata (catalogue information) must be spread in the community. A naive approach for metadata searching would be to distribute queries to all members, but it is obvious that this solution is not scalable. Hence, efficient metadata access and querying are very important challenges.

Access to content and data processing services must be regulated by access policies. These policies refer to virtual organizations, users, roles and operations on digital content. These can specify, for example, that a collection of objects are only visible to a particular group of users.

The users of a digital library require a good quality of service (QoS), i.e. an acceptable level of non-functional properties. Ensuring the desired QoS is not trivial. It involves many functions such as: *security*, e.g. authorizing of the request, encryption and decryption as required, validation; *logging* for auditing and *dynamic rerouting* for fail over or load balancing. QoS is also measured in the average response time of the system to complex queries and the precision or relevance of the returned results

But probably the most important aspects, which determine the quality of a digital library management system, are the search and retrieval services. Therefore section 5 is dedicated to this subject.

5 A DL Model for Scientific and Technical Purposes

In order to achieve the necessary requirements a system organized into three layers is proposed. Each layer consists of a number of components, as presented in Figure 2.

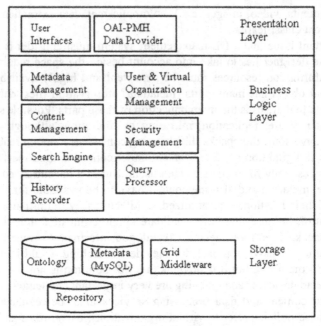

Fig. 2. Reference Architecture

The presentation layer contains components that communicate with the world outside the system. It contains the web user interface and the Open Archives Initiative protocol for metadata harvesting service.

The business layer deals with managing the content, the users and the virtual organizations. With the help of the history recorder one can track the user activities. This information can be used to improve the future search results. Security management deals with authorizing, authenticating and auditing the users.

The user and virtual organization management offers the support for authentication, authorization and auditing. The search engine deals with information retrieval, identifying documents or sub-documents that meet information needs expressed in the form of queries interpreted by the query processor.

Grid technologies allow creating distributed grid services to hide the complexity of the underlying resource network, which is the central concept of grid computing philosophy [7, 8]. The Grid offers new techniques that enable computational tasks on a set of distributed computers connected by a network. Combining information retrieval with the emerging Grid services information collections can be optimized. The Grid scheduler distributes the computationally-intensive operations (e.g. in-depth search, classification, etc.) on the available executor nodes in order to assure a minimum response time.

The physical storage layer is responsible for physical storage of metadata and content. It also contains the implemented ontology which contains the main concepts.

A relational database is used to store all the information about the organization of content, metadata, information about users and authorization. The system also uses the relational database in order to maintain indices that users can browse. These functionalities can be offered by any standard SQL database that supports transactions, such as MySQL.

6 Information Retrieval in DLs

From a user's point of view the main functionality of a digital library is to offer access to relevant information about subjects of interest. There are at least three ways to obtain access to the requested information:
- through key-word or index search
- through semantic Information Retrieval
- through non-semantic Information Retrieval

The first technique is looking for all the documents that contain a key-word or group of words. A number of experiments were made [3] with in-depth content, which revealed that this kind of search is computer intensive and it requires high performance computing infrastructures. Experiments showed that using GRID structures the search time may be reduced significantly until an acceptable level. More efficient techniques use index searching on metadata. This kind of search is faster and it can benefit from traditional database query functionalities. But in many cases the quality of the result depends very much on the ability of the user to express in a few words the essence of his quest. Synonym words may not be considered relevant or words with different meanings in different context may mislead the search. Therefore semantic search techniques try to solve this problem through context-aware and semantic-aware retrieval methods. Semantic web documents (SWD) are currently written in RDF (Resource Description Framework) or OWL(Web Ontology Language) and they contain semantic annotations and references to other SWDs. Semantic search engines are customized for such SWDs, especially for ontology, and they take advantage of these semantic annotations.

Non-semantic algorithms are alternatives for higher quality results. The idea is to make a search in the content of the digital documents (instead of catalogue) and to find statistical similarities between them. The user may give a document that best describes its interest and the system responds with other similar documents. This research was focused on two approaches: the Naive Bayes Algorithm [9] and the Topic-Based Vector Space Model Algorithm (TVSM) [10]. The first technique was used to classify unlabeled data using training documents while with the second technique the closest domain class for given documents was determined using vector spaces.

The following paragraphs contain a brief description of these algorithms and their interaction with the proposed system.

The *Naive Bayes algorithm*, being a learning algorithm has its foundations in the domain of artificial intelligence. The following equation represents the probability model, where the numerator is the product between the prior class probability and the likelihood probability, meanwhile the denominator is the probability of the training data:

$$p(C \mid F_1,..., F_n) = \frac{p(C)p(F_1,..., F_n \mid C)}{p(F_1,..., F_n)}. \quad (1)$$

where : C – document to be classified
F_i – a training document

The learning task is to estimate the parameters of a generative model (the numerator of the fraction) using labeled training data only. The parameters of a generative model can be represented as collections of calculated word probabilities.

In the next step the estimated parameters are used to classify new documents based on their similarity with the given classes. The construction of a classifier (U) using a probability model is presented below:

$$U = \arg \max_{V_j \in U} p(V_j) \prod P(a_j \mid V_j). \quad (2)$$

In the above equation $P(a_j \mid V_j) = \dfrac{e + s * p}{e + s}$ represents the probability of a_i, an attribute of the document , to be part of the model V_j; e is the number of examples for which $U = V_j$, s is the equivalent sample size and p is a prior estimate of U. A more detailed description of this algorithm can be found in [10,11].

In order to applying the Naive Bayes algorithm, a limited number of labeled examples were provided. Unlabeled documents were used to augment the available labeled documents. The introduced weighting factor dynamically adjusts the strength of unlabeled data. Although the Naïve Bayes algorithm considers words independent of their context the search results are reasonably good.

This method can be easily implemented on a Grid infrastructure obtaining notable performances regarding processing time, space distribution, response time and the identification of new documents.

The *Topic-Based Vector Space Model* [11] (TVSM) is a new vector-based approach for document classification. The approach does not assume independence between terms and it is flexible regarding the specification of term similarities. This model uses specific terms like stop-words, stemming and thesaurus.

A *Stopword-list* contains words, which are assumed to have no impact on the meaning of a document. Such a list usually contains words like "the", "is", "of", "a", etc. During preprocessing all words matching the Stopword-list are removed from the document.

Thesaurus Substitution is defined as the replacement of different synonymous words by one leading word. For example the synonyms "application" and "program" can be replaced by the leading synonym "software". The leading synonym is usually defined in an arbitrarily manner.

The term *Stemming* stands for the reduction of word forms e.g. "software", "networks" to word stems e.g. "soft","net" (also known as Strong-Stemming) or to basic word forms e.g. "software"," network" (also known as Weak-Stemming).

First a user defines a profile that associate a set of documents to predefined classes. The rest of the documents are classified by adopting the classification of the most similar documents. The newly classified documents are added to the profile. Figure 3 shows a possible representation of the vector space. Each axis intercept of this vector space may have only positive values (including zero) and represents an elementary topic (e.g. sports, computer, music).

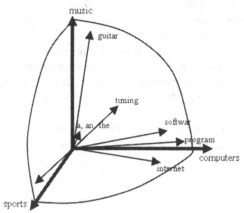

Fig. 3 TVSM vector space

Although the application of TVSM on given documents has real advantages over other classification methods, it requires an amount of interaction with the user. The enhanced TVSM algorithm proposed and tested in this paper reduces the user involvement (interaction) through an automatic vector weight computation. According to the proposed method the weight of a vector is computed as a function of its appearance frequency in the processed documents (e.g. a term with higher frequency in documents will get a higher weight).

7 Experimental Results

In order to evaluate the efficiency of the proposed model an in-depth word pattern search was made. This was implemented on a Condor GRID Framework. The goal was to build a digital content library with enhanced search facilities.

Most digital libraries offer very good search engines with real-time response, when the search is made on catalogs or on metadata. But, if the search must be made in all the documents of the library the execution time may exceed a few hours or even days, making the search un-feasible. In order to reduce the response time for in-depth search procedures a GRID solution was adopted.

Comparisons were made between search time made on a single computer and on a GRID architecture, with variable number of executor nodes. The test scenario was as follows:

- a set of computers were organized as a GRID infrastructure using the Condor middleware; the computers were connected through an Ethernet LAN (100Mbs)
- the content of the digital library was made of document files having different formats: TXT, DOC and PDF.
- the library had 1000 files with variable length, from 1KB to 1MB
- the search procedure was looking for a set of words in a frame with predefined length (the distance between any two words found in the file should not exceed the length of the frame)
- in some experiments all the files were in a single node and in others a random distribution of files was used

Figure 4 shows the relation between the execution time of the search procedure and the number of Executor nodes. The total execution time of a search is a sum between the scheduling and communication time (the time needed to distribute the tasks and the data files) and the search time (processor time). Two cases were considered:

- case 1 – the files are distributed between nodes
- case 2 – all the files are stored in a single computer

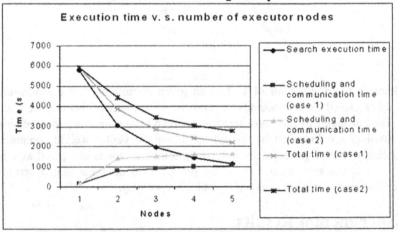

Fig. 4 The relation between the execution time and number of executor nodes

It can be seen that the search time is decreasing with the number of processors but the scheduling and communication time is increasing. However the total execution time is decreasing with the number of nodes. It is also interesting to observe that in the second case the communication time is higher because a greater amount of data has to be transferred through the network.

The graphics shows that in the above specified scenario if more than 5 GRID-nodes are used the results don't improve significantly. Probably in another scenario where the processing time has a more weight in the total time the optimal number of GRID-nodes would be higher. For instance in case of pattern search in multimedia files (audio or video) the execution time is significantly higher and the need for more nodes is evident.

The experiment showed that the search time depends significantly with the format of the files. For the same file length the PDF files requires 4 to 5 times more processor time than a TXT file. The search time for DOC files was approximately twice the time of a TXT file. Figure 5 shows the search time related to the dimension and type of the files. It can be seen that the search time varies for the same file dimension, but a proportional average time increase is obtained with the files' length. The search time does not include the scheduling and communication time.

An important drawback of the Condor implementation and of many other GRID implementations (e.g. Globus, EGEE) is the fact that the search tasks are performed in a batch style and not in an interactive mode. Maybe if the user would have a bigger involvement during the search process some less useful searches could be stopped in an earlier phase.

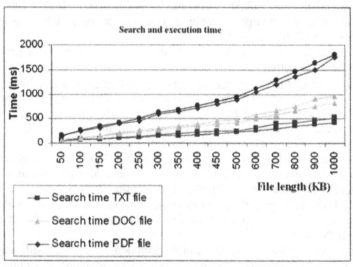

Fig. 5 The search times for TXT, DOC and PDF files

8 Conclusions

The paper presents a new vision on the design and implementation of a digital library management system. It defines the basic requirements, specifies its main functionalities and gives a general model of such a system. The proposed model is based on a technical and scientific document ontology used to obtain more relevant search results taking into account the relationships among the concepts. Some search protocols are outlined to facilitate communication between digital libraries. The presented architecture is based on Grid technology. This technology helps to implement data- and computationally-intensive tasks. The paper also gives a short description of the two classification algorithms used in the experiments.

Acknowledgments
The present paper presents the results of a national research project called SINRED funded by the Romanian Ministry of Education and Research through the Excellency Program.

References

1. "DELOS Digital library architecture (WP1) - Cluster Objectives.", 2004
2. H. Suleman, *Analysis and Evaluation of Service Oriented Architectures for Digital Libraries*, Digital Library Architectures: Peer-to-Peer, Grid, and Service-Orientation - Pre-proceedings of the Sixth Thematic Workshop of the EU Network of Excellence DELOS, 2004, pag. 165-176
3. Gh. Sebestyen, D. Banciu, T. Balint, A. Hangan, "Digital Content Management on GRID Structures", ICCP 2007 IEEE International Conference on Intelligent Computer Communication and Processing, Cluj-Napoca, 2007, pag. 259-262
4. C. Lagoze and H. V. de Sompel, "The open archives initiative protocol for metadata harvesting.",
   http://www.openarchives.org/OAI/openarchivesprotocol.html, 2002
5. Hao Ding, *A Semantic Search Framework in Peer-to-Peer Based Digital Libraries,* ISBN 82-471-8153-3 (electronic), 2006
6. "Dublin core medata initiative", http://www.dublincore.org, 1995
7. Ian Foster, *What is the Grid? A Three Point Checklist,* 2002
8. Ian Foster, Carl Kesselman, Steven Tuecke, *The Anatomy of the Grid: Enabling Scalable Virtual Organizations*, International Journal of Super-computer Applications, 15(3), Sage Publications, 2001, USA.
9. McCallum A., Nigam K.: *A comparison of event models for naive Bayes text classification,* In AAAI-98 Workshop on Learning for Text Categorization, AAAI Press, 1998
10. Nigam K. , McCallum A. , Thrun S., Mitchell T.: Text Classification from Labeled and Unlabeled Documents using EM, Machine Learning, Kluwer Academic Publishers, 1999
11. Yang Y., Pederson J. O.: Feature selection in statistical learning of text categorization, In Proceedings of the Fourteenth International Conference ICML-97 1997
12. Becker J., Kuropka D.: *Topic-based Vector Space Model,*Proceedings of the 6th International Conference on Business Information Systems, *2003*
13. EGEE – Enabling Grids for E-sciencE, http://public.eu-egee.org/
14. Diligent deliverables, http://diligent-training.isti.cnr.it/
15. BRICKS Project, http://www.brickscommunity.org/
16. OpenDLib Project, http://www.opendlib.com/

III

GRID RESOURCE MANAGEMENT AND SCHEDULING

Fair Execution Time Estimation Scheduling in Computational Grids

Eleni Dafouli, Panagiotis Kokkinos, Emmanouel A. Varvarigos

Abstract We propose a fair scheduling algorithm for Computational Grids, called Fair Execution Time Estimation (FETE) algorithm. FETE assigns a task to the computation resource that minimizes what we call its fair execution time estimation. The fair execution time of a task on a certain resource is an estimation of the time by which a task will be executed on the resource, assuming it gets a fair share of the resource's computational power. Though space-shared scheduling is used in practice, the estimates of the fair execution times are obtained assuming that a time-sharing discipline is used. We experimentally evaluate the proposed algorithm and observe that it outperforms other known scheduling algorithms. We also propose a version of FETE, called Simple FETE (SFETE), which requires no a-priori knowledge of the tasks workload and in most cases has similar performance to that of FETE.

Key words: grids, scheduling, fairness, task workload

Eleni Dafouli
Department of Computer Engineering and Informatics, University of Patras,
e-mail: dafouli@ceid.upatras.gr

Panagiotis Kokkinos, Emmanouel A. Varvarigos
Research Academic Computer Technology Institute, Patras, Greece,
e-mail: kokkinop, manos @ceid.upatras.gr

1 Introduction

Grids consist of geographically distributed and heterogeneous communication, computation and storage resources that may belong to different administrative domains, but can be shared among users. Since the sharing of resources is the "raison d' etre" of Grids, fairness is a concept that is inherent in Grid scheduling, and has been previously ignored. Fairness can be defined in a number of different ways, but an intuitive notion of fairness is that a task submitted to the Grid, is entitled to as much use of the resources as any other task. When the Grid serves different classes of users (e.g., users willing to pay different prices for the service they receive) the notion of fairness depends on the class of the user, with users belonging to the same class having "equal" access to the resources.

In this work we propose a fair scheduling algorithm for Computational Grids, which we call the Fair Execution Time Estimation (FETE) algorithm. FETE assigns a task to the computation resource that minimizes what we call its fair execution time estimation. This estimation is obtained assuming that the task gets a fair share of the resource's computational power. Though space-shared scheduling is used in the actual resource, the estimates of the fair execution times are found assuming time-sharing is used. We also propose a version of FETE, called Simple FETE (SFETE), which is a good approximation of FETE, and does not require a-priori knowledge (or estimates) of the task workloads. FETE and SFETE can be implemented both in a centralized and in distributed way. We perform an extensive set of experiments using the GridSim [7] simulator and show that FETE outperforms other known scheduling algorithms with respect to performance and fairness related metrics. The improvements obtained by using FETE are particularly important when the load in the Grid, in terms of tasks submitted, increases. Finally, it is observed that the FETE and the SFETE algorithms give similar results, and so in almost every case the latter version is preferable, since it has no need for the a-priori knowledge of the task workloads. These results strengthen our belief that SFETE can in fact be incorporated in a production Grid Middleware.

The remainder of the paper is organized as follows. In Section 2 we report on previous work. In Section 3 we describe the Grid environment used. In Section 4 we present the Fair Execution Time Estimation (FETE) and in Section 5 the Simple FETE (SFETE) scheduling algorithms. Performance results are presented in Section 6. Finally, conclusions and directions for future work are presented in Section 7.

2 Previous Work

A number of scheduling algorithms have been proposed so far, both for single- and for multi-processor systems, some of which have also been adapted for use in the Grid environment. Lately a number of scheduling schemes that are specific to Grids have also been proposed. [1][2][3][4][11] present centralized, hierarchical and distributed scheduling schemes for Grids. Most of the scheduling algorithms proposed so far try to minimize the total average task delay [3] and maximize resource utilization, while several other performance metrics are used. In [8] and in [9] scheduling algorithms that support deadline and budget constraints are proposed and implemented.

The fair scheduling of packets in Data networks is a concept quite well studied [5][6]. On the other hand fair scheduling algorithms for Grids have received relatively little attention until now. In [10] a fair packet-by-packet algorithm for the joint allocation of processing and bandwidth resources is proposed. In [12] game theory is used to prove that a strong community control is required to achieve acceptable performance in Grids, by comparing centralized and distributed fair scheduling algorithms. In [13] the authors propose a resource allocation scheme based on fair resource sharing in hierarchical Virtual Organizations (VOs). Simulation results show that the proposed scheme provides greater fairness than other schemes, as well as better performance. In [14] three different fair scheduling algorithms are proposed and evaluated in a centralized scheduling environment.

3 Grid Environment

We consider a Grid environment consisting of a number of users and a number of computation resources. By the term user we do not necessarily mean an individual user, but also (and probably more appropriately) a Virtual Organization (VO), or a single application, using the Grid infrastructure. Also a computation resource can be a cluster, a parallel computer or a Grid site.

Users generate atomic (undivisible and non-preemptable) tasks and every task i has workload w_i and non-critical deadline D_i. By the term "non-critical" we mean that if the deadline expires, the corresponding task remains in the system until completion, but it is recorded as a deadline miss. Upon creating a new task, the user sends the task characteristics to the central scheduler, in the form of a task request. The central scheduler works "offline" or "online". In the former case the central scheduler receives task requests by several users and stores them in a local queue. Periodically the scheduler orders the queued task requests (using an ordering policy) and assigns them to resources (using an assignment policy). In the "online" mode the central scheduler assigns tasks to resources immediately after the arrival of the corresponding task requests. Each resource j contains a number CPUs, of total computational capacity equal to C_j and uses a space-sharing policy. Tasks are served by the CPUs of a resource based on the order they arrive to it. At any time t there are $N_j(t)$ tasks in resource's j local queue or under execution in its CPUs.

The FETE and Simple FETE algorithms can work both in "offline" and "online" mode. However, these algorithms are presented, in this paper, in their "offline" mode and evaluated along with other "offline" algorithms. Finally, the FETE and Simple FETE algorithms do not use the task deadlines in their operation.

4 Fair Execution Time Estimation Algorithm

The Fair Execution Time Estimation (FETE) scheduling algorithm assigns task i to resource j that provides the minimum fair execution time X_{ij}. The fair execution time X_{ij} is an estimation of the time required for task i to be executed on resource j, assuming it gets a fair share of the resource's computational power. By fair share we mean that each time t the task gets a portion:

$$\frac{1}{N_j(t)+1},$$

of resource's j computational capacity C_j. That is, the estimates of the fair execution times are obtained assuming a time-sharing discipline, though space-shared scheduling is used in the actual resource. The parameter $N_j(t)$ is the total number of tasks already assigned (queued or executed) to resource j at the time t the assignment decision is made. The fair share of the resource's capacity each task gets changes with time, since $N_j(t)$ also changes with time, increasing by 1 every time a new task is assigned to resource j and decreasing by 1 each time a task completes service at resource j. For this reason, during the calculation of the fair execution time X_{ij} of task i on resource j, the fair execution time estimations of the tasks already assigned to resource j should also be taken into consideration.

In the example of Figure 1, we present two resources A and B that have the same computation capacity. At time 0 both resources have the same number of tasks N assigned to them, however the tasks assigned to resource B have smaller workloads. The first task completes its execution in resource A at time t_1^A, while in resource B at t_1^B, and $t_1^A > t_1^B$. Similarly, for the second task we have $t_2^A > t_2^B$, and so on. During the time periods $[0, t^A]$ and $[0, t^B]$, we assume that there are no new arrivals of tasks, so the last task, in both resources, utilizes the whole computational capacity of the corresponding resource. The last task in resource A finishes its execution at time t^A, while in resource B at time t^B, where $t^A > t^B$. These times, t^A and t^B, are also the fair execution time estimations of the corresponding tasks. We see that the fair execution time of a task depends not only on its workload, resource capacity and number of tasks assigned to resource, but also on the workloads of the other tasks.

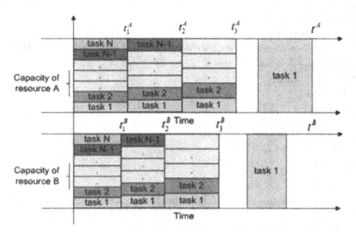

Fig. 1 Fair execution time estimation example.

For the calculation of the fair execution time X_{ij} of task i on resource j, we consider the fair execution time estimations of the tasks already assigned to resource j. However, in this calculation it is not possible to also consider tasks that may be assigned to the resource in the future, which would change the fair share of existing tasks. he fair execution time estimations of the tasks are calculated only once and are not re-estimated when new tasks arrive at the resource. So, the calculation of the fair execution time of task i on resource j is just an estimate and not the actual time that the task would complete its execution, even if it were executed using an ideal time-sharing (processor sharing) scheme.

The pseudocode of the centralized and "offline" implementation of FETE is presented in Algorithm 1. We assume that at the time a task arrives at the resource, there are N tasks assigned to it, having fair execution times t_n, $n = 1, \cdots, N$. Without loss of generality we also assume that $t_{n-1} > t_n$ for all n. A task i has workload equal to w_i and its remaining workload (defined in Algorithm 1) is denoted by $\widehat{w}_i$. In the end FETE algorithm assigns task i to resource j that provides the minimum fair execution time estimation X_{ij}.

5 Simple Fair Execution Time Estimation Algorithm

The FETE algorithm requires the a-priori knowledge of the task workloads for obtaining the fair execution time estimations. However, the task workloads, in practice, are often not known and may be hard to estimate. For this reason

---

Algorithm 1 Fair Execution Time Estimation - FETE

1: **for** each task i queued in the scheduler's ordered list **do**
2:   **for** each resource j in the Grid **do**
3:     Set $\widehat{w}_i = w_i$
4:     Estimate the fair execution time X_{ij} :
5:     Set $t = 0$, $n = N$ and $X_{ij} = 0$
6:     Estimate task's i temp fair execution time X_{ij} assuming it gets computational capacity $\frac{C_j}{N_j(t)+1}$ on resource j: $X_{ij} = \widehat{w}_i \cdot \frac{N_j(t)+1}{C_j}$
7:     **if** $X_{ij} < t_n$ **then**
8:       $X_{ij} = X_{ij} + t$
9:     **else**
10:      $\widehat{w}_i = \widehat{w}_i - \frac{C_j}{N_j(t)+1} \cdot (t_n - t)$
11:      $X_{ij} = X_{ij} + t_n$
12:      Set $t = t_n$ and $n = n - 1$
13:      Goto(6)
14:    **end if**
15:   **end for**
16:   Assign task i to resource j that gives the minimum fair execution time X_{ij}
17:   $N_j(t) = N_j(t) + 1$
18:   Send the scheduling decision to the user of task i
19: **end for**

---

we propose a version of FETE, called Simple FETE (SFETE), which requires no a-priori knowledge of the tasks workload.

The SFETE assigns task i to resource j that provides the minimum simple fair execution time $\widehat{X}_{ij}$. The simple fair execution time $\widehat{X}_{ij}$ is an estimation of the time by which task i will be executed on resource j, assuming it gets a fair share of the resource's computational power, without taking into account the fair execution times of the other tasks already assigned to the resource (Figure 2). So, when the SFETE is employed in the example of Figure 1, then the simple fair execution time estimations of the tasks are equal ($t^A = t^B$).

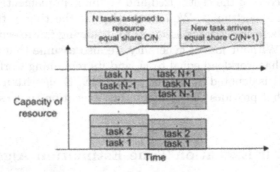

Fig. 2 Simple execution time estimation example.

The simple fair execution time $\widehat{X}_{ij}$ of task i on resource j, is defined as

$$\widehat{X}_{ij} = \frac{N_j+1}{C_j},$$

where C_j is the computational capacity of resource j and N_j is the number of tasks in the resource's queue, including the one being processed. It is once again important to note that the calculation of the simple fair execution time $\widehat{X}_{ij}$ of task i on resource j is only an estimate. New tasks may be sent to resource j, or existing tasks may complete their execution. This way the fair share of the computation capacity of the tasks already assigned to the resource changes, however their simple fair execution time estimations are not re-estimated.

The pseudocode of the centralized and "offline" implementation of the SFETE algorithm is presented in Algorithm 2.

Algorithm 2 Simple Fair Execution Time Estimation - SFETE

1: **for** each task i queued in the scheduler's ordered list **do**
2:    **for** each resource j in the Grid **do**
3:       Estimate the fair execution time: $\widehat{X}_{ij} = \frac{N_j+1}{C_j}$
4:    **end for**
5:    Assign task i to resource j that gives the minimum simple fair execution time $\widehat{X}_{ij}$
6:    $N_j = N_j + 1$
7:    Send the scheduling decision to the user of task i
8: **end for**

---

6 Performance Results

6.1 Simulation Environment

The proposed FETE and SFETE scheduling algorithms, along with other algorithms used for comparison (Table 1) were implemented and evaluated in the GridSim [7] simulator. The scheduling algorithms were implemented in a centralized and "offline" manner. FETE and Simple FETE algorithms were compared against some well-known algorithms presented in . In the Earliest Deadline First (EDF) ordering policy the task with the most imminent deadline is scheduled first, while in the Least Length First (LLF) ordering policy, the task with the smallest workload is given priority. The Earliest Completion Time (ECT) assignment policy, assigns a task to the resource where the task will finish its execution earlier. Also, the FETE and the simple FETE algorithms use the First Come First Serve (FCFS) ordering policy, where tasks are processed (assigned to resources) in the order they arrive to the scheduler.

All the scheduling algorithms were evaluated in a Uniform resource scenario, in which all resources have the same characteristics (number of CPU

Table 1 The scheduling algorithms compared with the FETE and the SFETE.

Algorithm	Ordering policy	Assignment policy
FCFS/ECT	First Come First Served (FCFS)	Earliest Completion Time (ECT)
EDF/ECT	Earliest Deadline First (EDF)	Earliest Completion Time (ECT)
LLF/ECT	Least Length First (LLF)	Earliest Completion Time (ECT)

and capacity) and in a non-Uniform resource scenario, in which the resources have different characteristics. The total computational capacity of the resources in both scenarios was the same. The tasks characteristics are defined probabilistically and the users task submission rate follows an exponential distribution, whose mean takes the following values: 12, 20, 25, 33, 40, 50, 55, 60, 65, 70 tasks/sec. Finally, in our simulations we assume that the communication delays are negligible compared to the execution time of the tasks, which is the case in Computational Grids.

6.2 Simulation Metrics

The algorithms are evaluated using the following metrics:

- Average Task Delay: The average of the delays of the tasks (task Delay = task Finish Time - task Creation Time).
- Task Delay Standard Deviation: The standard deviation of the task delays.
- Average Excess Time: The average time by which a task misses its non-critical deadline (task Excess Time = task Finish Time - task Deadline Expiration).
- Excess Time Standard Deviation: The standard deviation of the time by which the tasks miss their non-critical deadlines.
- Deadlines Missed: The number of tasks that miss their non-critical deadlines.

6.3 Simulation Results

For all the scheduling algorithms examined the average task delay increases as a function of the task submission rate (Figure 3). Specifically, for light load all the algorithms have similar behavior, however, when the task submission rate increases the FETE algorithms (FETE and SFETE) achieve smaller average task delay. This happens because the proposed algorithms treat the tasks and utilize the resources in a more fair manner, something that becomes more evident as the task load increases. We also observe that the FETE algorithms result in smaller task delay standard deviation than the other algorithms (Table 1). These results where confirmed both for the Uniform and for the non-Uniform resource scenario.

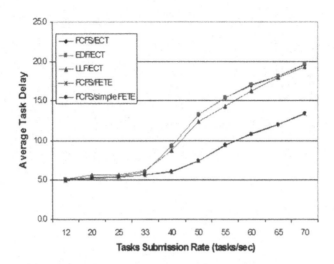

Fig. 3 Average task delay versus task submission rate in the Uniform resource scenario.

Figure 4 illustrates that the average excess time increases as a function of the task submission rate, for both resource scenarios. In the Uniform resource scenario (Figure 4.a) the increase is smaller when the FETE algorithms (FETE and SFETE) are used, meaning that the times by which the tasks miss their deadlines are also smaller. In the non-Uniform resource scenario (Figure 4.b) and for small task submission rates, the SFETE algorithm's performance is worse than that of the FETE and of the other algorithms examined. Next, as the task submission rate increases SFETE overpowers the other algorithms, whose performance deteriorates, while SFETE's remains almost constant.

SFETE does not have any knowledge of the task workloads and indirectly assumes a constant value for all the queued tasks fair execution times. On the other hand the FETE algorithm estimates more accurately the queued tasks fair execution times, whose values, however, are quite different due to the non-uniformity of the resources. When the submission rate increases, the number of tasks in the Grid also increases and the queued tasks fair execution times (estimated by FETE) approach on average a constant value. This is in accordance with the Law of Large Numbers and it is confirmed by Figure 4.b. Specifically, in Figure 4.b the average excess time achieved by the SFETE is almost constant and only increases in the very end when the Grid environment is almost saturated by the large number of tasks. On the other hand the average excess time of the FETE increases reaching that

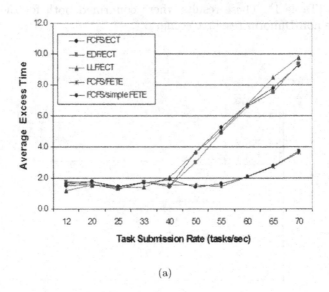

(a)

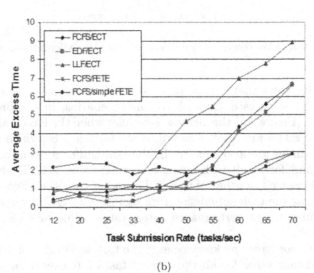

(b)

Fig. 4 Average excess time versus task submission rate, (a) in the Uniform resource scenario, (b) in the Non-Uniform resource scenario.

of the SFETE. Similar results were observed for the excess time standard deviation, for both resource scenarios.

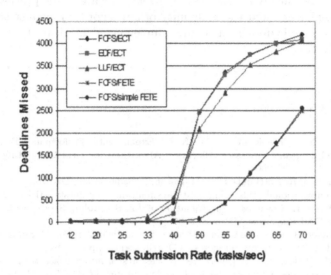

Fig. 5 Deadlines missed versus the task submission rate, in the Uniform resource scenario.

Finally, our performance results showed (Figure 5) that fewer tasks miss their deadlines when they are scheduled using the FETE algorithms than when they are scheduled with other algorithms. This is due to the fact that resources are utilized more uniformly, something that becomes more evident as the task load increases.

7 Conclusions

In this work we proposed two fair scheduling algorithms for Computational Grids, called Fair Execution Time Estimation (FETE) and Simple Fair Execution Time Estimation (SFETE). The FETE algorithms (FETE and SFETE) assign a task to the resource that minimizes what we call its fair execution time estimation. The fair execution time of a task on a certain resource is an estimation of the time by which a task will be executed on the resource, assuming it gets a fair share of the resource's computational power. The FETE algorithms where evaluated and compared against a number of known scheduling algorithms. The results indicate that in most cases and especially at large task submission rates, the FETE algorithms have similar performance and both outperform the other algorithms considered, with respect to performance and fairness related metrics. In addition, SFETE is more realistic, since it does not need the a-priori knowledge of task workload.

Based on these facts, we implemented SFETE in a production Grid Middleware and specifically in gLite [15]. Currently we are in the process of evaluating the efficiency and the scalability of our algorithm against the other, relative simple, scheduling algorithms implemented in gLite, by utilizing a real Grid Testbed.

References

1. I. Ahmad, Y.-K. Kwok, M.-Y. Wu, K. Li, Experimental Performance Evaluation of Job Scheduling and Processor Allocation Algorithms for Grid Computing on Metacomputers, IPDPS, 2004.
2. V. Subramani, R. Kettimuthu, S. Srinivasan, P. Sadayappan, Distributed job scheduling on computational grids using multiple simultaneous requests, HPDC, 2002.
3. Y. Cardinale, H. Casanova, An evaluation of Job Scheduling Strategies for Divisible Loads on Grid Platforms, HPC&S, 2006.
4. T. Braun, et al., A Comparison of Eleven Static Heuristics for Mapping a Class of Independent Tasks onto Heterogeneous Distributed Computing Systems, JPDC, 2001.
5. A. Parekh, R. Gallager, A generalized processor sharing approach to flow control in integrated services networks: the single-node case, IEEE/ACM ToN, 1993.
6. A. Demers, S. Keshav, S. Shenker, Analysis and simulation of a fair queuing algorithm, SIGCOMM, 1989.
7. R. Buyya, M. Murshed, GridSim: A Toolkit for the Modeling and Simulation of Distributed Resource Management and Scheduling for Grid Computing, Concurrency and Computation: Practice and Experience (CCPE), 2002.
8. R. Buyya, J. Giddy, D. Abramson, An evaluation of economy-based resource trading and scheduling on computational power grids for parameter sweep applications, Active Middleware Services, 2000.
9. R. Buyya, M. Murshed, D. Abramson, S. Venugopal, Scheduling Parameter Sweep Applications on Global Grids: A Deadline and Budget Constrained Cost-Time Optimization Algorithm, Journal of SPE, 2005.
10. Y. Zhou, H. Sethu, On Achieving Fairness in the Joint Allocation of Processing and Bandwidth Resources, IWQoS, 2003.
11. S. Zhuk, A. Chernykh, A. Avetisyan, S. Gaissaryan, D. Grushin, N. Kuzjurin, A. Pospelov, A. Shokurov, Comparison of Scheduling Heuristics for Grid Resource Broker, ENC, 2004.
12. K. Rzadca, D. Trystram, A. Wierzbicki, Fair Game-Theoretic Resource Management in Dedicated Grids, CCGrid, 2007.
13. K. H. Kim, R. Buyya, Fair Resource Sharing in Hierarchical Virtual Organizations for Global Grids, Grid Computing, 2007.
14. N. Doulamis, E. Varvarigos, T. Varvarigou, Fair Scheduling Algorithms in Grids, IEEE TPDS, 2007.
15. http://glite.web.cern.ch/glite/

Multiprocessor Task Scheduling using a new Prioritizing Genetic Algorithm based on number of Task Children

Marjan Abdeyazdan, Amir Masoud Rahmani

Abstract Due to optimal use of processors as well as spending less time, the task scheduling in multiprocessor systems is of great importance. This is one of the NP_hard problems and achieving the optimal schedule or finding the minimum schedule length, using the dynamic algorithm and back-tracking programming, would be time-consuming. Therefore, heuristic methods like genetic algorithms are suitable methods to schedule tasks in a multiprocessor system. In this paper, a new genetic algorithm is presented whose priority of tasks' execution is based on the number of their children. The results show that our developed algorithm finds the near-optimal schedule in a reasonable computation time, compared to other heuristics.

1 Introduction

A big program could not have been performed on a single processor in a reasonable time. Therefore, it has to be divided into several tasks and the schedule length should be minimized applying appropriate scheduling in a multiprocessor system.

For mathematical modeling of task scheduling problem, Direct Acyclic Graph (DAG) is used since each task is represented by its corresponding node in this graph. Presence of an edge from task t_i to task t_j means that while task t_i is not finished, task t_j can not start execution. The objective of scheduling a task graph onto a multiprocessor system is to allocate n tasks to m processors, as the priority task relations are observed and the completing time of the final task is reduced to minimum. Simply, if two tasks are scheduled on two different processors, the communication cost would be zero.

Scheduling in a multiprocessor system is an NP_Hard problem [1]. In traditional and dynamic methods, obtaining the best schedule is too time-consuming and often random execution of tasks needs less time. Then, in heuristic methods the best schedule is not necessarily obtained in a reasonable time; however the obtained solution is close to the best one. Many heuristic methods have been studied such as:

Marjan Abdeyazdan
Islamic Azad Universiy, Mahshahr branch, Iran. e-mail: marjanabdeyazdan69@yahoo.com

Amir Masoud Rahmani
Computer Engineering Department, Islamic Azad Universiy, Science and Research branch, Tehran, Iran. e-mail: rahmani@sr.iau.ac.ir

min–min, max-min, duplex, MCT (Minimum Completion Time), MET (Minimum Execution Time) [2], SA (Simulated Annealing) [3, 4], tabu search [5]. One of the best heuristic methods on task scheduling in multiprocessor systems is genetic algorithm [3, 6, 7, 8, 9, 11]. In this paper, a new genetic algorithm is introduced which executes tasks with respect to their priorities, based on the number of their children.

The paper is structured as followed. Section 2 presents priority-based task scheduling. In Section 3 a new method is explained that suggests prioritized tasks based on the number of their children. Section 4 elaborates on simulation and its result and Section 5 summarizes the achievements.

2 Priority-based task scheduling

2.1 Schedule length

The goal in scheduling problem is to minimize the schedule length. The time that the final task is completed on a processor is called the finishing time of that processor. The maximum finishing time between m processors is called TFT (Total Finishing Time) of the schedule or schedule length. TFT is calculated by Equation (1).

$$TFT= Max \ \{Finishing \ Time \ of \ Processor_j)\}; \quad for \ 1 \leq j \leq m \tag{1}$$

2.2 Prioritizing tasks based on their height

One of the common scheduling methods is prioritizing tasks based on their height [9] and it is as follows:

In a task graph, if there is a sequence of directed edges from t_i to t_j, then t_i is an ancestor of t_j and t_j is a child of t_i. If $PRED(t_i)$ is a set of preceded tasks of t_i, then the height of a task would be calculated as Equation (2) [9].

$$height(t_i) = \begin{cases} 0 & If \ PRED(t_i) = \phi \\ 1 + \max\limits_{t_j \in PRED(t_i)} height(t_j) & otherwise \end{cases} \tag{2}$$

In effect, the height function represents special precedence relations between tasks. If t_i is an ancestor of t_j, then t_i has to be executed before t_j and height(t_i) < height(t_j). If there is not any sequence of edges between two tasks, then there would be no precedence relation between them and they could be executed in any arbitrary order.

A schedule producing algorithm based on the task height is as follows:

1. Put tasks in a queue in ascending order according to their height.
2. Produce a random number r between 1 and m (m is the number of the processors).
3. Select the first task from the queue and allocate it to r^{th} processor and then delete it.

4. Repeat steps 2 and 3 until the queue is empty.

As far as the relations of task graph in Figure 1 are concerned, tasks are arranged with Table 1 based on their height and are scheduled on three processors by employing the above mentioned algorithm. A schedule with respect to Table 1 and Table 2 (execution time of tasks) is presented in Figure 2.

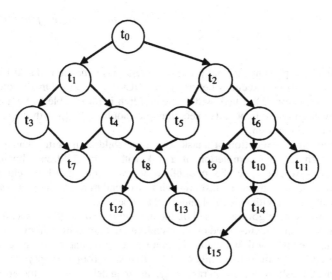

Figure 1 A task graph

Table 1 Height of tasks in Figure 1

t_0	t_1	t_2	t_3	t_4	t_5	t_6	t_7	t_8	t_9	t_{10}	t_{11}	t_{12}	t_{13}	t_{14}	t_{15}
0	1	1	2	2	2	2	3	3	3	3	3	4	4	4	5

Table 2 Execution time of tasks

t_0	t_1	t_2	t_3	t_4	t_5	t_6	t_7	t_8	t_9	t_{10}	t_{11}	t_{12}	t_{13}	t_{14}	t_{15}
3	2	4	1	10	3	6	9	7	11	5	5	8	10	15	2

P_1	t_0	t_3		t_9		t_{13}		t_{15}	

P_2		t_1	t_2	t_5		t_7		t_{12}	

P_3		t_4		t_6	t_8		t_{10}		t_{11}	t_{14}

```
     0   3  5   6  9   12  13   15  21  24    28  32 33    34  36  38        53
```

Figure 2 a schedule based on task height

2.3 Prioritizing tasks based on the number of their children

Our method of scheduling prioritizing is to assign tasks to each processor based on a higher number of their children. It means a task with more children would be scheduled earlier. In consideration of any task graph, the Number of Children (NC) for each task is calculated by Equation (3).

$$NC\,(t_i) = \begin{cases} 0 & ; if\ t_i\ has\ no\ child \\ \displaystyle\sum_{j=1}^{j=number\ of\ outgoing\ edges\ from\ task\ t_i} (1 + NC\,(t_j)) & ; as\ t_j\ has\ the\ direct \\ & incoming\ \ edge\ \ from\ t_i \end{cases} \quad (3)$$

The NC function represents special precedence relations between tasks. If t_j is a child of t_i, then t_i has to be executed before t_j and $NC(t_i) > NC(t_j)$. On the other hand, according to Equation (3), a task with more children is impossible to be a child of a task with fewer children; hence, its execution does not have to do with the completion of task with fewer children.

Logically, the earlier execution of a task with more children is better than a task with the lower height, as the completion of a task with more children - however with higher height - would raise the possibility of execution of all its children. For example, in Figure 1 there is task t_{10} with two children and height value of 4 compared with task t_3 with one child and height value of 3.

A schedule producing algorithm based on the number of task children is as follows:
1. Put tasks in a queue based on their children in descending order.
2. Separate tasks with the equal NC in a single group and perform steps 3 and 4 for all groups in order of higher NC until every group is empty.
3. Select a task from a group randomly, and then delete it from the group.
4. Allocate that task to one of the m processors based on EST (Earliest Start Time) method, in a manner that starting time of that task on that processor is less than other processors.

Finally, all tasks are assigned to the processors (completeness) and each task is allocated only once (uniqueness). Our suggested prioritizing algorithm is illustrated with an example with attention to the task graph in Figure 1. The NC of each task is presented in Table 3 and the tasks are arranged in descending order based on their NC in Table 4. The EST for each task is shown in Table 5. By applying the above algorithm, a schedule would be produced as shown in Figure 3.

Table 3 Relevant NC for each task of Figure 1

T_0	t_1	t_2	t_3	t_4	t_5	t_6	t_7	t_8	t_9	t_{10}	t_{11}	t_{12}	t_{13}	t_{14}	t_{15}
15	6	10	1	4	3	5	0	2	0	2	0	0	0	1	0

Table 4 Ordering tasks based on their NC

t_0	t_2	t_1	t_6	t_4	t_5	t_8	t_{10}	t_3	t_{14}	t_7	t_9	t_{11}	t_{12}	t_{13}	t_{15}
15	10	6	5	4	3	2	2	1	1	0	0	0	0	0	0

Table 5 EST for tasks

t_0	t_1	t_2	t_3	t_4	t_5	T_6	t_7	t_8	t_9	t_{10}	t_{11}	t_{12}	t_{13}	t_{14}	t_{15}
0	3	3	5	5	7	7	15	15	13	13	13	22	22	18	33

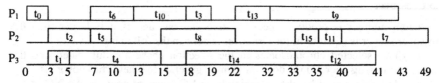

Figure 3 A schedule based on tasks' NC

3 The proposed algorithm

The genetic algorithm (GA) was developed by John Holland in 1975 [10] which is a search technique based on the principles of genetics and natural selection to find an optimal or sub-optimal solution. In GA, the term chromosome typically refers to a candidate solution to a problem. GA allows a population composed of many chromosomes to evolve under specified selection rules to a state that maximizes the fitness (i.e., minimizes the cost function). GA is a method for moving from initial population of chromosomes to a new population by using a kind of genetic operators like crossover and mutation. Each chromosome consists of genes. The selection operator chooses those chromosomes in the population that will be allowed to reproduce new generation. Crossover exchanges subparts of two chromosomes and mutation randomly changes the values of some genes in the chromosome.

The new genetic algorithm introduced in this paper has following six phases:

3.1 The fitness value and initial population producing

The cost function of each schedule (i.e., the fitness of each chromosome) is selected as schedule length or TFT based on Equation (1). By repetition of the schedule producing algorithm based on the number of tasks children, the initial population will be produced.

3.2 Selection

The selection phase has two steps:

1) Applying a roulette wheel to select two chromosomes:

After ascending ordering of chromosomes based on their fitness, a roulette wheel series is constructed based on their fitness [1]. Hence, the chromosomes with lower TFT (best fitness), occupy more slots in the roulette wheel. In this way the possibility of selecting chromosomes with best fitness is higher. Then two chromosomes will be selected.

2) Applying a roulette wheel for selecting a task:

A roulette wheel is constructed for tasks based on their NC. A task with more children has more chance to be selected compared to a task with fewer ones.

The genetic operators like crossover, mutation and load balancing will be applied on the current generation to produce the next generation.

3.3 Crossover

A random number is produced between zero and one and if it is larger than the crossover rate or is equal to it, the crossover is done in the following way:

1) Two selected chromosomes in the selection phase are duplicated and the following operation is done on them to generate two new chromosomes.

2) All tasks would be chosen which have NC lower or equal to the NC of the selected task in the selection phase. For every processor of the first chromosome, the chosen tasks are exchanged with the other tasks in the peer processor in the second chromosome.

For example, the chromosomes C_1 and C_2 and the task t_{14} with NC value of 1 have been selected. During the crossover, the tasks which have NC lower or equal to 1 e.g. tasks $\{t_3, t_{14}, t_7, t_9, t_{11}, t_{12}, t_{13}, t_{15}\}$ are selected in both chromosomes and then are exchanged on their relevant peer processors as shown in Figure 4.

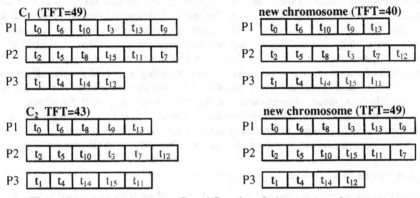

Figure 4 Applying crossover on C_1 and C_2 and producing two new chromosomes

3.4 Mutation

A random number between zero and one is produced and if it is larger than the mutation rate or is equal to it, the mutation operation is done in the following way:

1) Two selected chromosomes in the selection phase are duplicated and then the following operation is done separately on them.

2) For the first chromosome, the selected task in the selected phase is exchanged with another task on different processor which has NC equal to it. The same operation is done on the second selected chromosome.

For example, the chromosome C_1 and the task t_{13} with NC value of zero are selected for the mutation. Another task from chromosome C_1 in different processor that has the NC equal to t_3 e.g. t_{15} is selected and two tasks t_{13} and t_{15} are exchanged as shown in Figure 5.

Lemma 1. Since applying the mutation or crossover operators implies the uniqueness and completeness requirements have been met, after applying such operators, no task is missed and no task is added to the new chromosome. However, as all operators are based on tasks' NC, the tasks' execution precedence is met too.

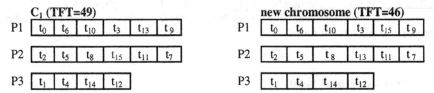

Figure 5 Applying mutation on C_1 and producing a new chromosome

3.5 Load balance

In this phase a new heuristic method called load balance is presented to reduce the TFT of chromosomes. The method involves following steps:

1) First, two selected chromosomes in selection phase are reduplicated and then the following operation is separately performed on two new chromosomes.

2) For one of the chromosomes from m processors, two processors which have the maximum and the minimum finishing time are selected (P_{max} and P_{min}). Then according to Equation (4), AVG is calculated as following:

$$AVG = (TFT(P_{max}) - TFT(P_{min}))/2 \qquad (4)$$

3) To balance the execution time of processors, task t_i is selected which is assigned to P_{max} and its execution time is equal or less than AVG. If such a task is not found, step 4 or load balance operation could not be performed.

4) Task t_i is deleted from P_{max} and then is added to P_{min} in a suitable place based on its NC in descending order, as all tasks' execution precedence is observed.

For example, the chromosome C_1 and the task t_{15} are selected for the load balance operation. As shown in Figure 6, applying the load balance guarantees improvement of the fitness of chromosome C_1.

After load balance operation, the uniqueness and completeness requirements are met based on Lemma 1.

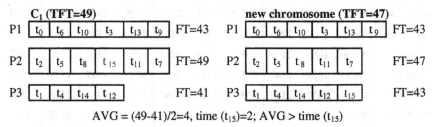

AVG = (49-41)/2=4, time (t_{15})=2; AVG > time (t_{15})

Figure 6 Applying load balance on C1 and producing a new chromosome

3.6 Reproduction

After applying all operators and producing new chromosomes, the former chromosomes along with new ones will be ordered based on their fitness and the next generation receives the most appropriate chromosomes (the chromosomes with lower

TFT or best fitness) at the number of population size. Then the phases 3-2 to 3-6 will be repeated as the number of generations. Finally, the best suitable chromosome is the optimal or near-optimal schedule.

4. Simulations and Results

A range of simulations is done using the Visual Basic .Net version 2005 on a computer Pentium IV, having AMD processor 2.8 GHz, and 512 MB memory of RAM to evaluate our suggested algorithm.

Using our developed program - producing a random task graph automatically - 57 task graphs are created. Each graph could have 30, 70, or 90 tasks with task dependency percentage between 20 and 90 and the execution time for each task is random between 1 and 100 seconds. These graphs are scheduled on a multiprocessor system with the number of 3, 5, or 7 processors for five heuristics: min–min, max–min, duplex, MCT (Minimum Completion Time) and MET (Minimum Execution Time) [2] and for two genetic-based algorithms: Genetic Algorithm whose Priority is based on Task Height (GAPTH) [9] and our proposed algorithm. The results are averaged over multiple runs for each algorithm.

For two genetic-based algorithms, the crossover rate is set to 0.7 and the mutation rate is set to 0.05. Other parameters such as initial population size and the number of generations are selected similarly for genetic algorithms to perform the scheduling at the same conditions.

Table 6 The schedules for seven scheduling algorithms

Algorithms	Total Finish Time (TFT) (seconds)									TFT Mean (s)
	Number of processors = 3			Number of processors = 5			Number of processors = 7			
	Number of tasks			Number of tasks			Number of tasks			
	30	50	70	30	50	70	30	50	70	
min–min	992.3	1689	2303	902.3	1561	2231	908	1485	2285	1595
max-min	975.3	1669	2206	835.3	1466	2220	850.6	1436	2183	1579
duplex	962.6	1669	2171	835.3	1466	2213	850.6	1436	2183	1572
MCT	988	1650	2148	836.6	1477	2271	858.6	1417	2177	1535
MET	966.6	1677	2164	835.3	1505	2268	890.3	1421	2178	1545
GAPTH	966.3	1634	2108	827.6	1447	2032	840.3	1410	2122	1487
Our algorithm	881.6	1560	2052	727	1418	2141	800	1296	2049	1436

Table 6 shows the schedules and TFT mean for each seven scheduling algorithms. The results indicate that our suggested algorithm finds better schedule with minimum TFT compared to the other heuristics. While the computation time of the two above genetic algorithms is more than the other five heuristics obviously, and is quite similar, as only their initial population producing step is different, the step is calculated once.

Table 7 illustrates the results of simulations with varying task dependency percentage. As shown here, if the number of tasks and processors, and the range of tasks' execution time are considered constant, then the higher percentage of the task dependency has better schedule for our developed algorithm compared with the other genetic algorithm, named GAPTH. The reason lies in the fact that the higher the task dependency is, the more number of children. Our scheduling algorithm is more efficient than the other one as it acts based on NC.

Table 7 Schedules for two genetic algorithms with varying task dependency percentage

Dependency percentage	Mean TFT for GAPTH (seconds)	Mean TFT for Our algorithm (seconds)	Efficiency of our algorithm to GAPTH
30	1503.4	1439.2	4.4
50	1586.2	1506.1	5.3
70	1466.3	1363.6	7.5

5 Conclusions

The task scheduling problem in multiprocessor systems is an NP_Hard problem. Hence, using heuristic methods instead of classic ones, the optimal or near-optimal schedule would be achieved in an acceptable time. Due to the higher potential of genetic algorithms in solving the complex problems, they have been vastly acceptable in the heuristic methods. In this paper, a new genetic algorithm was presented for task scheduling in a multiprocessor system. In this algorithm, the priority of execution of tasks is based on the number of their children, i.e., a task having more children will be scheduled earlier. Our developed algorithm was compared to the genetic algorithm whose priority is based on task height, and to the five well-known heuristics. The results showed that our suggested algorithm improves the achievement of the near-optimal schedule; however, the computation time of the two discussed genetic algorithms are quite the same.

References

1. Goldberg D. E.: Genetic Algorithms in Search, Optimization and Machine Learning, Reading. MA: Addison Wesley, (1989)
2. Braun T. D., Siegel H. J., Beck N. and et al.: A Comparison of Eleven Static Heuristic for Mapping a Class of Independent Tasks onto Heterogeneous Distributed Computing Systems. Journal of Parallel and Distributed Computing, vol. 61, pp. 810--837, (2001)
3. Rahmani A. M. and Resvani M.: A novel Static Task Scheduling in Distributed Systems by Genetic Algorithm using Simulated Annealing. 12th International CSI Conference, Iran, p. 83, (2007)

4. Bouffard V., Ferland J. A.: Improving simulated annealing with variable neighborhood search to solve the resource-constrained scheduling problem. Journal of Scheduling, Vol. 10(4), pp. 375--386, (2007)

5. Silva M. L. and Porto S. C. S.: An Object-Oriented Approach to a Parallel Tabu Search Algorithm for the Task Scheduling Problem. Proceedings of the 19th International Conference of the Chilean Computer Science Society, p. 105, (1999)

6. Shenassa M. H. and Mahmoodi M.: a novel intelligent method for task scheduling in multiprocessor systems using genetic algorithm. journal of Franklin institute, Elsevier, (2006)

7. Yoo M. and Gen M.: Scheduling algorithm for real-time tasks using multiobjective hybrid genetic algorithm in heterogeneous multiprocessors system. Computers and Operations Research, Vol. 34(10), P. 3084--3098, (2007)

8. Zheng S., Shu W. and Dai S.: Task Scheduling Model Design Using Hybrid Genetic Algorithm. in Proceedings of the First International Conference on Innovative Computing, Information and Control, Vol. 3, pp. 316--319, (2006)

9. Hou E. S. H., Ansari N. and Ren H.: A Genetic Algorithm for Multiprocessor Scheduling. IEEE trans. on parallel and distributed systems. vol. 5, no. 2, pp. 113--120, Feb. (1994)

10. Holland J. H.: Adaptation in Natural and Artificial Systems. University of Michigan Press, Ann Arbor, MI, (1975)

11. Zafarani Moattar E., Rahmani A.M., Feizi Derakhshi M.R., "Job Scheduling in Multi Processor Architecture Using Genetic Algorithm", 4th IEEE International conference on Innovations in Information Technology, dubai, pp. 248-251, (2007)

A Framework for Fair and Reliable Resource Sharing in Distributed Systems

Tarek Helmy, Irfan Ahmad and Aleem K. Alvi

Abstract Peer-to-Peer (P2P) and distributed systems are typically designed around the assumption that all peers/nodes will willingly contribute resources to each other. They thus suffer from freeloaders, that are, participants who consume many more resources than they contribute. For example, a peer/node may be willing to be a resource consumer and not a provider. Moreover a resource provider may not be providing efficient and reliable services to other peers/nodes and is just sharing resources for the sake of resource sharing. In this paper, we propose a framework for fair and reliable resource sharing in distributed/P2P systems. For fairness we use the concept of accounting systems; where the entities of the systems are bank accounts, salaries and resource rates. Every system can use the resources of other systems on payments from its salary and can select the resource in competitive environment. Reliability is implemented by using the trust model; where reliability levels are modeled for realization of reliability in the system. Experimental simulation used for evaluating and validating the performance of the proposed framework. Results show that the framework is very trustable for the resource sharing with fairness and reliability in distributed/P2P systems.

Tarek Helmy

College of Computer Science and Engineering, King Fahd University of Petroleum and Minerals, Dhahran 31261, Mail Box 413, Kingdom of Saudi Arabia. On leave at Tanta University, Egypt, e-mail: helmy@kfupm.edu.sa

Irfan Ahmad

College of Computer Science and Engineering, King Fahd University of Petroleum and Minerals, Dhahran 31261, Mail Box 413, Kingdom of Saudi Arabia., e-mail: irfanics@kfupm.edu.sa

Aleem K. Alvi

College of Computer Science and Engineering, King Fahd University of Petroleum and Minerals, Dhahran 31261, Mail Box 413, Kingdom of Saudi Arabia., e-mail: akalvi@kfupm.edu.sa

Keywords: Peer-to-Peer/Distributed systems, Fair and reliable recourse sharing.

1 Introduction

Recent years have seen the introduction of P2P systems, whose design relies centrally on exchange of resources between peers. Exchanged resources include content, as in popular P2P file sharing applications, and storage capacity or CPU cycles, as in computational and storage grid systems. Computation and storage are
the major resources in distributed systems. Resource sharing requires fairness and
reliability among the resources. Managing resources in terms of distribution
among the entities fairly either in non-distributed or in distributed environment is
one of the open challenges. The definition of a computational grid was primarily
centered on the computational aspects of grids [1]. Later iterations broadened this
definition with more focus on coordinated resource sharing and problem solving
in multi-institutional virtual organizations [10].

Two supposedly new approaches to distributed computing; P2P [12, 13,
14, 15, 22] and Grid computing [1, 3, 4, 5, 11, 21] have emerged in the past
few years, both claiming to address the problem of organizing large scale
computational resources; where, all resources are shared using the grids (like data
grids, computational grids, etc.). P2P technology is used to share the resources
among individual peers. The characterization of P2P is that, it is decentralized,
self-organizing, distributed systems, in which all or most communication is symmetric. This type of sharing is very dominant nowadays and may be the permanent
part of the future computing. At start, authorities criticized on this technique because of copyright problems. The one node (user or may say provider or consumer
on the other hand) can communicate and share a resource without any restriction
and monitoring by any authority. Majority of the resource sharing is developed [2]
for the copyrighted material (e-Books, audio and video). This capability gives the
power to individual peers to share resources and increases their utilizations. While
many P2P systems have implicitly assumed that peers will altruistically contribute
resources to the global pool and assist others, recent empirical studies have shown
that a large fraction of the participants engage in freeloading [15]. These issues de-
feat the purpose of resources sharing and cooperation originally intended by the
P2P/distributed systems. Thus there is an acute need for some frameworks and
mechanisms to be incorporated into these distributed systems so as to realize the
goal of fair and reliable sharing of resources among the systems in the distributed
environment.

We present a framework; as a solution to the above mentioned problem; of
fair and reliable resource sharing among the peers in the distributed environment.
In this framework, the goal of fairness is realized using concepts of bank account
and funds. The goal of reliability is realized by utilizing the concept of trusts.

Trust model is used for this concept, where the reliability of one supplier of a resource is measured by an input from all other consumers' satisfaction. Our semantics of trust is simple and easy to implement compared with other trust models [11, 17, 19]. The rest of this paper is organized as follows. Section 2 gives a brief overview of the related works. In Section 3 we provide a system model and specification for the proposed framework for resource sharing followed by an architecture description and the details of the mechanisms for fairness and reliability. Section 4 presents simulation results for evaluating and analyzing the performance of the implemented framework, while concluding remarks and future work directions are outlined in Section 5.

2 Related Works

A framework for providing incentives for honest participation in global-scale distributed management infrastructures is given in [7, 8]. The author's approach in [8] is given as (1) to provide rewards for participants that advertise their experiences to others, and (2) to impose the credible threat of halting the rewards; for a substantial amount of time; for participants who consistently provide suspicious feedback. From security point of view, the researchers developed frameworks for secure access and sharing among resources that prevent the malicious user from the network.

Anthill [14] is a novel framework for P2P application, it is development based on ideas such as multi-agent systems and evolutionary genetic programming. The goals of Anthill are to provide an environment that simplifies the design and deployment of P2P systems based on these paradigms, and to provide a test bed for studying and experimenting with complex adaptive systems-based P2P systems in order to understand their properties and evaluate their performance. Details of the design and implementation of Anthill as storage management and ant scheduling can be found in [14].

Ngan et al. in [20] present a design that enforces fair-sharing in P2P storage systems. Their goal is to ensure that the disk space; a user is willing to put up for storing other user's files; is greater than the space consumed by the user's files on other disks. This design makes use of the fact that the resource in contention is spatial in nature: any user's claim that s/he is storing files for other users can be verified after the claim is made.

The new Grid frameworks [9, 21] that implement the concept of dynamic trust and reputation adaptation of resources based on community experiences. It has harnessed the power of Web service technologies to allow communication and flexibility in the framework. Again for security point of view the decentralized P2P networks offer threats. Its open and decentralized nature makes it extremely susceptible to malicious users spreading harmful content like Viruses, Trojans or, even just wasting valuable resources of the network [10]. In order to minimize such threats, the use of community-based reputations as trust measurements is fast becoming a standard fact. The idea is to dynamically assign each peer a trust rating based on its performance in the network and store it at a suitable place. Any peer wishing to interact with another peer can make an informed decision based on such a rating [18].

Authors of paper [23] presented Credence, a decentralized object reputation and ranking system for large-scale P2P file sharing networks. Credence counteracts pollution in these networks by allowing honest peers to assess the authenticity of online content through secure tabulation and management of endorsements from other peers. The system enables peers to learn relationships even in the absence of direct observations or interactions through a novel, flow-based trust computation to discover trustworthy peers.

Czajkowski in [6] discusses the concept of directory service so as to identify different resources available as services across the network. The job of selecting a non-local resource for computation needs of a node in the network is carried by a super-scheduler. An agent is responsible for deciding if its local application needs some remote resources by monitoring the external resource availability. For managing security related issues, an information provider may specify; for each piece of information that it maintains; the credentials that must be presented to access that information.

3 The Proposed Framework

We propose a framework for fair and reliable resource sharing in distributed P2P environment. Resource implies any service offered by a system in the network like storage and/or computation. By "fair" we mean that we should not allow a system to just use resources from other systems but rather it should also provide its own resources to other systems in a proportional scale. Thus a system should not only be a consumer but also a service provider in the distributed P2P environment. We use the concept of the bank account and salary to model the goal of fairness. As illustrated in Figure 1, there is a global monetary agent in the system which will be acting as a bank for the systems in the network. This monetary agent unit will be responsible for maintaining the bank balances for each system in the network, to deposit regular salaries to each system at regular times, and to adjust the balance between systems whenever one of them takes service (consumes resource) from another system. By "reliable" we mean that the consumer of the resource (CPU time, Storage etc...) should get good service from other systems and that it was not "cheated". Moreover any particular system should not be overloaded by offering a lot of services to other systems. This will again be achieved by the concept of variable rates. Thus our framework not only promotes fair sharing of resources among the systems but also reliable resource sharing as it will be shown hereafter.

3.1 Proposed Framework Architecture

Systems in a network cooperate with each other and provide resource sharing, where we consider a system as an autonomous peer in the distributed systems. As shown in Figure 1, each system has Decision Making Units (DMU) to help itself in making decisions related to selection of services from other systems in the distributed systems. The decision for selecting resources is based on the value of reliability level and the resources rate of that particular system. Thus query to the decision unit will be of the form: Request (R_i , C, T) where, R_i = Resource context i, C = Maximum rate willing to pay, and T = Minimum trust level of the server node. Therefore the system requires a resource will shortlist the other systems based on the reliability level. Then it selects the system offering the cheapest rate among the listed systems by searching Global Bulletin Board (GBB).

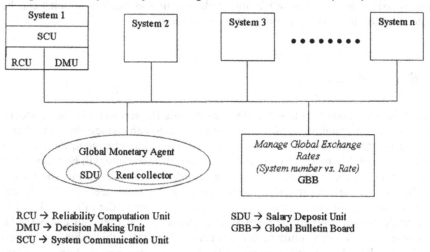

RCU → Reliability Computation Unit   SDU → Salary Deposit Unit
DMU → Decision Making Unit   GBB → Global Bulletin Board
SCU → System Communication Unit

Fig. 1: Overall system architecture

The proposed framework will have a GBB publishing the current resource rates offered by all systems in the network for different resource types. Each row in the table will have information for each resource type and the columns signify the system offering the service. Thus R (i, j) = x means rate offered for resource 'i' by server 'j' is 'x' units per time unit. As discussed before, there will be a global monetary agent in the network to manage monetary related information of the systems in the network. This global agent will deposit salaries to the accounts of respective systems in the network at regular time intervals so that they can use them in turn to avail the services from other systems in the network. A form of taxation has been implemented so as to avoid excessive accumulation of salaries by any system. A resource requirement by any system will be notified to the monetary agent. Now the monitory agent will deduct amount from this particular system's bank account and will deposit it to the server's bank account based on the resource context and the rate. Thus a system should have enough funds in its account so as to avail services from other systems in the network. If it has insufficient funds in its account than it can take one or more of the following decisions:

1. It can wait for until it receives its regular salary from the monetary agent.
2. It can encourage other systems in the network to use its shared resources by decreasing the resource rate. As more systems use this system's resources, its fund will increase.
3. It can make changes to its local policies so that it serves other systems more reliably. This will lead to better reliability levels and will encourage other systems to avail services of this system leading to increase the fund of this system.

We observe from the above discussion that systems in the distributed environment will be encouraged to share resources and offer better quality and service. Thus by using the rate and reliability levels, useful and flexible policies can be created by individual systems to suit there local needs.

3.2 Resource Rate

Each system in the network will offer resource rate for services to other systems. This rate can be dynamic in the sense that the system can change the current rate or willing to charge for one or more of its resources. Any change in the resource rate by a system has to be notified to GBB so that this new rate will be reflected to other systems in the network. The change in rate could be due to various factors like the current consumption/demand for the resource, local needs of the system, reliability level, and etc. To avoid very frequent changes in the rate, a policy has been implemented globally to restrict the systems so that they can change their rates only after "Δt" time units once it has changed the rate, (this value of "Δt" can be common based on some relevant criteria). In our experimentation, a system changes its current rate and willing to charge for a particular resource based on its current bank balance, the fraction of fund it has consumed and the fraction of time left before it will get its regular salary. Let "Δb" denote the fraction of balance left when compared to original balance and "Δt" denote fraction of time left before regular salary deposit. For any resource type, the current rate a system is willing to charge will be updated as:

$$new\ rate = old\ rate + (\Delta b - \Delta t)\%\ old\ rate$$

The resource rate is updated in regular interval of time. Thus a system having more balance fraction in comparison to time fraction (*it means that system's fund utilizations are very slow*) will increase the rate for resources. Therefore the second term of the equation will be positive. Whereas a system having less balance in comparison to time for salary dispatch to account (*it means that system's fund utilizations are very fast*) will require decreasing its rate. Therefore the second term of the equation will become negative. It means that if systems use their funds quickly and funds are exhausted so the system should decrease its local resource rate to attract clients for providing services. On the contrary it means that the system's local funds will increase and may be used for taking services from other systems. Hence the equation second term always keep balance in either the situation as mentioned.

3.3 Reliability Scale

Each system in the network will have a reliability value ranging in the scale of 1 to 7. Reliability values from 1 to 3 signify **"low"**, 4 to 5 signify **"medium"** and 6 to 7 signify **"high"** reliability levels. Reliability value for a particular system can be different than other systems based on the experiences of the observer system while dealing with the particular system. The reliability computation unit of the system will store the reliability levels of different systems in the network as perceived by itself. We introduce a term $\Omega(i)=x$ (reliability level of system i is x) as perceived by a system. Each system periodically inquires about the reliability level of other systems in the network. Let each system respond with a value Φ (i, j) meaning reliability level of system i is Φ as perceived by system j. Thus a particular system will update the reliability level of a target system x as follows:

$$R_i = \sum_{j=1}^{n} \Phi(i, j) \quad , where \quad n = no. \ of \ systems$$

$$\Omega_{t+1}(i) = \alpha * \Omega_t(i) + (1 - \alpha)R_i$$

Where $\alpha = 0.5$ gives equal weights to old and new information.

4 Experiments and Results

We conducted simulation experiments to demonstrate how the proposed framework satisfies the fairness goal. We simulated the distributed environment for 10 systems. Each system is initially given a salary of 500 units (this is the incentive given to the systems for joining the network). Salaries of 100 units are deposited to every system after Δt regular time interval. To avoid domination by any particular system in the network, we implemented a form of taxation where no system is allowed to exceed balance of 500 at the time as a salary deposit. In our simulation, context for resource sharing is CPU computation. Resource rate for each system is initially fixed at 250 units. It means to get service once; a system needs to pay 250 units. Individual resource rates can be varied by each respective system depending on its own local conditions of consumption and account balance. Rate updates are done much more frequently by each system as compared to salary deposits (in our simulation a system can change its rate 6 times between two salary deposits). There are upper and lower limits to the resource rates (250 and 50 respectively i.e. 1/2 and 1/10 of salary respectively). We conducted two experiments as follows:

Scenario 1:

In this scenario, there are 10 systems and requests for remote service are generated randomly. Thus each system will have about the same number of requests for shared resource. All the other condition and criteria (e.g. fairness) are used as described above. Simulation results of scenario 1 are shown in the following Figures. In Figure 2, we show the fairness results for each system. The number of times it receives service from other systems is shown against the number of times it offers its services to other systems. From the figure we can see that our framework does satisfy the fairness goal as there are small fluctuations between services availed verses services offered for each system.

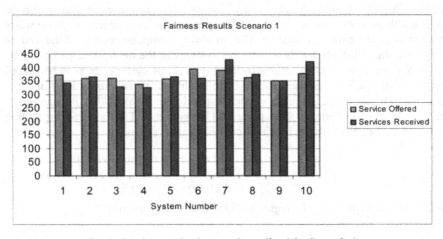

Fig. 2: Services received vs. services offered for Scenario 1

In Figure 3, we present the results for satisfaction. By satisfaction we mean the number of times a system needs a shared resource against the number of times it succeeded in getting served. We know from the framework discussion that, for a system to get a resource, it should have enough balance to pay the system offering the resource. From Figure 3, we can see that although satisfaction results for each system is high; still we are testing some mechanisms to increase the satisfaction rate further.

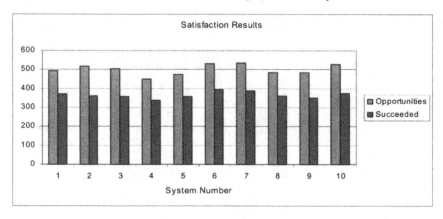

Fig. 3: Opportunity vs. success for Scenario 1

Figure 4 and Figure 5 show the trends in rates and funds for few systems between two time intervals.

Scenario 2:

In this scenario there are 10 systems and we choose two systems at random such that the need for shared resource for these two systems is twice in comparison of other systems in the network. We were interested to see how the proposed framework behaves in these conditions. All the other conditions are kept same as before. Simulation results of scenario 2 are shown in the Figures 6, 7, 8, and 9.

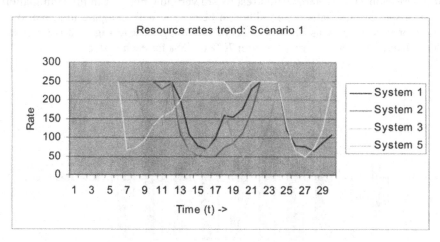

Fig. 4: Resource rates trend for Scenario 1

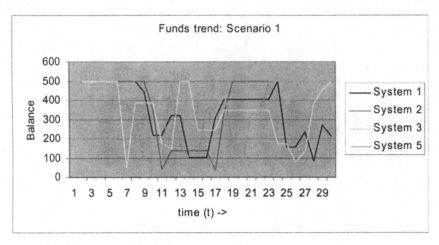

Fig. 5: Funds trend for Scenario 1

In Figure 6, we show the fairness results for scenario 2. We can see that the proposed framework satisfies the fairness goal as there is not much fluctuation be-tween services availed verses services offered for each system. Even though sys-tem 5 and system 9 have high requirements for shared resource as compared to other systems, still the overall conditions are balanced.

In Figure 7, we show the satisfaction results in case of scenario 2. We may get an impression that the satisfaction results are very low but on careful examination we can see that the satisfaction although being low with compare to scenario 1, however it is not low as initially understood. Going back to Figure 3 we can see that satisfaction rates are varying from 70% to 75% for each system.

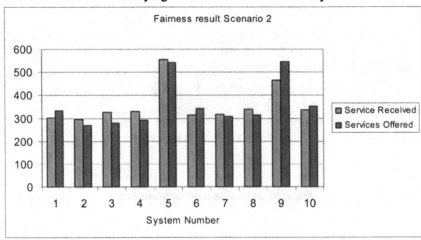

Fig. 6: Services received vs. services offered for Scenario 2

From Figure 7 we can see that except for system 5 and system 9 (systems having high shared resource needs), satisfaction rates are slightly higher than Scenario 1. Even for system 5 and system 9 the satisfaction rates are 66.23 % and 58.56 % respectively. We can see that the satisfaction rate dropped by around 10% and 15% respectively even though the resource requirement (shared) increased by around 76% and 64% respectively. Thus we claim that our framework successfully achieved its goals. However some work is under exploration to further increase the satisfaction rates in an unbalanced scenario.

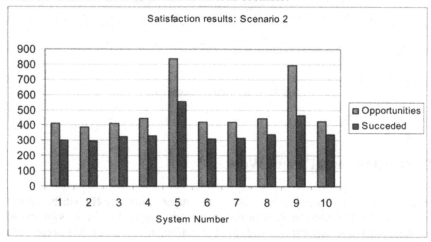

Fig. 7: Opportunity vs. success for Scenario 2

Figure 8 and Figure 9 show the trends in rates and funds for few representative systems between two time intervals.

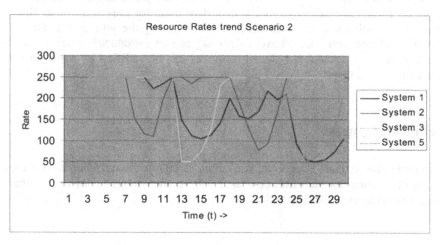

Fig. 8: Resource rates trend for Scenario 2

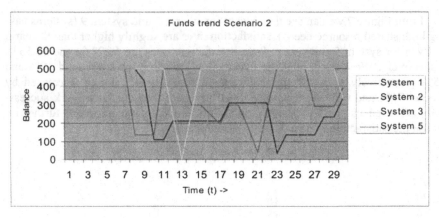

Fig. 9: Funds trend for Scenario 2

5 Conclusions and Future Work

Fair and reliable resource sharing is one of the major issues in P2P/distributed systems. To realize the intended benefit of resource sharing in distributed systems we need mechanisms to support fair and reliable sharing of resources. We presented a framework to realize these goals in this paper. The concepts of bank accounts, regular salary deposits and resource rates were used in the framework to achieve fairness. Reliability levels were used to model reliability. We have conducted experimental simulations to make a consistent evaluation of the framework's performance and to validate the claim. The results were promising but still there is scope of improvements. Some of the important areas for improvement as future work are as follows. Incorporate mechanism increasing the satisfaction rates for systems and concepts like "Borrow Criteria" can be introduced where systems which have high demand for shared resources can be satisfied by some sort of mechanisms like loans.

Acknowledgments

We would like to thank King Fahd University of Petroleum and Minerals for providing the computing facilities. Special thanks to anonymous reviewers for their insightful comments and feedback.

References

1. Alunkal K (2003) Grid Eigen Trust: a framework for computing reputation in grids. Master Thesis, Graduate College of the Illinois Institute of Technology.
2. Biddle P et al. (2002) The Darknet and the Future of Content Distribution. MSC 2002, http://msl1.mit.edu/ESD10/docs/darknet5.pdf
3. Bharadwaj V and Wong M (2004) Scheduling divisible loads on heterogeneous linear daisy chain networks with arbitrary processor release times. IEEE Trans Parallel Distributed Systems, 15:pp.273–288.
4. Banini C et al. (2004) Scheduling strategies for master-slave tasking on heterogeneous processor platforms. IEEE Trans Parallel Distributed Systems, 15: pp.319–330.
5. Chien A et al. (2003) Architecture and Performance of an Enterprise Desktop Grid System. Journal of Parallel and Distributed Computing, V 63, Elsevier Science, V. 36 no.5, pp.597–610.
6. Czajkowski K et al. (2001) Grid information services for distributed resource sharing. 10th IEEE International Symposium on High Performance Distributed Computing, pp.181-194.
7. Ernesto Damiani et al. (2002) A Reputation-Based Approach for Choosing Reliable Resources in Peer-to-Peer Networks, Proceedings of the 9th ACM conference on Computer and communications security pp.207-216.
8. Fernandes A et al. (2004) Pinocchio: Incentives for honest participation in distributed trust management, 2nd International Conference, iTrust, Oxford, UK, Volume LNCS 2995/2004, pp.64-77.
9. Foster I and Kesselman C (1998) The Grid: Blueprint for a New Computing Infrastructure. Morgan Kaufmann Publishers, San Francisco, CA.
10. Foster I et al. (2001) The Anatomy of the Grid: Enabling Scalable Virtual Organizations, Journal of High Performance Computing Applications, 15(3): pp.200-222.
11. Foster I (2002) The Grid: A New Infrastructure for 21st Century Science. Physics Today, pp.42-47.
12. Kevin Walsh and Emin Gun Sirer (2006) Experience with an Object Reputation System for Peer-to-Peer File sharing, Proceedings of the 3rd conference on 3rd Symposium on Networked Systems Design & Implementation - Volume 3, pp.1-1.
13. Oram A (2001) Peer-to-Peer: Harnessing the Power of Disruptive Technologies. O'Reilly.
14. O. Babaoglu (2002) A Framework for the Development of Agent-Based Peer-to-Peer Systems, In IEEE Proceedings of the 22nd International Conference on Distributed Computing Systems, pp. 15-22.
15. P. Krishna (2002) A measurement studies of Napster and Gnutella as examples of peer-to-peer file sharing systems, Multimedia Systems Journal, 9(2): pp.170-184.

16.   Runfang Zhou (2007) Power Trust: A Robust and Scalable Reputation System for Trusted Peer-to-Peer Computing. IEEE Transactions on Parallel Distributed Systems, vol. 18, no. 4, pp.460-473.
17.   Seti@home, "A system uses Internet-connected computers in the Search for Extraterrestrial Intelligence (SETI)", http://setiathome.berkeley.edu/.
18.   Shirky   C,   "What   is   P2P   and   what   isn't? http://www.openp2p.com/pub/a/p2p/2000/11/24/shirky1-whatisp2p.html
19.   Singh A and Liu L (2003) TrustMe: Anonymous Management of Trust Relationships in Decentralized P2P Systems. Proceedings of the 3rd IEEE International Conference on Peer-to-Peer Computing.
20.   T. Ngan et al. (2003) Enforcing Fair Sharing of Peer-to-Peer Resources, Springer LNCS, Volume 2735, pp.149-159.
21.   Van Moorsel and A P A, Grid, Management and Self-Management" The Computer Journal, Vol. 48, Issue 3, pp.325-332.
22.   Vivek Vishnumurthy et al. (2003) KARMA: A Secure Economic Framework for P2P Resource Sharing, http://www.sims.berkeley.edu/research/ conferences/p2pecon/index.html.
23.   Zhenggiang Liang and weisong Shi (2005) Enforcing Cooperative Resource Sharing in Un-trusted Peer-to-Peer Environment, Journal of Mobile Networks and Applications, Journal of Mobile Networks and Applications, Vol. 10, No.6, pp.971-983.

An Agent Based Architecture for DAG Scheduling

Catalin Leordeanu, Florin Pop, Corina Stratan and Valentin Cristea

Abstract This paper presents an efficient agent based DAG scheduling system. The proposed system has a decentralized architecture. It is able to manage tasks with dependencies, and bases its decisions on Grid resources' status captured dynamically and used at schedule time. Fault tolerance mechanisms can also be easily implemented, providing a great degree of certainty that the schedule results will be correct and delivered before the imposed deadline. The system has been integrated and tested with MonAlisa farms and the ApMon, which is a MonAlisa extension. The results obtained so far in the performed experiments show that the system introduces a reasonable overhead while producing higher quality mappings than the centralized ones.

1 Introduction

A Grid scheduler receives applications from users and determines the resources that will be used for each task. This is very difficult in Grid environments where we are dealing with shared resources in dynamic Virtual Organizations. In a Grid environment multiple schedulers could be deployed. The scheduling system is also responsible for the transfer of input data where and when they are required by the scheduled tasks. It also collects the results and presents them to the user who submitted the tasks. The Grid scheduler ensures that mapping the applications to resources satisfy some optimization criteria such as the average response time and the balanced resource utilization.

Grid schedulers take decisions regarding the resources, which are situated in several locations and are not directly accessible. As a result, Grid schedulers work with various agents or brokers[1], usually considered as part of a Grid scheduling system.

Catalin Leordeanu, Florin Pop, Corina Stratan and Valentin Cristea
Faculty of Automatics and Computer Science. University Politehnica of Bucharest, e-mail: {catalinl,florinpop,corina,valentin}@cs.pub.ro

The Grid scheduler needs accurate information on resource availability at different sites. This information is dynamically provided by a Grid Information Service (GIS), which is responsible for collecting and delivering resource state information such as CPU capacity and load, memory size, network bandwidth, and software availability. On the other hand, an Execution Service ensures the communication with multiple heterogeneous schedulers that operate at the level of resources that will execute the applications.

One solution for efficient and high performance execution of applications on distributed computing resources is breaking the problem into smaller pieces, which means partitioning the applications into smaller tasks. This can lead to dependent tasks, which ask for the design and use of more complex scheduling algorithms. The collection of tasks with dependencies that compose an application can be modeled as a Directed Acyclic Graph (DAG)[2] with weighted nodes and edges. Each node represents an individual task and its associated weight represents the execution time. An edge represents a dependency between two tasks; its weight represents the time needed to transfer data from the task producing it to the destination task before it can start execution.

The existing DAG scheduling systems have a centralized architecture. One of the most widely used instruments for DAG scheduling is DAGMan[9], which manages inter-job dependencies for Condor[13]. DAGMan works as a meta-scheduler, submitting the jobs to Condor in the order that corresponds to a topological sort of the graph; it also has fault-recovery capabilities. Other examples of workflow scheduling systems are the WorkFlow Enactment Engine (WFEE)[10], Pegasus[15] and Triana[16]. WFEE supports just-in-time scheduling, which permits resource allocation decision to adapt to changing grid environments. Current schedulers with decentralized architecture have been built to only schedule independent tasks. An example is Nimrod/G[11], which focuses on the management and scheduling based on the concept of computational economy.

As in many scientific applications the typical size of DAGs is of the order of thousands of nodes, the centralized approaches to scheduling have the disadvantage of poor scalability. In order to overcome this problem, we propose here a decentralized DAG scheduling system. The system is able to manage tasks with dependencies, and bases its decisions on Grid resources' status captured dynamically and used at schedule time. Like other Grid schedulers, it makes use of Grid services such as automatic resource discovery service, monitoring service, etc. It has been tested in experiments with complex jobs used for satellite image processing[8].

The remainder of this paper is structures as follows. In Section 2 we discuss the details about the architecture, describe the role of the major components, and presents the agents-brokers communication model. The advantages of choosing this architecture are also described here. In Section 3 we present the job description format, which is used to create the corresponding task graph and to submit new jobs for execution. In Section 4 we shortly describe the scheduling algorithms considered in the experiments and how the results relate to the scheduler's performance. The last part is dedicated to conclusions and further work.

2 Scheduling architecture

Generally, Grid scheduling involves three main phases: (1) discovery of available resources, which generates a list of potential resources; (2) gathering information about these resources and selecting a good sub-set of them; and (3) job execution, which includes file staging and cleanup.

Our project extends the DIOGENES architecture[12] for scheduling dependent tasks. DIOGENES uses a decentralized solution based on genetic algorithms for task scheduling in heterogeneous environments. It exploits the ability of parallel genetic algorithms, organized according to a replicated workers paradigm, to produce a near to optimal solution in a reasonable short time. In this new scheduling system, we use the same replicated workers model. This time, different workers run different scheduling algorithms that try to find an optimal schedule. Workers' results are passed to the master, which selects the best schedule.

The scheduling system's architecture is presented in Fig. 1 and is, in many respects, similar to that of DIOGENES.

The services included have the following roles:

- The *Lookup Service* detects the available hosts where it can run the scheduling algorithm.
- The *Grid Monitoring Service* returns, in real-time, information about the various site facilities, networks, and about the state of the current activities performed in the system, including data about the scheduled tasks that were sent for execution. The monitoring data is used by the scheduler to determine if a resource is available at a given time or if it meets the requirements for a particular task.
- The *Execution Service* receives the mappings returned by the scheduling algorithm, prepares and sends the tasks for execution on allocated resources. Since the Grid shcheduler doesn't have direct access to the resources this service submits the tasksto a local scheduler like Condor or PBS.
- The *Grid Service* accepts the new jobs submitted by users and direct them to the scheduler. The use of this service improves the system's flexibility as a user can submit a new job remotely, from any place, and at any time, doesn't matter if the scheduler is running or not.

There are two entities that compose the scheduling system: brokers and agents. A *broker* receives the scheduling requests from a client and sends the tasks to be schedule to the agents. The *agents* are responsible for running a scheduling algorithm for the jobs received from a broker using the monitoring information. Multiple scheduling requests can be sent at the same time. A broker can run on a different remote machine or on the same machine as an agent. In this way any available resources can be used to run the scheduling algorithm and at the same time all the computers can receive scheduling requests from users. Details about the format of the description files and the information they contain can be found in the next section of this paper.

In the experiments performed with this scheduler system, it has been demonstrated that the increased load due to the parallel execution of brokers and agents

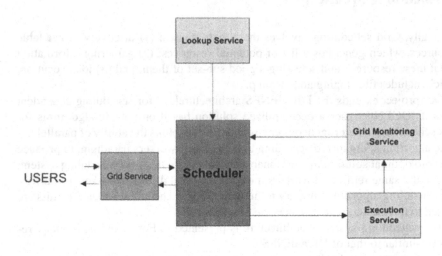

Fig. 1 Scheduling architecture

does not affect the overall performance in a significant way. In addition, with this approach, the number of available machines able to run a scheduling algorithm increases.

This scheduler has a decentralized, agent based architecture, which presents several important advantages. The main reason for such an architecture is the significant increase in fault tolerance of the scheduler. Since each task mapping is generated by a single agent, the system can easily recover from an agent failure by sending the scheduling request to another available agent. To further improve fault tolerance and also the quality of the mappings the broker can send the same request to two or more agents which will then generate the results independently using different algorithms. This will allow the broker to select the best task mapping from the results received from the agents, and if one of the agents stops functioning it will not affect the overall performance.

Using JINI technology for the lookup service makes it very easy to add new agents to the system. They are immediately recognized and can start running the job scheduling algorithm. Another important advantage is the support for fault tolerance: if any agent fails, the scheduling process can still be completed by one of the remaining agents. The parallel use of different scheduling algorithms and the selection of the best schedule improves the performance of the whole Grid scheduling system.

The scheduler has been integrated and tested with MonAlisa[14] farms and the ApMon, which is a MonAlisa extension.

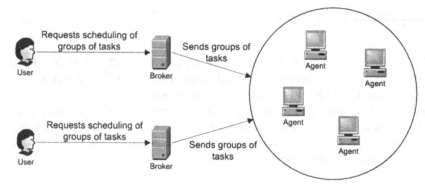

Fig. 2 The DIOGENES communication model

3 Job description

A client can submit an application by sending the job description in an **XML** format. This format was designed to be very easy to understand and edit when describing very complex jobs.

For each task, the description contains information about the estimated processing time, the links to other tasks, and the required costs associated with different links. For each task we can also set the memory and CPU requirements. The exact XML format can be seen in the example below.

```
< task >
    < taskId > 3 < /taskId >
    < path > /home/student/executabile/loop100.sh < /path >
    < arrivingDate > 2008/05/04 < /arrivingDate >
    < arrivingTime > 01 : 20 : 00 < /arrivingTime >
    < arguments >< /arguments >
    < parent >
        < Id > 1 < /Id >
        < Cost > 5 < /Cost >
    < /parent >
    < child >
        < Id > 5 < /Id >
        < Cost > 10 < /Cost >
    < /child >
    < requirements >
        < memory > 1024.0MB < /memory >
        < cpuPower > 2745.9404MHZ < /cpuPower >
        < processingTime > 1 < /processingTime >
        < deadlineTime > 2008/08/0920 : 59 : 30 < /deadlineTime >
        < schedulePriority > 1 < /schedulePriority >
    < /requirements >
```

$< nrexec > 1 < /nrexec >$
$< /task >$

The important elements of this format are the parent and child tags which are the difference tasks with dependencies and independent tasks. These tags are not necessary if the user wishes to submit a set of independent tasks.

In case of a complex job, for each task the user must specify a parent tag for each link with a parent task, and a child tag for each child task. Each of these tags contains the elements Id and Cost. The Id indicates the identity of the parent or child task; the Cost is the weight associated with the link.

4 Scheduling algorithms

For the experimental evaluation of the Grid scheduling system, two algorithms were chosen: ISH (Insertion Scheduling Heuristic)[5], and CCF (Cluster ready Children First)[3]

ISH is a list scheduling algorithm that tries to fill the gaps left in the mappings by previous scheduled tasks. The tasks are first ordered giving priority to the ones with higher blevel values. The blevel (bottom level) is the weight of the longest path from a node to an exit node of the DAG. The algorithm for computing the blevel is described below:

```
Create RTList, a list of nodes in reversed topological order.
foreach node n of RTList do
        max = 0
        foreach child c of n do
                if (blevel(c) + C_{n,c}) > max then
                        max = blevel(p) + C_{n,c}
                endif
        endfor
        tlevel(n) = τ_n + max
endfor
```

In the listing above τ_n is the cost of the node p and $C_{n,c}$ is the weight of the link between the nodes n and c. The blevel is a dynamic attribute and must be computed again after each task has been scheduled. This is done because the link between two tasks can be zeroed if they are mapped on the same resource. Ordering the tasks according to the blevel tends to schedule the nodes on the critical path first.

The ISH algorithm selects the next node that will be scheduled from a ready list which contains the nodes whose parents have already been mapped so they are ready to be scheduled. From this list the nodes with a higher blevel have the highest priority. The blevels of the nodes are computed statically at the beginning of the algorithm. The selected node is assigned to the processor that allows the earliest execution, using the non-insertion algorithm (the task is scheduled to the processor using a FIFO queue).

If the scheduling of this node causes an idle time slot, then the algorithm schedules as many nodes as possible into this idle time slot, providing that these nodes cannot be scheduled earlier on other processors. Then it selects a new ready node and repeats all these steps.

A task is scheduled to the resource that allows the earliest execution time. If this schedule causes an idle time slot on that resource then the scheduler tries to add as many tasks as possible in that idle time interval.

CCF is a dynamic list scheduling algorithm that assigns resources, at run-time, to tasks described by a DAG. The algorithm is described below:

```
Insert sourceTask into RUNNING_QUEUE
while (RUNNING_QUEUE is not empty) do
       task = extract (RUNNING_QUEUE)
       foreach child of task do
               Insert child into CHILD_QUEUE
       endfor
       while (CHILD_QUEUE is not empty) do
               childTask = extract(CHILD_QUEUE)
               if (childTask is ready) then
                       assignResource(childTask)
                       updateSuggestedResource(childTask)
                       Insert childTask into RUNNING_QUEUE
               else
                       suggestResource(childTask)
               endif
       endwhile
endwhile
```

The algorithm maintains RUNNING_QUEUE and a CHILD_QUEUE. The RUNNING_QUEUE contains the tasks that have already been mapped to a resource and the CHILD_QUEUE contains the children of the mapped tasks. At each step, the algorithm assigns a resource to the tasks in the CHILD_QUEUE and moves them to the RUNNING_QUEUE if they are ready to be scheduled.

Using this algorithm a child task with one parent is immediately assigned to a resource while children with multiple parents must wait until all its parents have been scheduled. After the child task has been mapped to a resource it is submitted for execution and placed in the running queue.

5 Experimental results

In order to test our scheduling system, an experimental cluster with 11 computing resources was configured. The first results (see Fig. 3) show the variation of the scheduling algorithm's completion time with an increasing number of tasks submitted for scheduling. In this figure, the completion time (in milliseconds) of the algorithm is represented on the vertical axis, while the number of tasks in the job is represented on the horizontal axis. The tests were made by submitting jobs of 10 to 1000 tasks.

In this experiment, the execution times of the two algorithms are very close to each other since the two algorithms have similar complexity.

Another element that contributes to the overall performance of the system is the time needed for the parsing of the input files used to specify the submitted job. The size of the input files depends on the number of tasks it contains and on the number of links between them. As we can see in this graph the parsing time may be small for files with few input files but it must be taken into account as it greatly limits the overall performance of the system.

Since an agent based architecture is used and jobs can be submitted remotely, we also took into account the communication time needed to send the job descriptions to an agent running a scheduling algorithm and the time to receive the resulting mappings. For example an input file with 1000 tasks may become as large as 7MB which can slow down the job submission process.

The results are presented in Fig. 4. The communication times become relevant only for very complex jobs and we can see that the overhead is within acceptable levels.

The scheduling completion time can be defined as the time passed between the job submission and the moment when the task mappings are generated and can

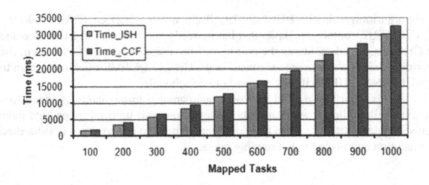

Fig. 3 Algorithm completion time

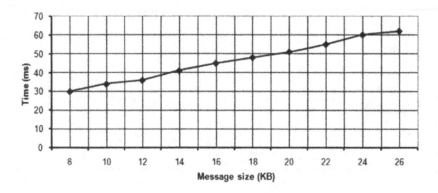

Fig. 4 Communication times

be sent to the Execution Service. This can also be seen as the sum of the delays described above:

$$T_i = t_c + t_p + t_{alg} \tag{1}$$

Using this formula we can calculate T_i which is the scheduling completion time. The delay t_c is the communication time needed to send the job description file to the agent that will run the scheduling algorithm and t_p is the time needed to parse this data. The final delay t_alg is the completion time of the scheduling algorithm. We can se from the first chart that this is the most time consuming operation and depends mostly on the algorithm used.

Another use for an agent based architecture is to provide a comparison between various scheduling algorithms. If more than one agent is idle when a new job is submitted then they can be used to run different scheduling algorithms for the same scheduling. In the example presented in Fig. 5, two agents are used to generate mappings for up to 500 tasks.

As we can see in this figure, the two agents complete the scheduling in nearly the same time. Because the algorithms are run on different agents the time that the broker needs to wait for the mappings is not much higher than in the case when just one agent was executing a single scheduling algorithm. The schedule lengths can be very different for the same group of tasks, depending on the number of dependencies between tasks, the communication costs and other parameters so another advantage in using this approach is that, after all the agents have finished, the broker has a number of mappings and can easily choose the one with the shortest schedule length.

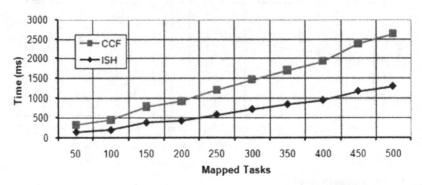

Fig. 5 Scheduling the same group of tasks using two agents

6 Conclusions and future work

This paper proposes a system for DAG decentralized scheduling. This approach has the benefit of being very efficient and fault tolerant due to the agent architecture. The architecture is also very flexible, as new computers can be set up to run agents, brokers or both. They are immediately recognized and ready to be used in the scheduling process.

The agents can be configured to run any scheduling algorithm, so the scheduling can be improved by a selection of the best schedule from the ones delivered by different agents.

After the task mappings have been generated the Execution Service asked to send the jobs to allocated resources. The execution service has been integrated with a number of local schedulers like Condor and PBS thus making it possible to work with different environments.

In the future, we intend to optimize the transfer of job description files and of the input files of different tasks in order to minimize the communication delays. This would be used to reduce the overhead and to improve the overall efficiency of the system. Building an efficient file transfer system would also solve the problem of co-scheduling, which is very important when submitting complex jobs with large input files.

We are also working on a checkpointing system that will improve the fault tolerance facility of the architecture. In case of an agent or resource failure, the broker will keep the mappings until the last checkpoint and so the rescheduling process will have a head start. The only tasks that will need to be rescheduled will be the ones that were mapped after the most recent checkpoint.

References

1. F. Berman, R. Wolski, H. Casanova, W. Cirne, H. Dail, M. Faerman, S. Figueira, J.Hayes, G. Obertelli, J. Schopf, G. Shao, S. Smallen, N. Spring, A. Su and D. Zagorodnov, Adaptive Computing on the Grid Using AppLeS (2003)
2. Yu-Kwong Kwok and Ishfaq Ahmad. Static scheduling algorithms for allocating directed task graphs to multiprocessors. ACM Computing Surveys (1999).
3. Alberto Forti, DAG Scheduling for Grid Computing Systems (2006)
4. Waldo, The Jini architecture for network-centric computing, Communications of the ACM, July 1999
5. B. Kruatrachue and T.G. Lewis. Duplication scheduling heuristics (dsh): A new precedence task scheduler for parallel processor systems. Technical report, Oregon State University (1987)
6. Florin Pop, Dacian Tudor, Valentin Cristea, and Vladimir Cretu, Fault-Tolerant Scheduling Framework for MedioGRID System (2007)
7. Florin Pop, Valentin Cristea Intelligent Strategies for DAG Scheduling Optimization in GRID Environments, CSCS16 Conference, May 2007, Bucharest, Romania
8. Marcela S. Boboila, George V. Iordache, Florin Pop, Valentin Cristea, A Framework for Scheduling Image Processing Applications in MedioGRID (2006)
9. Douglas Thain, Todd Tannenbaum, and Miron Livny. Condor and the grid. In Fran Berman, Geoffrey Fox, and Tony Hey, editors, Grid Computing: Making the Global Infrastructure a Reality, December 2002
10. J. Yu and R. Buyya. A Novel Architecture for Realizing Grid Workflow using Tuple Spaces. In 5th IEEE/ACM International Workshop on Grid Computing (Grid 2004), Pittsburgh, USA, IEEE CS Press, Los Alamitos, CA, USA, Nov. 8, 2004.
11. R. Buyya, D, Abramson, and J. Giddy. Nimrod/G: An Architecture of a Resource Management and Scheduling System in a Global Computational Grid, HPC Asia 2000.
12. G. Iordache, Marcela Boboila, F. Pop, Corina Stratan, V. Cristea, "A Decentralized Strategy for Genetic Scheduling in Heterogeneous Environments", in Lecture Notes in Computer Science, Springer Vol. 4276 "On the Move to Meaningful Internet Systems", Meersman, R.; Tari, Z. (Eds.) 2006, proceedings GADA, Montpellier, France, November 2-3, 2006, pp 1234-1251
13. Condor web page: http://cs.wisc.edu/condor
14. MonALISA Web page: http://monalisa.cacr.caltech.edu/
15. Ewa Deelman, Gurmeet Singh, Mei-Hui Su, James Blythe, Yolanda Gil, Carl Kesselman, Gaurang Mehta, Karan Vahi, G. Bruce Berriman, John Good, Anastasia Laity, Joseph C. Jacob, Daniel S. Katz. Pegasus: a Framework for Mapping Complex Scientific Workflows onto Distributed Systems, Scientific Programming Journal, Vol 13(3), 2005, Pages 219-237
16. I. Taylor, M. Shields, I. Wang, and A. Harrison. The Triana Workflow Environment: Architecture and Applications, in I. Taylor, E. Deelman, D. Gannon, and M. Shields, editors, Workflows for e-Science, pages 320-339. Springer, New York, Secaucus, NJ, USA, 2007

IV

GRID PROGRAMMING ENVIRONMENTS

Workflows in a secure environment

Norbert Podhorszki and Scott Klasky

Abstract. Petascale simulations on the largest supercomputers in the US require advanced data management techniques in order to optimize the application scientist time, and to optimize the time spent on the supercomputers. Researchers in such problems are starting to require workflow automation during their simulations in order to monitor the simulations, and in order to automate many of the complex analysis which must take place from the data that is generated from these simulations. Scientific workflows are being used to monitor simulations running on these supercomputers by applying a series of complex analysis, and finally producing images and movies from the variables produced in the simulation, or from the derived quantities produced by the analysis. The typical scenario is where the large calculation runs on the supercomputer, and the auxiliary diagnostics/monitors are run on resources, which are either on the local area network of the supercomputer, or over the wide area network. The supercomputers at one of the largest centers are highly secure, and the only method to log into the center is interactive authentication by using One Time Passwords (OTP) that are generated by a security device and expire in half a minute. Therefore, grid certificates are not a current option on these machines in the Department of Energy at Oak Ridge National Laboratory. In this paper we describe how we have extended the Kepler scientific workflow management system to be able to run operations on these supercomputers, how workflows themselves can be executed as batch jobs, and finally, how external data-transfer operations can be utilized when they need to perform authentication for their own as well.

Norbert Podhorszki
Oak Ridge National Laboratory, USA, pnorbert@ornl.gov

Scott Klasky
Oak Ridge National Laboratory, USA, klasky@ornl.gov

1   Introduction

Supercomputer centers, like the National Center for Computational Sciences (NCCS) at the Oak Ridge National Laboratory, have strict security policies. Users have to login with a One Time Password (OTP), using an RSA SecurID token to have access to the computers. Once the users log into the machine, they can edit, compile, and submit their programs as batch jobs. If they want to check the status of a running job later, they have to login again and run commands locally. In the framework of the Center for Plasma Edge Simulation (CPES) project we have developed a workflow [1] that watches a simulation from a remote host, transfers the simulation's output on-the-fly to another resource where it analyzes the data and creates plots from the data and archives the data. Another workflow [2] modeling the complex multiphysics nature of plasmas in tokamak reactors, couples several codes running on different resources and transfers the data among them, keeping track of the provenance during the simulation.

It is impractical for our workflows to run on the supercomputers, since the software infrastructure of the workflow is not supported on these machines, so we run the workflows on a different machine. Therefore they need to connect to the supercomputer regularly to access data and status information. Any authentication is always performed interactively (i.e. the user must be present) and relies on short-lived OTP expiring in 30 seconds. In section 2, we describe how the Kepler scientific workflow management system [3] has been extended to be able to deal with these workflows.

With the increase of the users monitoring their simulations with our "monitoring workflows", we need to run the workflows themselves on separate machines; therefore we have to submit them as batch jobs on our local cluster to avoid problems. In section 3, we describe how these workflows that require interactive authentication with the user, can be executed as batch jobs.

For transferring data from the simulation host to another host, external transfer tools have to be used. Currently we must have a password-less authentication method (host-based method or public-key method with a private key that has no passphrase) to be able to run external tools. In section 4, we show how we have extended Kepler so that it can provide a traditional password or passphrase to the external tool that can establish its own connection using it.

2   Remote operations with SSH

A scientific workflow, which works with codes which run on supercomputers, usually contains operations that should be executed externally to the workflow's own runtime environment. This is necessary because, of several reasons: they are costly operations, their codes are available in another language, they must be run on another system, or the computation should be delivered to the (remote) data and not vice-versa, or simply because the workflow has been built to orchestrate the many operations on a set of hosts. The external operations can be realized as *jobs*, which are to be submitted to a job manager on a remote host, as *services*, which can respond to requests from the workflow, or as direct execution of programs on the local or on remote machines. In case of all remote actions, some form of authentication is required.

The Grid Security Infrastructure [4] has been designed to allow users to "login" once and use a certificate to authenticate the user to different resources and repeatedly to the same resource. However, NCCS and other supercomputing centers and academic institutions, do not allow the use of certificates, requiring an OTP for authentication which allows connections from outside computers only by SSH. Because jobs must be submitted only from the supercomputer's login nodes, a workflow has to login to the machine first and then submit a job locally. Our goal is to run and monitor supercomputer simulations, so we have extended Kepler to use SSH to access such secure resources. Because of the OTP, the workflow has to perform the authentication interactively with the user, unlike Grid infrastructures where the workflow gets a proxy certificate ready to use from the workflow system/portal, and the interactive part is performed prior the workflow execution. Since the OTP expires in 30 seconds it is not feasible to ask the user in advance and to store the password offline and then to start up the Kepler workflow on a remote resource, which then would initiate a connection to the supercomputer and use the password for the authentication.

By design, Kepler actors [5] are separate entities (Java object instances), so an actor's variables cannot be shared among other actors. We created a Java package underlying Kepler that can keep the established connections open and can be used by any actors in the workflow. There are ongoing developments for generic SSH support for Java applications, like JSch [6] and Ganymed SSH-2 [7]. Kepler developers have already had experience with JSch, which provides support for all kinds of authentication (except for host-based authentication), password, public key, and most importantly the keyboard-interactive method used for one-time-password authentication. JSch provides an interface to open several channels within one established SSH session to execute different operations concurrently. The *org.kepler.ssh* package is built on JSch to be able to share a connection among different actors in a workflow. The identifier of a connection is the *user@host:port* string, which is delivered either through links in the workflow graph from one actor to another or through parameters given to all actors. This Java package provides the following remote operations:

- open or close a connection,
- copy files from a remote host to the local host,
- copy files to the remote host from the local host,
- execute a command,
- create a directory,
- remove files.

A set of Kepler actors have been created that provide the above remote operations in a workflow (SshDirectoryCreator, SshDirectoryList, SshExecuteCmd, SshFile-Copier, etc). The *SshSession* actor opens an SSH session using this package. This actor is used to let the workflow ask the user for password at the beginning of the workflow run instead of at the very first remote operation at the given host. However, the underlying *org.kepler.ssh* package does not require the use of this actor to explicitly open a session. Before any remote operation is started, it checks whether the connection to the requested host is opened. If it is not, a new connection is established (and if necessary, a password prompt is displayed) before performing the action. The connection is kept open until the end of the workflow run, so that any actor can use it to perform its remote operation. Other Kepler actors and a monitoring workflow are described in detail in [1].

The authentication is performed either through a pop-up dialog, if the workflow is executed within the Kepler GUI, or on the standard input/output if it is executed from command line, as usually our current users do it.

Futhermore, the *org.kepler.ssh* package implements all of the operations on the local host with Java runtime, and all of the SSH related actors can actually perform operations locally, too. For example, if a host is named *local*, no SSH session is established to the local host but local operations are performed. This makes deployment of a workflow to a host, where many of the operations are to be performed, simple by replacing the host's name to *local* in one parameter of the workflow.

An application of the above package is that the job-oriented actor set (that submit and controls computational jobs as part of a workflow) in Kepler is capable of submitting jobs to job managers (like PBS, SGE, LoadLeveler, Condor) of non-Grid resources using an SSH connection.

3 Running workflows on a cluster as jobs

In order to become appealing for a wide range of users, a workflow system should hide the hassle of workflow execution on a specific machine. The simple solution is that the system runs the workflow locally on the same host; however, this is not scalable on compute clusters with a limited number of login nodes. As the number of users and workflow runs increases, the workflows need to spread over several machines, since the performance of the workflows will slow down. We can maintain a round-robin scheduling of workflows on the login machines, but this is not scalable: our workflow execution cluster has only 2 login nodes for 80 compute nodes. The only scalable solution that we found is when workflows are executed on the compute nodes of the cluster, which is managed by a job manager.

A Kepler workflow is basically a Java application, which can be executed as a job without further investigation on the workflow cluster. The problem with running this as a batch job is that the workflow needs to connect to the simulation host with ssh and perform authentication with a one-time-password, i.e., it has to have an interactive connection back to the user; which contradicts the concept of a batch job. We have extended Kepler to support user interaction through a socket instead of the standard input/output and have created a job submission script that forwards communication between the user and the Kepler job as shown in Fig. 1.

The *SshSession* class of the *org.kepler.ssh* package has been extended to support a third type of communication to the user besides pop-up dialogs and stdin/stdout. Through environment variables, a socket connection can be specified for the workflow, so that *SshSession* establishes a socket to write/read when requesting the passcode to a secure host.

The other end – the listening party – has to be created as well. Since the users currently just run a script to start the workflow and expect the communication with the workflow through the standard input/output, we have created a python wrapper script that

- opens a listening socket,
- creates the job script to be submitted (containing the Kepler workflow and the socket information),
- submits the job and
- forwards all socket communication to the standard input/output.

Using this approach, the job submission procedure is hidden from the user, who has the same experience as running the workflow locally. The workflow performs the authentication at the beginning of its run, so the user can leave it after providing the one-time-password interactively.

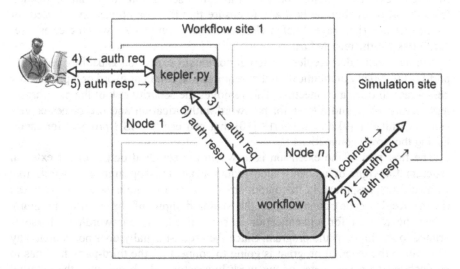

Fig. 1 The steps of authentication after the workflow starts and connects to a remote host. These steps are repeated for each remote connection.

Currently, we are investigating the security flaw introduced by sending the pass-code through a socket between two nodes of the workflow cluster between the python script and the Kepler workflow. We are also investigating how to support the submissions of such workflows from a web interface, when the user is sitting in front of a web browser at a remote desktop.

4   Third-party data-transfer with authentication

The monitoring workflow moves data from the simulation host to the processing host. We designed this workflow such that it was able to run from a third machine and orchestrate the workflow actions. Although the java ssh package in Kepler has the capability to transfer files to and from the host where Kepler is running (and is used by the workflow when jobs are staged on remote hosts), its performance is insufficient to move large simulation data. Therefore, we have been using external tools (SCP and BBCP [8]) to transfer the files. The requirement to be able to do this has been always that those tools can establish their own connection in one direction without asking for passwords, which is a strict requirement that limits the set of hosts that can be used for our workflow runs. In case of JAGUAR, the Cray XT4 supercomputer at ORNL, where the plasma fusion simulations are executed, the administrators of EWOK, a small infiniband cluster where the workflows run, were asked to allow host-based authentication from it, which was acceptable for them because JAGUAR is in-house and is defended by one-time-password authentication. In case of external systems, the user is asked to set-up public-key authentication from EWOK to the remote host and to ensure that there is no passphrase used for the private key (i.e. leave it defenseless on the disk on EWOK), which creates a security risk for the remote host.

We have extended Kepler's external command execution capability with support for third-party authentication that requires a normal password or a private-key passphrase to open a connection. This removes the security risk of the passphrase-less private keys, and allows for password authentication and use of newer versions of GRIDFTP [9] and SRM-LITE [10] that can use the SSH protocol for establishing their own connections.

The first part of the extension is to watch the standard output of the external program for signs of authentication requests, i.e. the appearance of words like password or passphrase in the output stream, and to create a Java *OutputStream* (in the Kepler code) connected to the standard input of the external program. When the request for authentication is recognized, the password/passphrase is printed to the input of the program. Since the request usually does not contain any clue where the external program is going to connect to, the third-party host has to be declared as a parameter of the workflow actor, which executes the external program. Since the parameter can be updated (its actual value at the time of firing of the actor is used), it is not a limitation for dynamic workflows that may choose a third-party at runtime. However, this means that the workflow must know in advance where the external tool is going to connect.

The interactive part of the authentication is performed by the Kepler workflow at a well-defined point of the workflow (usually at the very beginning) or when the request arrives as shown in Fig. 2. Kepler establishes a connection to the third-party host itself and performs the authentication in the same way as it does with other hosts. It then remembers the password or passphrase used for the authentication and sends it to the external program's standard input. This means, that the third-party host must be reachable from Kepler's local host and the method of authentication must be the same as from the host of the external program. This is somewhat of a limitation because this technique cannot be used when the third-party is not directly reachable from the workflow, e.g. when the external program is to be executed on a proxy host between the workflow and a remote host. This third-party support was not designed for such scenarios.

Kepler keeps the password in memory in order to feed it later to the external programs. The password is requested and remembered by the *SshSession* class while the external command execution methods that need the password are in the *SshExec* and *LocalExec* classes in the same *org.kepler.ssh* package.

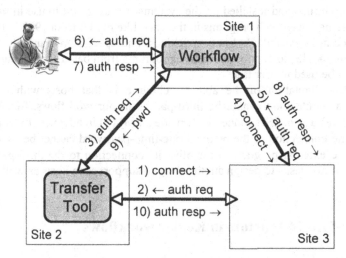

Fig. 2 The steps of authentication after the external tool connects to the third-party. If the workflow performs the authentication to Site 3 earlier (steps 4-8), than step 3 is followed by step 9 immediately

The last part of the extension is to deal with programs that ask for the password directly on a terminal device instead of their standard input/output, e.g. SCP, or any python program that uses the *getpass* module to ask for a password. When executed non-interactively, no terminal is there for their use, so they fail if forced to perform an authentication interactively. Pseudo-terminals have been always the solution to let programs believe they are interactive. OpenSSH itself provides an option (-t), and similarly the JSch package provides a method Channel-Exec.setPty(), to force pseudo-terminal allocation for the remote program. We found two problems in Kepler in using this option. First, it has a side effect that none of the user's profile files are executed at login, and therefore we do not have access to certain commands when connecting to the remote host. Second, Kepler must provide the same functionality through LocalExec when executing commands locally then through SshExec when executing the same commands remotely. Java has no concept of pseudo-terminals at all and the Java Runtime environment cannot be forced to allocate one. Therefore, we have refrained from using the above option for the remote connections.

Instead, we have created a small C program, which executes arbitrary commands through a pseudo-terminal. It allocates a pseudo-terminal first and then forks a new process that executes the original command. The master process forwards the standard input and output traffic of the command's process between its own standard output and input, respectively, which can be connected to the Java streams in the Kepler execution class. When the command finishes, it retains the exit code of the command and exits with this code. Therefore, this program is transparent for both parties of the operation, although it is a compromise since it has to be compiled and installed on the systems we are going to use in the workflow. There had been such programs in the past, like pty4.0 from 1992 [11], which does not compile on today's Linux machines, and special programs, like expect [12] and empty [13] to control interactive programs from batch scripts, but none of them could be used for our task.

The clear limitation of the above technique is that hosts with one-time-password authentication cannot be third-parties in our workflows. Since Kepler establishes (a) a Java SSH connection (inside JVM) (b) in advance (c) from its local host, the connection or the retained one-time-password cannot be used by the local/remote external program to establish its connection to the third-party. It is one of our future tasks to design another way to support such hosts as well.

5   Use of the SSH actors in Kepler workflows

The methods described in the previous sections have enabled us to create various workflows that can monitor supercomputer simulations by transferring their output to another resource on the fly (as generated timestep by timestep) and by performing additional operations like conversion, analysis, plotting etc. All simulation and processed data are archived automatically on tapes by the workflow. Users welcome the automation of the labor of post-processing, plot generation and data archival, and this is the main cause for the acceptance of workflow technology. We have been also developing a dashboard [14], which (among other functions) allows users looking at the generated plots (i.e. monitor the simulation), see

Fig. 3. Another workflow is used to couple two plasma fusion codes on two different supercomputers by using two other fusion codes as well to check the stability of the simulation [2]. Another workflow has been used to transfer 10 TB of archive data between the storage systems of two supercomputer centers [15].

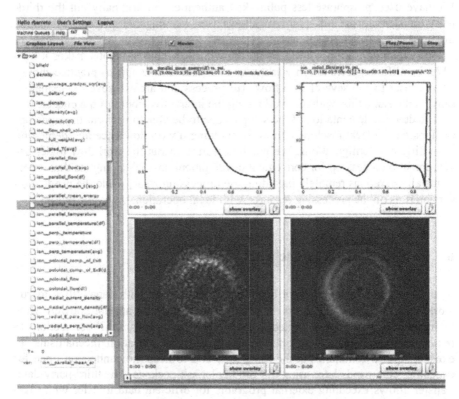

Fig. 3   Dashboard that displays movies generated from 1D and 2D plots of simulation variables from the XGC plasma fusion code.

Without describing the workflows in detail, here we enumerate the operations that were enabled by the development of the SSH actors in Kepler. First of all, the watching for the simulation output requires regular listing of the output directory of the simulation for new data. Keeping the connection (authenticated at the beginning of the workflow run) open allows performing this regular directory listing as well as executing external commands to transfer the data to the other resource or perform conversion and plotting. The Kepler job actors use the ssh package to submit and control jobs. Thus, in the monitoring workflow, we can submit an AVS/Express visualization job on another node of the workflow cluster, wait until the job starts (note that not until it finishes as usually job-oriented workflows do), send service requests to the visualization service whenever new data is available for plotting and finally stop the visualization job at the end of the workflow run.

Data transfers between two hosts are usually performed with host-based authentication inside NCCS but in case of the coupling workflow, we need to transfer data from NCCS to another center where the second simulation is executed. We have used passphrase-less public-key authentication originally but the third-party transfer support in Kepler now allows users keeping their private keys on the disk encrypted with a passphrase.

The capability to run workflows on the workflow cluster as jobs makes it possible for different users to run workflows at the same time and, as practice shows, for one user to run several workflows (to process and archive several simulation runs) at the same time without overloading the interactive nodes of the cluster.

The dual implementation of the ssh package to be able to perform the same operations on the local machine allows for building a workflow once and deploying it on different configurations. We use this feature to run the workflow under development on a desktop for convenient development and debugging, so that it performs all operations remotely including the processing steps, while the production version runs on the processing resource with local operations wherever possible.

6   Conclusion and future work

In the past two years we have been extending Kepler with capabilities to run workflows in an HPC environment where Grid certificates are not allowed while the number of resources is limited. Kepler is able to establish SSH connections to remote hosts defended with one-time-password authentication mechanisms, to execute several commands at the same time and to keep the connection open for executing commands later using our org.kepler.ssh package. The third-party data-transfer allows executing external programs for efficient data transfer while Kepler provides the passwords needed to establish the connection between the parties. Now Kepler workflows are executed as batch jobs even though they ask for one-time-passwords interactively from the user. This has allowed numerous scientists working on the ORNL supercomputers to run monitoring workflows of their simulation.

In the future, we will work on launching workflows from our web interface [14]. We are going to make sure that users can type in their one time password, and pass this through the web interface and over to the workflows. We are going to design a secondary way to provide passwords to external programs from the workflow as well, to enable data-transfer to hosts defended with one-time-passwords and/or a proxy login host. ORNL will also be incorporating grid certificates for data transfers in the future, and we will modify the workflows to use them locally, but we will still need to move data over to our collaborators machines, which do not support these.

References

1. N. Podhorszki, B. Ludäscher and S. Klasky. "Workflow Automation for Processing Plasma Fusion Simulation Data", 2nd Workshop on Workflows in Support of Large-Scale Science (Monterey, CA, June 2007), pp. 35-44
2. J. Cummings et al., "Plasma edge kinetic-MHD modeling in tokamaks using Kepler workflow for code coupling, data management and visualization", to appear in *Communications in Computational Physics* special issue for the 20th International Conference on the Numerical Simulation of Plasma (Austin, TX, Oct 2007).
3. B. Ludäscher, I. Altintas, C. Berkley, D. Higgins, E. Jaeger-Frank, M. Jones, E. Lee, J. Tao, Y. Zhao. "Scientific Workflow Management and the Kepler System", Concurrency and Computation: Practice & Experience, 18(10), pp. 1039-1065, 2006.
4. I. Foster et al., "A Security Architecture for Computational Grids". 5th ACM Conference on Computer and Communications Security, pp. 83-92, 1998
5. E.A. Lee and S. Neuendorffer. "Actor-oriented models for codesign: Balancing reuse and performance". In *Formal methods and models for system design: a system level perspective*, ISBN:1-4020-8051-4, pp. 33–56, 2004.
6. JSch – Java Secure Channel. http://www.jcraft.com/jsch
7. Ganymed SSH-2 for Java. http://www.ganymed.ethz.ch/ssh2
8. BBCP. http://www.slac.stanford.edu/~abh/bbcp/.
9. GridFTP. http://www.globus.org/grid_software/data/gridftp.php
10. SRM-Lite data transfer tool. http://datagrid.lbl.gov/srmlite
11. Daniel J. Bernstein. pty4.0 from comp.sources.unix archive: http://www.isc.org/index.pl?/sources/utils/terminal/pty4.php
12. D. Libes. "Automation and Testing of Interactive Character Graphic Programs", *Software - Practice and Experience*, Vol. 27(2), p 123-137, February 1997.
13. Mikhail E. Zakharov. empty: http://empty.sourceforge.net
14. S. Klasky, et al., "Collaborative Visualization Spaces for Petascale Simulations", accepted at 2008 International Symposium on Collaborative Technologies and Systems May 19-23, 2008.
15. Norbert Podhorszki, Bertram Ludäscher, Scott Klasky: Archive Migration through Workflow Automation, Intl. Conf. on Parallel and Distributed Computing and Systems (PDCS), November 19–21, 2007, Cambridge, Massachusetts.

High-level User Interface for Accessing Database Resources on the Grid

Tamas Kiss and Tamas Kukla

Abstract Data access in Grid systems and applications focused on managing flat files only, until recently. However, many scientific and industry applications rely on data stored in relational or other databases. The OGSA-DAI project developed a widely utilised middleware tool that enables accessing and managing a various database products through uniform Web service interfaces. As OGSA-DAI is a middleware level solution, it cannot be utilised by end users directly. Although research projects have developed user interfaces for specific OGSA-DAI based applications, these cannot be applied for more ad-hoc tasks. In order to fill this gap, a set of comprehensive and function-rich user interfaces were developed to expose OGSA-DAI functionalities. The portlets can be used in a wide range of applications and enable a much wider take-up of OGSA-DAI, as it is illustrated on the example of a data mining application on a UK National Healthcare database.

1 Introduction

The Grid, besides facilitating the access to large computing power, also provides capabilities to store and process huge amounts of data. Grid related research and development activities mainly concentrated on systems until recently where data was stored in flat files. Examples for widely utilised distributed file storage systems in the Grid environment include the Storage Resource Broker (SRB) [15] or the Storage Resource Manager (SRM) [7] protocol. SRB is available as a service in several production Grids including the TeraGrid [20] in the US, or the UK National

Tamas Kiss
University of Westminster, 115 New Cavendish Street, London, UK W1W 6UW
e-mail: kisst@wmin.ac.uk

Tamas Kukla
University of Westminster, 115 New Cavendish Street, London, UK W1W 6UW
e-mail: kuklat@wmin.ac.uk

Grid Service (NGS) [21], while SRM forms the basis of the Logical File System (LFS) [3] of the EGEE Grid [17].

However, many scientific and industrial applications rely on database management systems to provide a more structured access to mass amounts of data. The DAIS (Data Access and Integration Services) [14] working group of the OGF (Open Grid Forum) is specifying generic interfaces to expose database operations in a Grid environment. The aim of the group is to develop standards for providing consistent access to existing, autonomously managed databases from Grid data services. Working together with the DAIS, the OGSA-DAI (Open Grid Services Architecture Data Access and Integration) project [18] aims to develop a reference implementation for the OGF specification. OGSA-DAI is a middleware layer that provides data access, data management and data integration capabilities for various types of data resources such as structured (relational) and semi-structured (XML) databases [2]. In order to support end-users, higher level tools should be built on top of OGSA-DAI to provide the necessary level of abstraction.

Several research projects have utilised OGSA-DAI as their middleware-level data access solution. For example, in the LEAD (Linked Environments for Atmospheric Discovery) [5] project, that aims to improve the forecasting of medium-scale weather phenomena such as tornados and severe storms, OGSA-DAI is the basis of a metadata catalogue and provides a rich search space for end-users. Built into these highly complex systems OGSA-DAI could fulfil its role by providing access to heterogeneous distributed data resources.

On the other hand, sometimes more ad-hoc access to databases is also desired by individual researchers and smaller projects. The most important aspect in this case is to provide database access utilising already existing tools and to avoid long development processes. Unfortunately, the take-up and utilization of OGSA-DAI in these latter scenarios remained rather low. As OGSA-DAI is a middleware level tool it is not suitable to be used by end-users directly.

The end-user interface for Grid applications is typically provided in the form of Grid portals [22]. The set of OGSA-DAI portlets described in this paper are the first comprehensive set of end-user interfaces that provide rich and high-level functionality to access generic OGSA-DAI services. Utilising this portlet set, users can access databases exposed by OGSA-DAI, and can manage and manipulate the data stored in these collections. As the portlets are implemented using the JSR-168 [8] standard, they can easily be integrated to any JSR-168 compliant portal framework opening the way for a much widespread utilization of the OGSA-DAI middleware.

The remaining part of this paper is structured as follows. Section 2 reviews related work, while Section 3 describes the developed OGSA-DAI portlets in detail. Section 4 illustrates the usage of the portlets based on a real-life scenario, and finally Section 5 outlines future developments.

2 Related work

OGSA-DAI is a middleware that provides query, update, transform and delivery capabilities for a wide range of databases through web service interfaces. The latest stabile release at the time when our portlet development started was OGSA-DAI version 2.2. Therefore, the portlets described in this paper utilise this release.

OGSA-DAI exposes data (database or file) resources through a data service. Each data service is capable to expose multiple data service resources each connecting to a physical data resource. Data service resources are responsible for the execution of perform documents and the generation of response documents. Perform documents are generated by clients and describe a pipeline of activities (e.g. queries, updates, data transformations etc.) in XML format. After executing the perform document the service returns a response document that contains information on the execution status and the ID of the session. It may also include the result dataset if for instance a database query was executed. Graphical user interfaces to OGSA-DAI can be developed as either 'thick' client applications, or as a portlet by following the thin client approach.

An example for the former is the First Data Service Browser [6] developed originally by the First DIG (First Data Investigation on the Grid) project and then added to future OGSA-DAI releases. This is a java client application that supports interaction with various databases by providing a user-friendly interface to browse and run queries on selected data resources. Although the client comes with rich functionality it has some disadvantages compared to the portlet approach. The application requires installation from the user and does not integrate well with existing Grid portal interfaces.

Portal-based interfaces to OGSA-DAI can be divided into two different categories. Large projects, such as the LEAD project mentioned earlier, has developed application specific portals that provide access to large databases through OGSA-DAI. These portals, for example the LEAD portal [4], do not provide generic OGSA-DAI interfaces. Rather, they support their specific applications with low-level OGSA-DAI services. As such, they cannot be utilized by other projects seeking to expose OGSA-DAI functionalities through portlet interfaces. The second category, where the portlets described in this paper also belong to, are portlets exposing generic OGSA-DAI functionalities. Although some projects aimed to develop reusable OGSA-DAI portlets in the past, they all provided only very limited functionality and have not reached production quality. The Alliance OGSA-DAI Portlet [11], for example, takes a perform document as the input and returns a response document as the output of the operation. The portlet also shows query results in a table format in case of relational databases. The OGSA-DAI portlet in a previous version of the NGS Portal [24] allowed defining a query statement and then returned the results in pure XML format. This portlet, due to its limited functionality, is not included in the NGS Application Repository [12], the current version of the portal. The Sakai VRE Demonstrator project [16] has also developed a limited functionality portlet prototype with similar features to the NGS portal.

The set of portlets described in this paper are the only OGSA-DAI portlets that offer rich functionality to end-users from database browsing to complex queries, data delivery and transformation. This unique portlet set can easily be integrated to Grid portals opening the way to easy utilization of OGSA-DAI functionalities avoiding long development processes.

3 Grid portal interface for OGSA-DAI

When identifying the functional requirements towards the portlets, the aim was to provide high-level functionality and abstraction for the user. All existing OGSA-DAI portlets, as we have seen in the previous section, require the creation and interpretation of XML-based perform/request documents. This level of abstraction is clearly not convenient for an average database user. Our aim was expressing OGSA-DAI operations through widely used database tools such as SQL queries, and also providing user friendly interfaces for additional OGSA-DAI operations and transformations such as data compression and delivery.

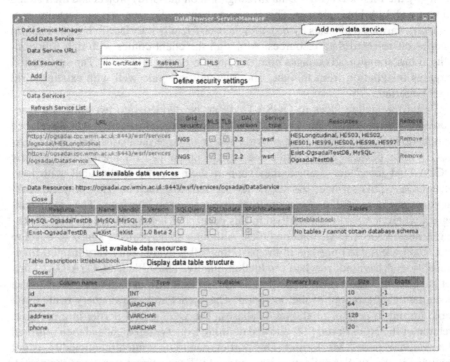

Fig. 1 OGSA-DAI Service Manager Portlet

The desired functionalities can be divided into 4 main categories:

- Managing data services where existing services can be listed with their relevant properties, services can be removed and new services can be added.
- A database browser interface where users can explore the content of available services and resources.
- Executing advanced queries allowing data to be displayed on the screen or to be delivered to a set of files for further processing.
- Updating the content of a database through queries or by delivering data from a set of files.

The above described functionalities have been implemented as four different portlets. The advantage of this design is the flexibility when integrating to Grid portals and allowing administrators to select only the desired portlets. Functional extension is also easier by developing and adding a new portlet to the set. Next we describe the implemented portlets in detail.

The *ServiceManager* portlet is illustrated on Figure 1. The portlet allows adding new data services by specifying their URL and the required security settings. Both transport and message level (using Grid certificates) security can be defined. Selecting an active service will display its database resources and their allowed operations (SQL query/update or XPath statement). In case of relational databases the table structure can also be displayed showing attribute names, types and additional information such as size, primary key, etc.

The *DataBrowser* portlet provides bulk data browsing capabilities. After selecting the data service and resource, the whole content of an XML or relational database is displayed on the screen, broken down to displayable pages.

The *QueryManager* portlet enables running queries on selected databases and either displaying results on the screen or delivering them to a set of files via GridFTP [1]. Figure 2 illustrates both options. The result of an SQL select query is displayed in table format at the bottom of the figure. The output of the same query is also converted into files and delivered via the means of GridFTP to a remote location. The file can be compressed and the results can also be divided into several files (in this example the results are divided into 4 files). Converting query results into files and dividing them allow utilising them as inputs to single or parameter sweep computational Grid jobs or workflows, as it will be illustrated in Section 4.

Finally, the *ManipulationManager* portlet, following a similar logic, allows the user to run update queries, and also to convert and deliver a set of files from a remote location to a database. Results of computational Grid jobs or workflows can this way be converted and stored in relational or XML databases.

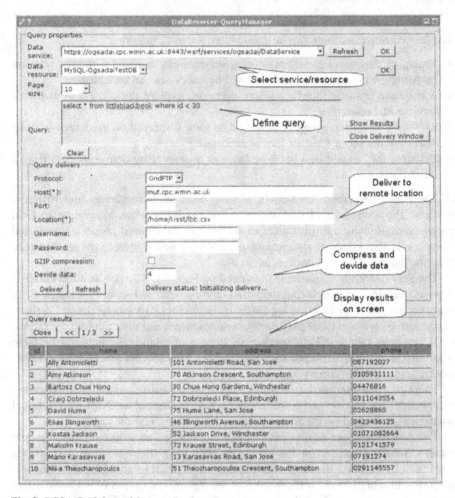

Fig. 2 OGSA-DAI Query Manager Portlet

4 The OGSA-DAI Portlets in Action

In order to demonstrate the usability of the OGSA-DAI portlets they have been integrated into the P-GRADE Grid portal [10]. P-GRADE is a workflow oriented Grid portal that enables the execution of parameter sweep workflow applications spanning multiple Grids and resources. P-GRADE was built on top of the Grid-Sphere portal framework [13] facilitating the easy integration of new portlets. The OGSA-DAI portlets provide useful extension to this portal allowing users to query databases, convert query results into files and feed them to parameter study work-flows, as illustrated by the following example. The portlets are available within the NGS PGRADE portal, one of the production portals of the UK National Grid Service.

The Department of Health in the UK releases annually its national database, the Hospital Episode Statistics (HES). The HES dataset contains a seven financial year period and approximately 80 million records in total, and forms the basis of a performance rating framework for hospitals. In the context of profiling hospitals, using the complete dataset is not practical. Therefore, a hierarchical cluster analysis is performed to group all patients with similarities based on the shape of the cumulative distribution function of length of stay (LOS) in the community before readmission. Hence, a very large dataset is decomposed into clustered sub-groups of patients that experience similar LOS. These clustered patient sub-groups are then sampled and a rank value (based on the multilevel transition model) is assigned to each hospital in every sample. Finally, the results coming from the different samples are aggregated to give a final score. In order to achieve the desired level of accuracy the sampling and ranking procedure is repeated many times, typically in the range of thousands for a production run, and can take hours to complete on a single processor machine.

The HES dataset is stored in a MySQL database. The clusters are extracted using select queries and different proprietary algorithms, and provided in the form of CSV (Comma Separated Variables) files for sampling and analysis. The analysis of the samples uses R [19], a language and environment for statistical computing and graphics.

The Grid enabled implementation utilises the independent nature of the samples and runs the R algorithms on different nodes of a cluster or on several clusters in the Grid. Each node receives the same input file containing the selected cluster of data, randomly samples it and runs the R analysis program. The input data cluster is extracted form the MySQL database using the OGSA-DAI portlets. The user runs the required select queries or named procedures from the portlets and delivers the results to a file. This file is then fed into a parameter study workflow. The P-GRADE portal automatically generates the number of required sampler and analysis jobs and distributes them on Grid resources [9]. Finally, a special 'collector' job in the workflow collects and aggregates the results of the analysis and stores them in a CSV file. The application is currently running on the UK National Grid Service utilising an OGSA-DAI service set up at Westminster, and compute nodes from the Rutherford and Westminster computing clusters where the required version of R application package is deployed. More information on this application can be found at [23].

5 Future Work

The portlet set presented in this paper is the first comprehensive Grid portal-based interface for the OGSA-DAI middleware. The portlets provide a function rich environment for end-users to access and manipulate distributed data resources.

Future work is two-folded. On one hand, the portlets are migrated to the latest version of OGSA-DAI, version 3.0. As OGSA-DAI 3.0 represents a significant reengineering of previous releases, the portlets require substantial changes too. On the other hand, the integration of OGSA-DAI to Grid workflow engines would also significantly increase the usability of the tool. For example, the manual process of data extraction described in the example of section 4 can be automated and the extracted data can be automatically fed into the parameter sweep workflows. Work is currently ongoing to specify and implement this workflow level integration and will be published in a forthcoming paper.

References

1. Allcock, W., Bester, J., Bresnahan, J., Chervenak, A., Liming, L., Tuecke, S.: GridFTP: Protocol Extension to FTP for the Grid, March 2001, http://www-fp.mcs.anl.gov/dsl/GridFTP-Protocol-RFC-Draft.pdf
2. Antonioletti, M., et al.: OGSA-DAI Usage Scenarios and Behaviour: Determining, good practice, Proceedings of the Third UK e Science All Hands Meeting, pp. 818-823, 2004, ISBN 1-904425-21, 31st August - 3rd September 2004, Nottingham, UK.
3. Baud, J., et. al.: LCG Data Management from EDG to EGEE, In the proceedings of the UK E-Science All Hands Meeting, 19 - 22 September 2005, Nottingham, UK, ISBN 1-904425-534
4. Christie, M., Marru, S..: The LEAD Portal: A Teragrid Gateway and Application Service Architecture, Concurrency and Computation: Practice and Experience, Volume 19, Issue 6, pp 767-781, Oct 2006, John Wiley & Sons.
5. Droegemeier, K.K., et.al.: Linked Environments for Atmospheric Discovery (Lead): Architecture, Technology Roadmap and Deployment Strategy, 21st Conference on Interactive Information Processing Systems for Meteorology, Oceanography, and Hydrology, January 2005, http://www.cs.indiana.edu/dde/papers/droegemeierIIPS2005.pdf
6. Graham, P.J.: First Data Service Browser User Guide, http://www2.epcc.ed.ac.uk/ first-dig/DISSEMINATION/FirstDIGBrowserUserGuide.pdf
7. Gu, J., Sim, A., Shoshani, A.: The Storage Resource Manager Interface Specification ver 2.2 http://www.ogf.org/Public_Comment_Docs/Documents/2007-10/OGF-GSM-SRM-v2.2.pdf Cited 9 May 2007
8. Introduction to JSR 168-The Java Portlet Specification, Sun Microsystems White Paper, 2003, http://developers.sun.com
9. Kacsuk, P., Farkas, Z., Sipos, G., Toth, A., Hermann, G.: Workflow-level parameter study support for production Grids, ICCSA'2007, (proc. in Springer LNCS), Kuala Lumpur, 2007, ISSN: 0302-9743 (Print) 1611-3349 (Online) ISBN 3-00-011592-7, DOI: 10.1007/978-3-540-74484-9_74
10. Kacsuk, P., Sipos, G.: Multi-Grid, Multi-User Workflows in the P-GRADE Grid Portal, Journal of Grid Computing Vol. 3. No. 3-4., 2005, Springer,1570-7873, pp 221-238, DOI: 10.1007/s10723-005-9012-6
11. Kodeboyina, D., Plale, B.: Experiences with OGSA-DAI: Portlet Access and Benchmark, Global Grid Forum Workshop on Designing and Building Grid Services, October 8, 2003, Chicago, Illinois, USA.
12. Meredith, D. et.al.: A JSDL Application Repository and Artefact Sharing Portal for Heterogeneous Grids and the NGS, Proceedings of the UK e-Science All Hands Meeting 2007, Nottingham, UK, 10th-13th September 2007, pp 110-118, ISBN 978-0-9553988-3-4
13. Novotny, J., Russell, M., Wehrens, O.: GridSphere: an advanced portal framework, Euromicro Conference, 2004. Proceedings. 30th Volume , Issue , 31 Aug.-3 Sept. 2004 pp: 412-419
14. Open Grid Forum Data Access an Integration Services Working Group (DAIS), http://forge.ogf.org/sf/projects/dais-wg
15. Rajasekar, A., et. al.: Storage Resource Broker - Managing Distributed Data in a Grid, Computer Society of India Journal, Special Issue on SAN, Vol. 33, No. 4, pp. 42-54, Oct 2003.

16. Sakai VRE Demonstrator project, http://acet.rdg.ac.uk/projects/vre/index.php
17. The EGEE Web page, http://public.eu-egee.org
18. The OGSA-DAI Website, http://www.ogsadai.org.uk
19. The R Project Website, http://www.r-project.org
20. The TeraGrid Website, http://www.teragrid.org
21. The UK National Grid Service Website, http://www.ngs.ac.uk/
22. Thomas M.P., et. al.: Grid Portal Architectures for Scientific Applications, Journal of Physics: Conference Series 16 (2005), pp. 596-600, SciDAC 2005, doi:10.1088/1742-6596/16/1/083
23. W-GRASS (Westminster Grid Application Support Service), http://wgrass.wmin.ac.uk
24. Yang, X., Chohan, D., et.al: A Web Portal for the National Grid Service, In the proceedings of the UK E-Science All Hands Meeting, 19 - 22 September 2005, Nottingham, UK, ISBN 1-904425-534

V
MISCELLANEOUS GRID-RELATED ISSUES

A supporting infrastructure for evaluating QoS-specific activities in SOA-based Grids

Ignacio Blanquer, Vicente Hernández, Damià Segrelles and Erik Torres

Abstract Despite the advances that have been made in Grid acceptance and adoption, further efforts are needed to ensure that the required level of service predictability is achieved. QoS issues require close attention, especially those aspects related to the evaluation of specific service activities with the aim of ensuring that the execution of a task produces an outcome according with its expectative behaviour. In this paper we present a supporting infrastructure to enable organisations to tackle the lack of tools for evaluating QoS-specific service activities. Additionally, we describe a case study that illustrates the applicability of the proposed model to general-purpose service management issues. The model has been tested in a controlled environment with promising results.

1 Introduction

Grid technologies are at the top level of the organizations attempt to become agile by allowing the abstraction of application logic from technology. This approach is a development in Service-Oriented Architecture (SOA) with the ability to access information technology devices as services over a network.

Despite the advances that have been made in Grid acceptance and adoption, further efforts are needed to ensure that the required level of service predictability is achieved. Quality of Service (QoS) issues require close attention, especially those aspects related to the evaluation of service activities with the aim of ensuring that the execution of a task produces an outcome according with its expectative behaviour.

In most of the current deployments, users see the Grid from the outside as a "black box" where requests go in and responses come out, but they do not see what is done (when something is done) for guaranteeing that a task fulfils a set of user-defined QoS requirements. Furthermore, users have no means for specifying a desired QoS attribute.

Ignacio Blanquer, Vicente Hernández, J. Damià Segrelles and Erik Torres

Institute for the Applications of Advanced Information and Communication Technologies (ITACA), Polytechnic University of Valencia (UPVLC), Camino de Vera S/N, 46022-Valencia, Spain, e-mail: {iblanque, vhernand}@dsic.upv.es, {etorres, dquilis}@itaca.upv.es

The objective of this paper is to present a supporting infrastructure to enable organisations to tackle the lack of tools for evaluating QoS-specific service activities with the aim of bringing predictability to SOA-based Grids.

The rest of this paper is organized as follows. Section 2 presents a workload balancing model which facilitates the compliance of QoS requirements in Grid. Section 3 describes an architecture implementing the model. Section 4 presents a review of the related works. Finally conclusions and future works are presented.

2 A workload balancing approach

A QoS-based workload balancing model for SOA-based Grids provides a set of components and mechanisms for allocating services, in order to execute the requests submitted by the clients with an optimal utilization of the resources. Such a model must assist the rest of the components of the Grid with the aim of fulfilling the service levels agreed with the clients, at the same time that guarantee the accomplishment of the service provider policies.

The workload balancing model presented in this paper implements four major concepts. First, it defines a simple set of Service Level Indicators (SLI). Secondly, it defines a set of measurable QoS indicators that can be used by clients to indicate their QoS requirements. Thirdly, it defines a Service Container Health Indicator, which describes the workload of the service containers at any time, and finally, it defines a workload distribution algorithm, which can be used to allocate services for executing tasks that demands specific QoS (e.g. a deadline).

2.1 Service Level Indicators (SLI)

A set of SLI enables the services with a means for expressing their QoS condition, so the workload balancing algorithm can match the client requests with the services. Through these indicators, the system differentiates the services into groups with similar performance.

The SLI can be applied to different entities. In our model, we aim to evaluate the Operation (the basic implementation unit of a service), the Service (the group of externally visible operations supported by a Grid service), the Activity (a logical unit of work completed by a collection of services) and the Service Provider (the organization that provides consumers access to the services in a Grid).

This fine-grain differentiation of the entities facilitates the characterization of the services at different levels, with the aim of providing users and resource administrators with a flexible framework for testing and evaluating the services and determining the possible points of failure or slows down.

The SLI defined in our model are described in the Table 1.

Table 1 Service level indicators and Measurable QoS indicators.

Name	Description	Measurable Items	Applicable Entity
Availability	Describes the availability of an entity, usually quantified by a dedicated tester.	The number of requests completed per requests submitted, or the total time that an entity is available.	Service, Activity, Service Provider.
Response Time	It can be notified by the supervised entity at the end of each request execution.	The time it takes to an entity to respond a request and send a response to the requester.	Operation, Activity.
Throughput	Depends on the request. It should be measured by dedicated testers and fixed tests.	The number of equivalent requests completed within a time frame.	Operation, Service, Activity.
Security	Security levels should be agreed between the participants and propagated to the service providers.	It could be measure in two quality scales: true/false, or high/medium/low.	Operation, Service, Activity, Service Provider.

2.2 Measurable QoS Indicators

A set of indicators explicitly distinguish requests on the basis of their QoS objectives. Through these indicators, a client specifies the QoS requirements of his or her application.

The QoS indicators are described in the Table 1. The measurable items coincide with those used in the section 2.1.

2.3 Service Container Health Indicator

Services are commonly grouped in service containers. Moreover, they share the resources of a server, a system, and frequently of a virtualization platform. Besides service level indicators, any model dealing with QoS needs to take into account the availability and the load of the underlying resources. The resources of the service container take part in the execution of every request. The condition of these resources must be monitored and integrated in the workload balancing algorithms, in order to allocate services in a more realistic way.

In this work, we have used the functions proposed in [1, 2].

2.4 Algorithm for workload distribution

The workload distribution algorithm determines which service (or group of services) executes a client request. A reasonable workload distribution can be based in a classification of the services in dependency to the predisposing of a service to deliver a service level, and to be free or occupied with other tasks. In this paper, we are proposing a clustering method for classifying the services in three groups of possible candidates for the execution of request. The three groups of candidate services are listed below:

- Services strongly predisposed to execute the request complying with the QoS requirements, but strongly predisposed to be mostly occupied with other tasks.
- Services predisposed to execute the request complying with the QoS requirements, and predisposed to be mostly free of load.
- Services known to execute the request without meeting the QoS requirements of the request, but strongly predisposed to be mostly free of load.

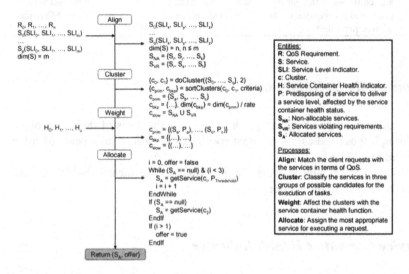

Fig. 1 Workload distribution algorithm.

The workload balancing consists in selecting the most appropriate service for executing a request in such a way that the fulfilling of the QoS requirements of the request affects as less as possible the performance of the whole system.

The distributing decision depends on the request requirements and the health status of the service containers. Requests will be typically assigned to the strongly predisposed services to meet the QoS requirements. To deal with this, the decision is modulated by the service container health function. The most a service is predisposed to be occupied with other tasks, the most the health function will penalize the selection of that service if the health status of the service container is unfavourable. In such a way, the services in the first cluster will be the primary source of service allocation, whereas the services in the second cluster will perform as a backup for the services in the first cluster. The services in the third cluster will be selected only when no other possibility exists, and always will be offered instead of allocated. The selection of one service or another in the same cluster occurs in a randomly fashion, prioritizing those services that feature a health status below a predefined threshold.

The Figure 1 presents a diagram for the workload distribution algorithm. The first step in the algorithm consists in aligning the requirements of an incoming request with the set of SLI monitored in the system. The Figure 1 represents this step in the algorithm with the block *Align*, at the top of the figure. *Align* takes a vector (R) of requirements and a matrix of services $(S_0 ... S_p)$ as its arguments and produces a new matrix with the services complying with the requirements $(S_0 ... S_q)$, and two vectors with the rest of the services $(S_{NA}$ and $S_{VR})$. The result matrix has the same element distribution as the initial matrix. In this matrix, the columns representing SLIs $(SLI_x, SLI_y, ... , SLI_z)$ that do not match any requirement in the request can be optionally removed. The services that do not have all the SLIs needed to match the requirements are grouped in the vector S_{NA}. These services will be referred as non-allocable services. In the same way, the services that do not meet one or more requirements are grouped in the vector S_{VR} and called services violating requirements.

In the second step (represented as *Cluster* in the Figure 1), the services are classified in three clusters: primary (C_{prim}), backup (C_{bckp}) and slow (C_{slow}).

A clustering algorithm is applied to the services that meet the requirements of the request in order to find the primary and backup clusters. SLIs have been taken as the coordinates for the cluster analysis (*doCluster* in Figure 1). An extra procedure allows the algorithm to unambiguously differentiate between the two clusters (*sortCluster* in Figure 1). The impact of the clustering algorithm in the differentiation procedure is weighted through a sorting criterion (represented as *criteria* in the Figure 1). For instance, when the objective of a cluster analysis is the accurate prediction of the most appropriate service for executing a request within a deadline, the decision relies particularly on the response time and on the availability indicators, and the influence of the other indicators is either minimal or null.

It is worth to mention that the number of elements in the primary cluster can be reduced by a rate of backup coverage (represented as *rate* in the Figure 1) in order to guarantee a defined number of elements in the backup cluster.

The C_{slow} cluster is formed by the union of the non-allocable services with the services violating requirements.

In the third step (represented as *Weight* in the Figure 1), a Service Suitability Index (SSI) is calculated for each service in the primary and backup clusters. In this step, the clustering information is weighted according to load balancing rules. The algorithm takes into account the basic load metrics (e.g. CPU utilization, available memory and available space in disk) of the service containers in order to know the service's availability and performance.

While all the other steps are important, this step avoids the overloading of the services in the primary cluster (the services with the best SLI). This step modulates the allocation decision by the service container load condition. The most a service is predisposed to be occupied with other tasks, the most the *Weight* step will penalize the selection of that service, if the load of the service container is unfavourable.

The last step is the allocation of services (represented as *Allocate* in the Figure 1). It consists on allocating a service on the primary cluster. Only when there is no possibility to allocate a service in the primary cluster, services are allocated on the backup cluster. In such a way, the services in the primary cluster will be the principal source of service allocation, whereas the services in the backup cluster will support the services in the primary cluster. The services in the slow cluster will be selected only when no other possibility exists, and always will be offered instead of allocated, e.g. the process can refuse the offer. The selection of one service or another in the same cluster occurs in a random fashion (*getRandomServ*).

With the aim of ensuring that the provision of a service does not imply that the resource allocation in the container penalizes the performance of other processes in the same container, only the services deployed in service containers which have load indicators bellow the threshold of availability defined for the resources, are considered to allocate services.

The procedure described in this section will be repeated every time a request is made, and the SLI or the load indicators had to be updated. For that reason, the cluster analysis placed primary emphasis on speed.

3 A QoS-aware workload distribution architecture

Figure 2 presents a scenario which illustrates the use of the workload distribution architecture presented in this paper for addressing a QoS-based allocation task. In this point, first it is described how the services of this architecture are set up to manage the QoS requirements of a Grid Service *S* in the VO. After that, the service-level indicators of the services are explained, and finally how a user can interact with the architecture in order to submit jobs to most appropriate services.

In the top left corner of the figure 2, a VO administrator creates a *QoS requirements* document for the service *S*, and submits the document to one of the Active Repository of Service Information and Configuration (*ARSIC*) services in the VO. The document specifies a threshold for the execution time of the operation *O* –exposed in *S*– which must be observed by all implementations of *S* deployed by any service provider in the VO, in order to be considered a correct instance. The document also defines the input and output values for the test "*T*" – which evaluates the availability of the service *S*–, and allocates the tester in the VO, which is the Service Level Monitoring Agent (*SLMA*) –a component of the *ARSIC*– of the domain where the instance of *S* is deployed.

The Service Provider (*SP*) decides to offer the service *S*. It deploys an implementation of *S* in the Service Container (*SC*) on the domain D, and the Service Management System (*SMS*) deployed in the same *SC* subscribes the service *S* to the *ARSIC* of the domain D. In a few seconds, the *SLMA* bound to the *ARSIC* runs the first test T in the service S, and broadcasts the results to the rest of the *ARSIC* services of the VO, which updates the *SMS* in their domains.

One client requests the execution of a task that involves the operation O in a service S. The client specifies a set of QoS requirements R, which the service provider should guarantee for its execution. The *SMS* that receives the request from the client executes a workload balancing algorithm for allocating a service S for the execution of the task. The Service Level Evaluation Agent (*SLEA*) bound to the *SMS* provides an evaluation of the instances of the service S in the VO. The *SLEA* uses the last SLIs collected from the *ARSIC* and requests a fresh copy of the service container health status information to the Provider Condition Information System (*PCIS*).

Finally, the *SMS* sends a response to the client, indicating the endpoint of an S instance that could be used by the client to execute the task, and specifying whether the instance S is able to fulfill the set of QoS requirements R or not.

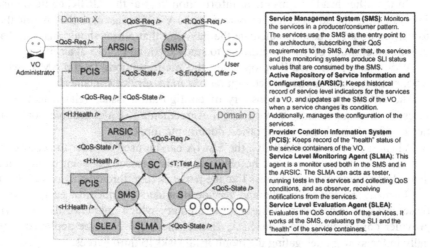

Fig. 2 A workload distribution example. Gray arrows represent the flow of the data through the architecture and black arrows represent association relationships.

3.1 Supporting QoS-specific management activities

The stack of components of the workload balancing architecture facilitates the achievement of QoS-specific management activities in SOA-based Grids. The SMS is a Grid service deployed by a service container. In this way, the SMS can access to container-level indicators that make possible to characterize a service at the endpoint with better detail.

The SMS collects SLI of the services with which it shares the service container. This data is spread throughout a network of ARSIC services that federate the information for the VO. Each SMS keeps a copy of the last condition observed in the VO, and the ARSIC keeps historical records over time. ARSIC links the SMS services of the VO, and keeps them updated with the last condition seen.

Depending on the QoS characterization made for a specific service, the load balancing achieved by the SMS can be focussed to allocate services in the VO for the execution of a task, and to the reuse of previous orchestrations, among others.

The SLI stored in the SMS can be used by the service provider for monitoring the services. These SLI can also be used for debugging as well as for checking the integrity of the internal dependencies of the services. The identification of which of the subjacent systems is causing a failure in a service orchestration is a challenge that can be addressed with this approach.

The capability of our system for describing and monitoring service levels enables service provides to examine specific service activities, in contrast to the general report generation tools. This capability is enhanced by the fact that the SMS can access to the error traces caught by the service container.

On the other hand, the historical information kept at the ARSIC could be used for evaluating the utilization of resources in the VO. For instance, the historical information could be used to calculate the payment that a user should make in base to the consumption of the resources, or to study the load pattern of a service.

Additionally, the ARSIC propagates the configurations to the SMS, which tests, evaluates and applies the configurations in its service container.

The ARSIC provides a repository of configuration issues related to the services: QoS requirements, Service Level Agreements (SLA), resource configurations, software packages and libraries, documentation, etc.

When deployed in the ARSIC, the SLMA can be used in order to acquire collectible indicators that can not be obtained at the service endpoint or indicators that rely on external dependencies like the network (e.g. throughput, availability).

On many occasions, clients and service providers do not trust each other. In these cases, it is necessary a trusted intermediary which guarantee that a service provider continuously meet the SLA. Hence, the SLMA can be deployed externally to the system, delegating the monitoring tasks to third parties.

4 Related Works

Erradi et al [3] propose a service-differentiation strategy based on prioritization, which uses profiles to classify requests, and offers different service levels to different clients. A component classifies incoming requests and places them into priority queues. This approach relies on centralized-decision making, which suffers from some loss in scalability. Our work focuses on providing tools for better process composition in SOA applications, through the analysis of metrics from services and service providers. Our solution is designed to be added on top of the existing middleware, relying in distributed components rather than in a centralized control.

Recent progress has been made in advance reservation of resources. Netto et al [4] present a scheduling strategy for advance reservation of resources that evaluates the flexibility of the requests in relation to the starting and completion time. The goal of their approach is to reduce the fragmentation generated by advance reservations, while improving resource utilization.

Service discovery using QoS properties has received increased attention due to its many application possibilities. An UDDI registry with extended capabilities to publish QoS information is proposed in [5]. A reputation manager assigns scores to the services based on customer feedback of their performance. Web services that match the consumers' requirements are then selected from the repository according to the QoS information and to the reputation scores. The effectiveness of this approach to service discovery has been demonstrated in a prototype implementation.

In [6] a semantic framework for Web services discovering based on QoS properties is described. Through the use of ontologies, customers can specify their preferences for service selection according to functional and quality properties. One of the goals of this work is the implementation of the processes in discovery algebra, facilitating the optimization and customization of the method presented by the authors.

In another approach, several authors have proposed strategies focusing on load balancing in service oriented environments. For instance, a distributed scheduling model is presented in [1]. With this work, the authors aim to provide a mechanism for allocating the workload among a group of Grid services in order to enhance the fault tolerance of the system. In this model, agents are applied to enable load balancing based on estimations of the probability of success of a request in a specific service.

Other projects have attempted to address issues related to the management of service levels with minimal resource consumption. Reich et al [2] present an extension for Web services that addresses to monitor and rectify the QoS of the services in order to satisfy their Service Level Agreements (SLA). This work introduces a structured P2P overlay network that monitors the SLA compliance, reacting to runtime conditions and redistributing services to find a QoS condition.

Other works have addressed the reconfiguration and the migration of services in service-based systems. Li et al [7] present such a study, where services are migrated when resource bottlenecks occur. They conclude that migration is a heavyweight exercise and should be avoided whenever possible and that migrating services to satisfy the minimal resource consumption can lead to unnecessary overhead.

Chen et al [8] proposes a framework for QoS-based service management in a Grid environment. Authors of this paper, present a model strongly focused in resource reservation, and provides mechanisms for negotiating SLA between client applications and service providers. In contrast to their work, we explore a workload balancing approach, considering that QoS management in Grid environments must also addresses the problem of optimizing the utilization of the resources.

Finally, Lee et al [9] proposes also a framework for managing SLA in a service-oriented environment. In this work, the authors define the components and functionalities that the framework must have.

5 Conclusions and Future Works

Large Grid deployments have become more common in research. Although the power of these approaches is enormous, the throughput of the processes driven by these initiatives is limited by the absence of QoS-specific management tools. In this work, we are concerned with the problem of bringing predictability to Grid applications, ensuring an optimal utilization of the resources.

Through the introduction of a new workload balancing model for requests with user-defined QoS requirements, we plan to improve the user experience in SOA-based Grids, at the same time that we provide developers and service providers with a means for getting more out of the infrastructure that is already deployed.

Our model has been tested in a controlled environment with promising results, in which, for simplicity, we considered an array of service containers (i.e. GT4 Web Services Container [11]) and two services that perform a set of combinable operations. In this experience, resource provisioning is handled by the SMS. The SLMA monitors the load of the servers running the service containers. SLI enables the entities with a means for expressing their QoS condition. Through these indicators, the SMS differentiates the entities into groups with similar performance and match the client requests with the most appropriate services for executing the request. The possible evaluable entities are: Operation, Service (both standalone or composed) and Service Provider. To keep things simple, we have used a set of straightforward operations to run tests. This particular set of operations, exposed in Grid services, transmits data via the network, storages data in disk and executes CPU consuming tasks. In conjunct, the operations implement a procedure for calculating the average of a reduced list of elements. This procedure takes place in three steps: first the list of elements is filtered with certain threshold value, second, elements selected are ordered by ascending value; finally, the average of the elements in the reduced list is calculated.

TRENCADIS (Towards a Grid Environment for Processing and Sharing DICOM Objects) [10] is a software architecture developed by our group for managing DICOM Objects in OGSA-based Grid environments. TRENCADIS is a software architecture developed by our group for managing DICOM Objects in OGSA-based Grid environments. This architecture splits into five layers, from basic services located in the Infrastructure Layer to object-oriented components focused in facilitating the abstraction of service functionalities through object interfaces, located in the Middleware Component Layer. The Valencian Cyberinfraestructure of Oncological Medical Images (CVIMO) is a project funded by the Ministry of Enterprises, University and Science of the Valencia Region. CVIMO was built on TRENCADIS with the main goal to deploy a cyberinfrastructure to organize and share selected and relevant Medical Imaging studies among five hospitals, in a secure way and using the radiological structured reports coded in DICOM-SR [12] to semantically organize the information. Relevant cases are organised into three communities related with oncology. At present, there are several functional processes for digital imaging implemented on TRENCADIS. The deployment of these processes is objective in CVIMO project. Some examples are the process for the calculation of parametric images for contrast-enhanced Magnetic Resonance [13], and the medical image registration process [13].

The current implementation of TRENCADIS allocates the services for process execution without considering the probability of a service to complete a request in a given time. Furthermore, users have no means for specifying a desired execution time, nor have the means to estimate the time it will delay a request to be resolved. Currently we are working in the evaluation of the benefits introduced by the model in the use case of functional processes on TRENCADIS. Future efforts must be done in order to extend the use of the model to more complex scenarios.

This first experience shows how useful is the introduction of the proposed solution in a real environment. Complementary works are now in progress to consolidate this result.

Acknowledgments The authors wish to thank the financial support received from The Spanish Ministry of Education and Science to develop the project "ngGrid - New Generation Components for the Efficient Exploitation of eScience Infrastructures", with reference TIN2006-12890. This work has been partially supported by the Structural Funds of the European Regional Development Fund (ERDF).

References

1. Wang J., Wu Q., Zheng D., Jia Y.: Agent based load balancing model for service based grid applications. In: Int. Conf. on Computational Intelligence and Security, (2006)
2. Reich, C., Bubendorfer, K., Buyya, R.: A SLA-Oriented Management of Containers for Hosting Stateful Web Services. In: 3rd IEEE Int. Conf. on e-Science and Grid Computing, (2007)
3. Erradi, A., Padmanabhuni, S., Varadharajan, N.: Differential QoS support in Web Services Management. In: IEEE Int. Conf. on Web Services, Vol. 00, (2006)
4. Netto, M. S., Bubendorfer, K., Buyya, R.: SLA-based Advance Reservations with Flexible and Adaptive Time QoS Parameters. In: LNCS, Vol. 4749, Springer Verlag, (2007)
5. Xu, Z., Martin, P., Powley, W., Zulkernine, F.: Reputation-Enhanced QoS-based Web Services Discovery. In: 5th IEEE Int. Conf. on Web Services, (2007)
6. Vu, L-H., Porto, F., Hauswirth, M., Aberer, K.: An Extensible and Personalized Approach to QoS-enabled Service Discovery. In: 11th IDEAS, (2007)
7. Li Y., Sun K., Qiu J., Chen Y.: Self-reconfiguration of service-based systems: A case study for service level agreements and resource optimization. In: IEEE ICWS, (2005)
8. Chen, H., Jin, H., Mao, F., Wu, H.: Q-GSM: QoS Oriented Grid Service Management Framework. In: LNCS, Vol.3399, Springer-Verlag, (2005)
9. Lee, B.-Y., Lee, G.-H.: Service Oriented Architecture for SLA Management System. In: 9th ICACT, Vol. 2, (2007)

10. Blanquer, I., Hernandez, V., Segrelles, D.: TRENCADIS – A Grid Architecture for Creating Virtual Repositories of DICOM Objects in an OGSA-based Ontological Framework. In: LNCS, Vol. 4345, (2006)
11. Foster I.: Globus Toolkit Version 4: Software for Service-Oriented Systems. IFIP International Conference on Network and Parallel Computing, Springer-Verlag LNCS 3779, pp. 2-13, (2006).
12. D. A. Clunie. "DICOM Structured Reporting", PixelMed Publishing, ISBN 0-9701369-0-0, (2000).
13. V. M. Runge, J. A. Clanton, C. M. Lukehart, C. L. Partain, A. E. James. "Paramagnetic agents for contrast-enhanced NMR imaging: a review", American Journal of Roentgenology, Vol 141, Issue 6, pp. 1209–1215, (1983).

Checkpointing of Parallel Applications in a Grid Environment

Kreeteeraj Sajadah, Gabor Terstyansky, Stephen C. Winter and Peter Kacsuk

Abstract Jobs in Grid workflows are exposed to different types of failure. It is important to develop fault tolerant mechanisms to ensure a good level of reliability during the execution of Grid jobs. While checkpointing is the most common method to achieve fault tolerance, there is still a lot of work to be done to improve the efficiency of the mechanism. This paper gives an overview of a checkpoint solution for checkpointing parallel applications executed on multiple sites in the Grid environment. The checkpointing mechanism is an improvement of the PGRADE checkpointing solution.

Key words: Checkpointing, First Order Approximation, Natural Synchronisation Points, Critical Region.

1 Introduction

The Grid environment is generic, heterogeneous, and dynamic with lots of unreliable resources making it very exposed to failures. It is vital to develop efficient tools to make applications that are executed on multiple Grid sites more fault tolerant.

Kreeteeraj Sajadah
University of Westminster, 115 New Cavendish Street, London, UK W1W 6UW, e-mail:
K.Sajadeh@westminster.ac.uk

Gabor Terstyansky
University of Westminster, 115 New Cavendish Street, London, UK W1W 6UW, e-mail:
G.Z.Terstyanszky@westminster.ac.uk

Stephen C. Winter
University of Westminster, 115 New Cavendish Street, London, UK W1W 6UW, e-mail:
S.C.Winter@westminster.ac.uk

Peter Kacsuk
MTA SZTAKI. H-1518 Budapest, P.O. Box 63, Hungary, e-mail: kacsuk@sztaki.hu

One of the research challenges in Grid computing is to find mechanisms to ensure successful execution of applications in the presence of failures.

Section 2 gives a brief explanation about fault tolerance and checkpointing. Section 3 summarises some existing projects. Section 4 explains the research work carried out, with a proposed checkpointing solution. Section 5 describes the test bed on which the checkpointing mechanism has been tested.

2 Fault Tolerance

Fault tolerance is the ability of an application to continue its operation after the application, or part of it, fails in some way [18]. In the Grid environment, there are several techniques to achieve fault tolerance. The most common ones are Retrying, Replication and Checkpointing. Retrying enables a failed job to be re-executed a certain number of times. Replication enables replicas of a given job to be executed on different resources simultaneously. Checkpointing is a process during which the state of an application is saved, usually to a storage device, so that it may be reconstructed later in time. In distributed applications, it is harder to achieve fault tolerance because there are lots of inter-process communications among the processes during the execution of an application [17]. A failed process will affect the whole application even if other processes are still running, thus making the whole application inconsistent in many cases.

In the Grid environment, Retrying is not the best option because the expected completion time for a job using this mechanism is very big due to the high rate of failure. Replication requires extra processing power which is not always readily available in the Grid environment. Checkpointing is appropriate because it is very efficient in environment where the rate of failure is high.

3 Related Work

The two main checkpointing techniques are transparent checkpointing and non-transparent checkpointing [10]. In transparent checkpointing, the placement of checkpoints as well as the recovery process is transparent to the programmer. In general, global checkpoints are generated by suspending the whole application at the checkpointing time. A coordinator orchestrates the checkpointing process ensuring that the global checkpoint is consistent by instructing processes to perform synchronisation of messages to ensure that all the in-transit messages are dealt with conveniently. Once the processes have saved their checkpoint image, they are instructed to resume execution. Examples of transparent checkpointing mechanisms are the CoCheck [13, 15] system and the User-Triggered checkpointing system [6]. P-GRADE [7, 12] is an extension of CoCheck which contains a parallel checkpoint and migration module that enables the checkpoint and migration of generic PVM programs either inside a Grid site, like a cluster, or among Grid sites when the PVM programs are executed as Condor or Condor-G jobs. P-GRADE checkpoints an application periodically. The checkpointing procedure is controlled by a GRAP-NEL library. A GRAPNEL Server performs a consistent checkpoint of the whole application. Checkpoint files contain the state of the individual processes including in-transit messages, and are stored on a Checkpoint Server. The checkpointing process and application migration is achieved without the need to modify the user code or the underlying message passing library. When node loss is detected user processes are resumed from the last checkpoint.

The non-transparent checkpointing mechanism provides support for checkpointing through a run-time library. This approach is not transparent to the user. The developer can specify the data that should be included in the checkpoints as well as where checkpoints should be taken within the application code [10]. Dome is an example of a non-transparent checkpointing mechanism. It runs on top of PVM and supports application-level fault-tolerance in heterogeneous networks of workstations [1]. Another example is the 2PCDC checkpointing algorithm [2] which was integrated into an MPI environment. A coordinator process triggers the checkpointing mechanism by requesting each process to take a checkpoint. Together with the checkpoint files, the mechanism also ensures that no in-transit messages are lost by capturing them using a counter-based approach. During recovery, the coordinator sends information to each process instructing them to retrieve their state from the checkpoint server, including in-transit messages. When done, they notify the coordinator which then instructs the processes to proceed [2].

The solutions above produce large overheads due to synchronisation of messages to achieve a consistent global checkpointing state. The checkpoint intervals are either user-defined with no regular pattern or are periodic. Not too much effort has been made to define techniques to calculate optimal checkpointing intervals. This is an important criterion as it affects the overall performance of an application. Our proposed solution ensures a well defined and effective pattern of checkpointing by eliminating the need to deal with the communication layer where possible, keeping in mind the necessity of taking checkpoint at the best possible intervals.

4 Proposed Solution

In parallel applications, inter-process communications can cause inconsistent checkpoints due to lost messages or orphan messages [4]. To achieve a global consistent checkpoint, many mechanisms require processes to block their computation to perform synchronization [9]. Extra communications among processes are required to achieve a synchronous state. The mechanism has to either log in-transit messages or wait for them to be delivered before checkpoints can be taken. Because our research is focused on fault tolerance of parallel applications, we used the checkpointing solution implemented at the SZTAKI Laboratory of Parallel and Distributed Systems, Hungary as a base [7, 12].

4.1 First Order Approximation

To improve the PGRADE checkpointing mechanism, the first step is to adopt a methodology to calculate an optimal checkpointing interval. The First Order Approximation proposed by John W. Young (Fig. 1) is a very good technique to calculate the optimal checkpointing intervals. His research is based on how frequently checkpoint should be taken during the execution of an application. He said that the occurrence of failures is essentially random (a Poisson process), with failure rate λ. The mean time T_f between failures is $1/\lambda$ [8].

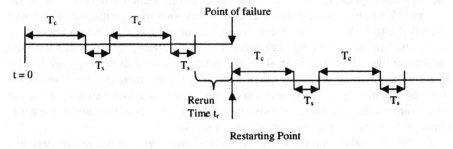

Fig. 1 First Order Approximation

The following data are needed to calculate the optimum checkpoint interval:

- The number of hours the program will run on the machines (T_h).
- The known failure rate during that time (λ_k).
- The time required to save information at a checkpoint (T_s).

From these information, the mean time between failures (T_f) can be calculated:

$$T_f = T_h/\lambda_k \tag{1}$$

Using this value, the optimum checkpoint interval (T_c) can be calculated using the following formula:

$$T_c = \sqrt{2T_sT_f} \tag{2}$$

The P-GRADE portal contains a toolset called PROVE [7, 12] which enable users to visualise the execution of any parallel application launched by PGRADE running on different Grid sites. Using this tool, we can measure both the execution time and the checkpointing time of an application.

Nagios [3] is an open source host, service and network monitoring program. We can find out the failure rate of Grid resources using Nagios.

4.2 Natural Synchronisation Points

To improve the PGRADE checkpointing mechanism, we tried to eliminate the overhead incurred due to the synchronization process involved during checkpointing. A parallel program generally executes as a sequence of parallel steps separated by synchronizations points. Each step is usually composed of three ordered phases; a local computation phase, a global communication phase and a synchronization phase [14]. There are several existing synchronization points such as barriers, the top or the bottom of the main loop and collective operations that represent natural consistent global states. At these points, we do not need to force a global consistent state because the processes are already in a consistent state. There are no interprocess communications involved. Therefore, there is no need to be concerned with the state of the communication channels or possible in-transit messages.

Barriers are functions that block a current execution until all prefix-operations have been completed. When a process calls a barrier function, it stops executing. A coordinated process ensures that all processes have called the barrier function before execution can continue. That is, all processes should reach the synchronisation point before they are allowed to proceed past it. Therefore, calls to barrier functions mark potential checkpoint locations where a process may be saved. Similarly, many parallel applications have the following program structure: they start with some initialization procedures and then enter a program loop executing a large number of iterations [11]. If we insert a checkpoint at the top or bottom of the loop, we constrain the exchange of messages to within an epoch. This ensures no lost and no orphan messages [2]. Collective operations also represent natural consistent global states for checkpointing. Examples are broadcast, scatter, gather and reduction. The functions for collective communication are collective, which implies that they have to be called by all processes before the processes can continue execution [5].

4.3 New Checkpointing Approach

Taking checkpoints at intervals defined by the First Order Approximation still involves synchronisation of messages and capturing in-transit messages. On the other hand, taking checkpoint at natural synchronisation points only may not be very effective because there are no patterns in their occurrences. There can be situations where a set of natural synchronisation points occur in quick successions. It is not efficient to take checkpoint at each of these points because it will affect the performance of the application. There can also be situations where we have long periods between two successive synchronisation points and not taking a checkpointing for a long period reduces the reliability of the application.

A better solution would be to use a combination of both the natural synchronisation points and the First Order Approximation before making a checkpointing decision. Using this technique, we can select the most appropriate places to take checkpoints. The solution takes checkpoints at natural synchronization points which are closest to the optimal checkpoint intervals. Once a checkpoint is taken, the next checkpointing interval is calculated from that checkpoint location.

The Fig. 2 below explains how the checkpointing intervals are chosen. The vertical lines represent the optimal checkpointing intervals and the natural synchronization points. The bracket represents the critical region; a region within which a checkpoint may be taken.

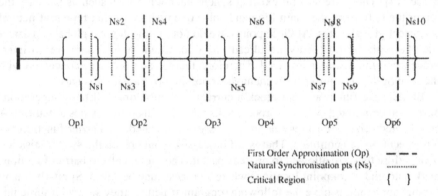

Fig. 2 A Checkpointing Mechanism

The decision to select a checkpoint is based on the optimal checkpoint interval, the natural synchronisation points and the critical region. Whenever the coordinated process receives a checkpoint signal from a given process, we may need to take a checkpoint. The checkpointing process is triggered by signals sent to the coordinated process whenever synchronization points are encountered. Once the coordinated process receives a signal, it checks to see if this signal is within the critical region. If not, no checkpointing is performed.

However, if the signal is within the critical region, we will need to take a checkpoint. Within that region, there may be more than one natural synchronization points and the one closest to the optimal checkpointing interval is the best choice. For our purpose, we will save the checkpoint image at the first natural synchronization point encountered and reset the clock. This is because we cannot predict if we will get a better solution further along the execution line within that critical region. If no natural synchronization points are met within the critical region, we will have to force a checkpointing at the end of the critical region. In such cases, the checkpointing mechanism will perform synchronization to ensure there are no lost or orphan messages. The coordinated process will make sure that the checkpointing images together with the in-transit messages are saved. Once the checkpoint is taken, all the processes will resume their normal execution. In case of a failure, the Mercury monitor [7, 12] will notify the coordination process which will initiate the rollback mechanism by terminating the execution of all other running processes. If the checkpoint to be restored was taken at a natural synchronization point, the rollback mechanism will load each process image from the checkpointing file and the execution process is resumed. We do not have to worry about the in-transit messages. However, if the checkpoint to be restored was not from a natural synchronization point, then we will need to restore the in-transit messages as well to ensure consistency.

5 The Test Bed

MadCity is a simulation tool that simulates traffic on a road network and shows how individual vehicles behave on roads and at junctions. It models the movement of vehicles in a road system described in a network file and turn file. The MadCity traffic simulator can be parallelised using P-Grade. We can create a workflow that will execute the parallel simulation of MadCity where each node will execute a particular road partition to provide simulation locality and allow efficient parallelisation of the simulator [16]. As an experiment, an executable of the MadCity simulator was executed through the command line and our proposed checkpointing mechanism was tested. See Fig. 3 below. Through the First Order Approximation, the calculated optimal checkpoint interval was 8 minutes. A critical region of 2 minutes range from the optimal checkpoint interval was defined.

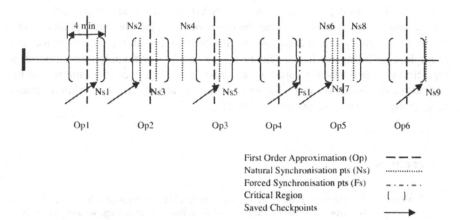

Fig. 3 The Checkpointing Solution

Based on our proposed methodology, the first checkpoint that is stored is Ns1 (9.5 min). As execution continues, we reach Ns2 (14.5 min) where a decision has to be taken on whether or not to take the checkpoint. Ns3 (17 min) is a better solution because it is nearer to the optimal checkpoint interval Op2. However, since we cannot forecast what will happen, it is best to take a checkpoint at Ns2. As we move towards Op3, we get the natural synchronisation point Ns4. Because it is outside the critical region it is dropped. As we move on, we enter another critical region and store the checkpoint at Ns5 (25 min). Unfortunately, within the fourth critical region there are no natural synchronisation points. In that case, we need to force a checkpoint (Fs1 - 32 min) as soon as we leave that critical region. The program continues execution and enters another critical region which contains the natural synchronisation points Ns6 (38.5 min), Ns7 (39 min) and Ns8 (41.5 min). However, a checkpoint is taken at the first synchronisation point, Ns6. As the program continues, another checkpoint is taken at Ns9 (50 min).

From the figure above, the First Order Approximation enables checkpointing at an interval of 8 minutes. If checkpoints are taken at selected points explained above, the average time between checkpoints is 8.3 minutes. However, here, less time were involved in saving the checkpoints.

6 Conclusions

The checkpointing mechanism provides a better and more efficient way to save checkpoint images. The next step is to integrate the checkpointing solution in PGRADE to provide an efficient fault tolerant solution to applications executed as Grid workflows.

In the worst case scenario, the mechanism will behave as the base PGRADE checkpointing mechanism where the process will take checkpoints at the end of each critical region thus requiring processes to perform synchronisation of messages.

The mechanism itself can further be improved to select the best options among the set of natural synchronisation points that may exist within a critical region. For example, a buffering mechanism can be used to buffer a checkpoint file temporarily, replacing it with the better option as we move along the execution line within the critical region. When we reach the end of the critical region, the checkpoint image in the buffer is stored on the storage device.

References

1. A. Beguelin, E. Seligman, P. Stephan: Application level fault tolerance in heterogeneous networks of workstations. Journal of Parallel and Distributed Computing, volume 43, issue 2, pp. 147 - 155, June 1997.

2. A. Nguyen-Tuong: Integrating Fault-Tolerance Techniques in Grid Applications. A Dissertation Presented to the Faculty of the School of Engineering and Applied Science at the University of Virginia, p. 170, August 2000.
3. D. Josephsen: Building a Monitoring Infrastructure with Nagios. Prentice Hall, February 2007.
4. E.N.Elnozahy, D.B.Johnson, Y.M.Wang: A Survey of Rollback-Recovery Protocols in Message Passing Systems. ACM Computing Surveys (CSUR) Volume 34,issue 3, pp. 375 - 408, September 2002.
5. G. Bronevetsky et al.: Collective operations in application-level fault-tolerant MPI. International Conference on Supercomputing. Proceedings of the 17th annual international conference on Supercomputing, USA, pp. 234 - 243, 2003.
6. G. Deconinck, R. Lauwereins: User-triggered checkpointing: system-independent and scalable application recovery. In Proceedings Second IEEE Symposium on Computer and Communications, pp. 418 - 423, July 1997.
7. J. Kovacs, P. Kacsuk: A Migration Framework for Executing Parallel Programs in the Grid - all 6 versions, 2nd European Accross Grids Conference (Nicosia, Cyprus), Springer LNCS, pp. 80 - 89, 2004.
8. J. W. Young: A first order approximation to the optimum checkpoint interval. Communications of the ACM, volume 17, issue 9, pp. 530 - 531, September 1974.
9. K.M.Chandy, L. Lamport: Distributed Snapshots: Determining Global States of Distributed Systems. ACM Transactions on Computer Systems, volume 3, issue 1, pp. 63 - 75, February 1985.
10. L.M. Silva, J.G. Silva: System-Level versus User-Defined Checkpointing. Proc. of the 17th Symposium on Reliable Distributed Systems, pp. 68 - 74, October 1998.
11. P.E. Chung, Y. Huang, S. Yajnik: Checkpointing in CosMiC: a User-level Process Migration Environment. Pacific Rim International Symposium on Fault-Tolerant Systems, pp. 187 - 193, December 1997.
12. P. Kacsuk et al.: P-GRADE: A Grid Programming Environment. Journal of Grid Computing, volume 1, issue 2, pp. 171 - 197, 2003.
13. P. Stefán: The Hungarian ClusterGrid Project. Proc. of MIPRO'2003, Opatija, 2003.
14. R.Y. de Camargo et al.: Checkpointing BSP parallel applications on the InteGrade Grid middleware. Concurrency and Computation: Practice & Experience, volume 18, issue 6, pp. 567 - 579, May 2006.
15. R. Ribler, J. Vetter, H. Simitci, D. Reed: Autopilot: Adaptive Control of Distributed Applications. Proc. 7th IEEE Symposium on High Performance Distributed Computing, Chicago, Illinois, pp. 172 - 179, July 1998.
16. T. Delaitre et al.: Traffic Simulation In P-Grade As A Grid Service. 5th Austrian-Hungarian Workshop on Distributed and Parallel Systems, DAPSYS, pp. 129 - 136, 2004.
17. V. Dialani et al.: Transparent Fault Tolerance for Web Services based Architectures. In the proceedings of the Eighth International Europar Conference (EURO-PAR'02). Padeborn, Germany, pp. 889 - 898, August 2002.
18. W. He: Recovery in Web service applications Proceedings of the 2004 IEEE International Conference on e-Technology, e-Commerce and e-Service (EEE'04), pp. 25 - 28, March 2004.

The Grid Data Source Engine Batch Query System

Giuliano Taffoni, Edgardo Ambrosi, Claudio Vuerli, Fabio Pasian

Abstract The interest in grid-databases integration has been steadily increasing in recent years and several projects provided different grid middleware components or tools trying to face this challenge. Among them the Grid Data Source Engine is offering native access to relational and non-relational data sources in a grid environment. In this paper we present its asynchronous query mechanism and we focus on the ability of this GSI/VOMS based middleware component to be integrated in workflow management systems.

Key words: grid, database, workflow, data management, grid architecture

1 Introduction

Modern e-Science projects have a broad perception of the grid, as their applications require not only traditional computations, but also the use of complex data operations that require on-line and off-line access to pre-existing heterogeneous and independently operated databases (DB). For example, some of the data accessed from a grid infrastructure by the BioinfoGRID project come in the form of relational DB. Another important example regards the Astronomical community that is using DB management systems (DBMS) to structure and store important data sets [11, 8].

Giuliano Taffoni, Claudio Vuerli, Fabio Pasian
INAF-OATS, via Tiepolo 11, 34143 Italy, e-mail: taffoni@oats.inaf.it

Edgardo Ambrosi
CNR, IASI, Viale Manzoni 30, 00185 - Roma, Italy e-mail: ambrosi@gmal.com

Claudio Vuerli
INAF-OATS, via Tiepolo 11, 34143 Italy, e-mail: vuerli@oats.inaf.it

Fabio Pasian
INAF-OATS, via Tiepolo 11, 34143 Italy, e-mail: pasian@oats.inaf.it

Fig. 1 Resource level protocols overview for a Globus Toolkit 2 GDSE. The picture presents the different components and layers involved in the SQL statement processing. The query manager manages the query execution. The QueryWrapper is in charge of the GDSE and gLite WMS interations.

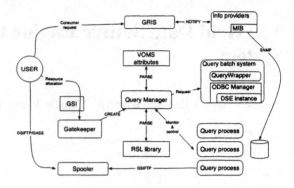

In this paper we present the advances of the GDSE. The GDSE provides security, transparency, robustness, efficiency and dynamic mechanisms to manage standard, relational, flat and xml DBMSs. Here, we focus on its capability to manage off-line queries that can be used to design workflows involving the use of DBMSs and standard computational resources. The outline of the paper is as follows: in Sect. 3 we summarize the GDSE architecture and features, while in Sect. 4 we discuss the design and implementation of the batch query system for off-line queries in a Globus environment [5]. Sect. 5 is dedicated to gLite [7] implementations and workflow capabilities. Finally, in Sect 6, we draw our conclusions and highlight future work.

2 Related Work

The need to integrate DBs and DB technology in the grid environment has already been recognized as a core research activity by the grid community and some tools and services have been developed for this purpose: (i) the Grid Relational Catalog (GRelC) [4]; (ii) the Grid Data Source Engine (GDSE) [1, 9]; (iii) the OGSA data access and integration middleware [2]. The OGSA-DAI project addresses the data virtualization and its underlying data resources [2]. OGSA-DAI developed a set of composable components that encompass uniform access to data sources. It is actually a new Grid middleware specialized for data access and integration that from an architectural point of view matches the Open Grid Service Architecture, it implements GSI security and data encryption. On the contrary we propose a different but complementary approach, we extend the computational capabilities of the standard computational resources so they interact with DB on the basis of an SQL job execution. Our approach is based on the idea that actual middleware implementation used to access computational resources should not be modified. The GRelC Project has developed a gSOAP based service that acts as front-end for database access on the Grid. It is designed on a client/server approach, security is based on GSI. An evaluation test campaign [10] has been done to compare performance and capabilities of G-DSE, AMGA [6], OGSA-DAI and G-DSE. According to those tests G-DSE demonstrates to be fast and versatile.

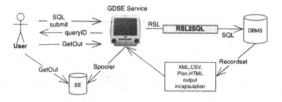

Fig. 2 The GDSE batch query mechanism.

3 Grid Data Source Engine: concepts, features and Queries

The GDSE is a grid component that inherits all the CE capabilities and capacities. Previous works on GDSE addressed architectural design aspects, related to middleware components, synchronous query mechanisms, integration in Globus (>2.4.3 and 4) and gLite, efficiency and performance [1, 9, 10] (Fig. 2).

In analogy with a CE, the G-DSE publish its status, contents and contact information of each DB in the Grid Information Service [5, 7] and a **Query Manager** (QM) is in charge of managing remote queries. The GDSE is able to direct statements regarding queries, updates, loads or schema change operations to any SQL data source. The authentication is based on GSI. Moreover it supports a global authorization level (by means of VOMS) that ensures scalability, manageability and flexibility in role and policies management. GDSE implements two kind of queries: synchronous and batch queries. Synchronous queries wait for the query to be completed and, since control is hidden in the query submission, neither the applications nor the GDSE are able to estimate the query execution time. Many applications do not want to block waiting for the query to be completed, but to proceed and eventually check whether the query ends successfully. Moreover, queries may last for long time, for example when performing complex statistical computations using DBMS computing capabilities and statistical functions. In this case the query may become part of a complex workflow that involves both DBMS and classical computation resources. In all those cases a batch approach is mandatory. GDSE implements data encryption to protect the information in WAN connections and channel protection based on GSI or SSL. Using a batch approach we are able to decouple Application-DBMS connections consequently increasing reliability against possible WAN instabilities.

4 Grid Data Source Engine Batch Queries

In Globus and gLite implementations the Globus Resource Allocation Manager (GRAM) is in charge of processing the requests for remote query execution thanks to the QM [5, 9]. In practice we use the Resource Specification Language (RSL) to encapsulate an SQL statement that is "executed" by a DBMS (Fig. 2).

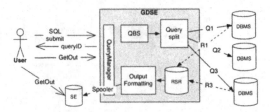

Fig. 3 GDSE DB Virtualization. We present the main component used to make the DB virtualization.

To manage query execution, we introduce a DB local resource manager: the Query batch System (QBS). It is a simple scheduler that enqueues the queries and that can be configured to assign a maximum number of contemporary queries. The QBS accepts queries from the query manager and invokes DBMS execution remotely through UnixODBC APIs. The query result is staged in the *query spooler* and then remotely accessed by the application (see Fig. 2) via GRIDFTP or GASS[5]. The spooler can be configured on a remote grid storage element (SE) or on the GDSE itself.

In practice, the execution of a query is expressed in terms of a job submission, for example to select columns A and B from table *T* of *TEST* DB, a client may use the command:

globusrun -r hostname:2119/dbmanager-odbc '&(executable="SELECT A, B FROM T;") (queue="TEST")'

This example highlights the modification done on the GRAM protocol and the RSL–SQL encapsulation. RSL "file_stage_in" and "file_stage_out" attributes can be used to access remote spoolers to read the SQL statements from a file or to write the result. The user can retrieve the output either using the *globus-get-output* command or from the storage resources using the GSIFTP APIs or commands.

When working in the gLite environment, we use the gLite data management service as GDSE spooler. We modify the GRAM Jobmanager component to copy and register files in the LCG File Catalogue [7] and to assess files stored in the LCG on the basis of their Logical File Name [7]. An important feature concerning the GDSE is the DB virtualization (Fig. 3). The GDSE is able to aggregate different DBMSs that appear to the user as one single (virtual) resource. The QBS coordinates the requests to the DBMSs and organizes the output (read/write operations are permitted). At this stage no distributed JOIN is supported, DBs should have dentical DB schemas, and the QBS addresses the issue of simple conflicts as identical entries.

5 Asynchronous and Workflow queries in gLite infrastructure

The gLite grid middleware provides common high level services; one of them is the Workload Management Service (WMS), the grid job scheduler. This collective service directs all the job submission phases, coordinates computational and storage

Fig. 4 Astronomical Reduction procedure. We present a DAG schema and its JDL description.

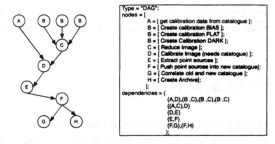

```
Type = "DAG";
nodes = [
    A = [ get calibration data from catalogue ];
    B = [ Create calibration BIAS ];
    B = [ Create calibration FLAT ];
    B = [ Create Calibration DARK ];
    C = [ Reduce Image ];
    D = [ Calibrate Image (needs catalogue) ];
    E = [ Extract point sources ];
    F = [ Push point sources into new catalogue];
    G = [ Correlate old and new catalogue ];
    H = [ Create Archive];
];
dependencies = [
    (A,D),(B ,C),(B ,C),(B ,C)
    ((A,C),D)
    (D,E)
    (E,F)
    (F,G),(F,H)
];
```

resources, handles workflow [7]. Once the GDSE resources are published in a BDII using the modified GLUE schema, they become valid grid resources for the WMS. So the WMS can be used to submit asynchronous queries (no WMS modifications are necessary). However, a *QueryWrapper* component must be introduced in the GDSE that manages the interaction between the GDSE and the WMS, in analogy with the JobWrapper.

In practice, when a client requires the execution of a query, it specifies that the executable parameter of the JDL is the SQL string. For example to select all data from table *A* of *TEST* database we use the gLite command: *glite-wms-job-submit -a query.jdl* where query.jdl is:

```
[
Executable="SELECT * FROM A"; Arguments="-xml"; StdOutput="sqlresults";
StdError="stderr"; OutputSandbox={"sqlresults","stderr"}; Requirements =
(other.GlueDSEName="TEST") && (other.GlueDSEInfoLRMSType="PostgreSQL");
]
```

The user submits the query getting back the queryID. Files to be transferred between GDSE and WMS, after the job execution, can be specified as attributes of the OutputSandbox parameter. In this particular case, the result set of the query is collected in the *sqlresults* file that is then transferred to the user interface using the *glite-wms-job-output* command.

The query result is formatted in XML format; the user can specify different formats: XML, CSV, plain text and HTML. Different result set formats are suggested by different needs: (i) the XML format is preferable for application-application or GDSE-application interactions; (ii) the Comma Separated Version is a common exchange format between different DBMSs; (iii) plain tabular format is useful for human visualization; (iv) HTML is preferable when interacting with portals.

Query Workflow: a use case

The gLite WMS framework naturally implements jobs aggregation in the form of Directed Acyclic Graphs (DAGs). DAG capability can be used to create a simple workflow that involves both classical computation and data access. As a test case, we use DAG workflows to process Astronomical Images and create a new archive. As shown in Fig. 4 this operation requires various steps. Some of them require image processing computations, others interaction with DBs. In particular, we process images from the Galileo Telescope using the GSC2 catalogue. The catalogue has been divided in 8 DBs and is virtualized by the GDSE.

6 Conclusions

In this paper, we described the batch query mechanisms provided by the GDSE. The GDSE can be integrated in any workflow pattern that supports interaction with grid computational resources; no modification in the workflow framework is necessary, queries (insert/select/management) are executed as a standard job. In fact, the GDSE implementation is based upon Globus ($¿$2.4.2 and 4) and gLite standard protocols and APIs (C, C++, JAVA, Python etc.). Future work is related to the extension of this approach to more complex workflow managers such as the one implemented in the PGrade portal and to the extension of the DB virtualization capabilities. IGI, the Italian grid Infrastructure (partner of the EGEE grid), will officially distribute the GDSE as a DB access middleware component from summer 2008.

References

1. Ambrosi, E., Ghiselli, A., Taffoni, G.: GDSE: A New Data Source Oriented Computing Element for Grid. In: Parallel and Distributed Computing and Networks 517:53-57 (2006)
2. Antonioletti, M., Atkinson M. P., Baxter R., Borley A., Chue Hong N. P., et al.: The Design and Implementation of Grid Database Services in OGSA-DAI. Concurrency and Computation: Practice and Experience 17(2-4): 357376 (2005)
3. Alfieri, R., Cecchini R., Ciaschini V., dell Agnello L, Frohner A.: From gridmap-file to VOMS: managing authorization in a Grid environment. Fut. Gen. Comp. Syst. 21(4): 549558. (2005)
4. Fiore, S., Negro, A., Vadacca, A., Cafaro, M., Mirto, M., Aloisio, G.: Advanced Grid DataBase Management with the GRelC Data Access Service. In: Proc. of the 5th International Symposium on Parallel and Distributed Processing and Applications (ISPA07), 2007, LNCS 4742, 683-694 (2007)
5. The Globus project website, http://www.globus.org. Cited 20 Mar 2008
6. Koblitz, B., Santos, N., Pose., V.: The AMGA metadata service. In J. Grid Comput. 6(1), 61-76 (2008)
7. Laure, E., Fisher, S.M., Frohner, A., et al.: Programming the Grid with gLite. Comp. Meth. in Science and Technology 12(1), 33-45 (2006)
8. Pasian, F., Taffoni, G., Vuerli C., Interconnecting the Virtual Observatory with Computational Grid infrastructures. In: IAU Prague, SPS3: 33 (2006)
9. Taffoni, G., Ambrosi, E., Vuerli, C., et al.: The Query Element: grid access to databases. In: Grid Computing Research Progress, Nova Publisher, New York, isbn: 978-1-60456-404-4, (2008)
10. Taffoni, G., Fiore, S., Donvito, G., Jain A., et al.: How to access databases from EGEE-II grid environment: a comparison of tools and middleware. In Proceedings of the Third Conference of the EELA Project R. Gavela, B. Marechal, R. Barbera et al. (Eds.) CIEMAT: 34-54(2007)
11. Taffoni, G., Maino, D., Vuerli, C., Castelli, G., et al: Enabling Grid technologies for Planck space mission. In. Fut. Gen. Comp. Syst. 23(2): 189-200 (2007)

Reputation-Policy Trust Model for Grid Resource Selection

Yonatan Zetuny, Gabor Terstyanszky, Stephen Winter and Peter Kacsuk

Abstract Grid systems are gradually shifting into a dynamic pool of services providing user access to heterogeneous resources spanning multiple security domains. In such systems, where it is necessary to share resources between potentially unknown parties, dynamic trust establishment becomes crucial factor for qualifying resources for selection. This paper argues that a reputation-policy based approach should be considered in order to provide complete resolution for dynamic trust establishment between Grid resources. The trust model presented in this paper introduces a novel paradigm for evaluating resources, as it allows subjective trust based resource selection to be based on client reputation policy statements.

Key words: Grid Security, Reputation, Policy, Trust Model, Resource Selection

1 Introduction

Grid research has traditionally focused on supporting large-scale scientific collaborations where resources from trusted entities were pooled together in order to form a VO [4]. However, as Grid systems are increasingly being developed for business

Yonatan Zetuny
Centre for Parallel Computing, University of Westminster, 115 New Cavendish Street, London W1W 6UW, UK, e-mail: yzetuny02@wmin.ac.uk

Gabor Terstyanszky
Centre for Parallel Computing, University of Westminster, 115 New Cavendish Street, London W1W 6UW, UK, e-mail: terstyg@wmin.ac.uk

Stephen Winter
Centre for Parallel Computing, University of Westminster, 115 New Cavendish Street, London W1W 6UW, UK, e-mail: s.c.winter@wmin.ac.uk

Peter Kacsuk
MTA SZTAKI, 1111 Kende utca 13, Budapest, Hungary, e-mail: kacsuk@sztaki.hu

purposes, more questions are being raised in regards to how to share resources between unknown, untrusted business parties [5]. In particular, resource selection becomes a great concern, as users may engage with uncertain workflows increasing potential execution risk. Grid security research has initially addressed trust through security mechanisms [7]. These mechanisms enabled single sign-on (SSO) for an entity in the system, considering that the entities belonged to the same trusted domain. Authentication mechanisms were provided through certificates, which entitled the nodes belonging to the trusted organizations, to join the Grid. As a result, trust creation and management has involved human-coordinated process. For example, when a new organization wished to join the Grid, it had to fulfill the requirements set by the certification authority and wait for its approval before it was able to participate in the computation. Once the organization was approved by the certification authority, it was considered trustworthy by the other resources.

However, as the the Grid shifts to ubiquitous and pervasive computing models, there is an increasing demand to be able to evaluate and manage the reputation of all entities in terms of their quality capabilities once they joined the Grid [6]. Currently, there are very few reputation model approaches applied for Grids. These approaches, such as GridEigenTrust [8] and PathTrust [9], are one of the first attempts to incorporate reputation-based trust management systems into Grid computing, based on earlier developments and requirements identified in P2P systems. At present, all Grid reputation-based trust models propose a central reputation service providing deterministic, predefined metrics for selecting a trusted resource from a list of possible alternatives. These approaches are limited as that they do not allow user involvement in the trust evaluation process. Grid clients are not able to calculate the trust value of a Grid resource by specifying their own evaluation criteria and as a result, they have to rely on a central reputation algorithm to compute trust values. These limitations stimulated the motivation behind the *reputation-policy* trust model for Grid resource selection. This model allows Grid clients (users and applications) to carry out a *heuristic* involvement in the trust and reputation evaluation process. This is achieved by enabling Grid clients to augment their existing reputation queries with a set of reputation-policy requirements expressed as policy statements. These requirements, rectified as a trust decision strategy representing quality aspects and relationship rules, provide complete trust metrics for the reputation algorithm, thus enabling fine-grained resource selection. The philosophy behind this approach is that reputation is a subjective matter and context dependent. Moreover, reputation should be consolidated with opportunistic trust based decisions allowing clients to predefine a threshold of trustworthiness reflecting on their individual attitude to risk. For example, two clients may have different opinions and decision actions regarding the trustworthiness of the same Grid resource, given their job requirements and evaluation criteria. This paper is structured as follows. Section 2 defines the core concepts behind trust, reputation and policy. Section 3 presents the principles of the reputation-policy trust model and its main contributions. Section 4 describes in details the reputation-policy trust model and its internal artifacts Trust Decision Strategy (TDS), Opinion Matrices (OM) and the Correlation Process (CP). Finally, section 5 summarizes current work and discusses future work.

2 Trust Concepts

This section defines the basic terminology that will be used throughout the rest of this paper.

2.1 Trust

Trust is a complex concept which had been a subject of research in different fields including sociology, business, law and computing. In the context of this paper, trust is based on Gambetta's [1] theoretical work, and envisions trust as the subjective belief a trusting agent[1] has in the capability of a trusted agent to deliver a quality service in a given context and time slot. This belief is based on the trusting agent's direct and indirect experiences with the trusted agent. In the scope of the work described in this paper, trust is regarded as benchmarking mechanism used for managing workflow execution risk.

2.2 Reputation

Reputation is a concept closely related to trust, as it is considered as a measure of trustworthiness. In the context of this paper, reputation is based on Abdul-Rahman and Hailes [2] theoretical work and envisions reputation as the aggregation of all the recommendations from the third-party recommendation agents about the service quality of the trusted agent in a given context and time slot. The recommendations are testimonies for different quality factors which aggregate both direct and indirect experiences with the trusted agent.

2.3 Policy

Policy is defined as a statement of the intent of the owner or controller of some computing resources, specifying how he wants them to be used. However, in the scope of the work described in this paper, policy is regarded as reputation requirements expressed by trusting agents depicting their intrinsic view on trust and the type job they wish to submit.

---

[1] Agents are communication facilitators. The remainder of this paper refers to users, resources and services as agents.

3 Toward Reputation-Policy Based Trust Management in Grid Computing

The reputation-policy trust model presented in this paper is based on theoretical work made by [1] and envisions trust is as subjective belief a trusting agent has in the capability of a trusted agent to deliver a quality service for a given job context and time slot. The main argument for this model concentrates on the notion that a trusting agent should be able to define a trust decision strategy representing subjective and opportunistic view on trust in order to manage workflow execution risk. The trust decision strategy is comprised of two aspects:

Evaluation Model (EM)   Ontology modeled by set of opinions, each of which represents subjective building block of trust (availability, reliability, cost, etc) and their relationships.

Decision Rules (DR)   Set of rules modeled by a map potential outcomes and correspondent opportunistic decisions.

There are five research contributions derived from the reputation-policy trust model propagating the presented argument into different aspects of a trust management system:

1. **Reputation-Policy Trust Mechanism** - Combined mechanism of policy statements for describing reputation evaluation and a reputation algorithm for calculating trust metrics based on the policy statements.
2. **Metrics Pool (MP)** - Mechanism for correlating opinions defined by trusting agents and opinions defined for the VO. For example, if a trusting agent defines availability and response time as opinions, the metrics pool will correlate these opinions to the ones available in the VO.
3. **Revised Feedback Methodology** - Segregated feedback methodology allowing trusting agents to rate executions with trusted agents based on opinions previously defined in the reputation-policy. The methodology records a segregated value for each opinion.
4. **Aggregated Reputation-Policy Algorithm** - Allowing the reputation algorithm to support global trust context. This allows obtaining the trust and reputation values for an entire VO based on the individual trust of its members using global scope reputation-policy statements.
5. **Reputation Meta-Model** - Semantic descriptions for ontologies defined in the reputation-policy model, such as opinions, sources and rules, in order to support strong knowledge sharing among trusting agents, the reputation-policy model and trusted agents.

These contributions extend the boundary of current trust and reputation research in Grid computing as they form the initial model which allows fine-grained resource selection based on policy augmented reputation queries constituting as complete trust metrics for the reputation algorithm. The following section describes the reputation-policy trust model in further details.

4 Reputation-Policy Trust Model

The reputation-policy trust model is a distributed data model where trust data is divided between the trusting agent and the reputation algorithm. As previously described, the trusting agent defines its reputation-policy in the form of a trust decision strategy while the reputation algorithm exploits opinion matrices for storing and manipulating historical execution data. The correlation between the two artifacts involves reconciliation of each opinion element in the trust decision strategy with it's historical information counterpart in order to compute trust values. The following subsections describe the trust decision strategy, the opinion matrices and the correlation process in further details.

4.1 Trust Decision Strategy (TDS)

The Trust Decision Strategy is represented by a fuzzy tree model (FTM) consisting of a finite set of opinions and relationship rules. An *opinion* is a subjective building block of trust (e.g. availability, reliability, data accuracy, etc.). The MP defines a set of opinions applicable for the VO. Therefore, the opinion elements defined in the FTM must be a subset of the opinions in the MP. Let x denote an opinion, let F denote a set of opinions defined in the FTM and let M denote a set of opinions defined by the MP. The opinion inclusion constraint is defined as:

$$\forall x(x \in F \rightarrow x \in M) \tag{1}$$

So that all opinions x in set F must be a correspondent opinion x in set M in order to be considered for correlation (residual opinions are ignored by the MP). Every opinion is dependent on one or more sources. A *source* is a reference for information such as reputation or experience. Let O define an opinion, let S denote a source set, let e denote an experience source and element let r denote a reputation source element. The following constraint can be defined:

$$S = \{e, r\}, O = \{x | x \subseteq P(S) \wedge x \notin \oslash\} \Leftrightarrow \{\{e\}, \{r\}, \{e, r\}\} \tag{2}$$

So that an opinion O can be based on either experience or reputation or both experience and reputation, denoted by the following predicate: $(e \vee r) \vee (e \wedge r)$. Sources for an opinion can have a weight factor, indicating the importance of a source over another source. In general, weight factors form part of a larger concept known as relationship rules. *Rules* are general constraints which can be attached to elements (e.g. decisions, opinions and sources) or group of elements. Rules are modeled using fuzzy logic, indicating a degree of influence of one rule over another. For example, let S denote a source set and let WR denote a weight rule set for S. The following condition must be met: $f : WR \rightarrow S$, so that the number of weight rules must be equal to the number of sources and that each source must be referencing only one weight rule. The *weight* for a source is modeled using a fuzzy value indicating the degree of importance where 1 represents complete importance, and 0 for irrelevance. Therefore, the weight membership function $\mu(WR_s)$ maps WR_s to the interval $[0,1]$, so the following constraint can be defined:

$$WV_s = \mu(WR_s), 0 \leq WV_s \leq 1 \wedge \sum_{i=1}^{2} WV_s = 1 \qquad (3)$$

This implies that a weight value for a source WV_s is a decimal in the range of $[0,1]$ and a summary of weight values (e.g. reputation and experience) is equal to 1. In conclusion, the following can be generalized for permissible values for an opinion:

$$O = \{\{S_e, WR_e\}, \{S_r, WR_r\}, \{(S_e, WR_e), (S_r, WR_r)\}\} \qquad (4)$$

However, if exists only one source of opinion, it can be assumed that the weight value $WV_s = 1$. Therefore, the weight rule can be discarded and it can be simplified to:

$$O = \{\{S_e\}, \{S_r\}, \{(S_e, WR_e), (S_r, WR_r)\}\} \qquad (5)$$

Similarly to sources, opinions can have weight factors associated with them, indicating an importance of an opinion over another. A set of n opinions constitutes as an evaluation model forming the ontology aspect of the reputation policy. Let EM denote an evaluation model, let O denote an opinion and let WR_o denote a weight rule on O. The evaluation model can be defined in the following way:

$$EM = \{\{(O_1, W_1R_o), (O_2, W_2R_o), \ldots, (O_n, W_nR_o)\}\} \qquad (6)$$

The evaluation model is combined together with decision rules to form a complete trust decision strategy. The decision rules, modeled as a decision tree, are used as a decision tool for analyzing trust metrics outcomes and possible courses of action. For example, at a basic level, a decision rule is supplied to denote a threshold value for trusting a resource. A value of 0.8 means that any resource(s) quantified at this value and above will be considered trustful for a job execution. Let TDS denote a trust decision strategy and let DR denote a decision rule. The trust decision strategy can defined in the following way:

$$TDS = \{EM, (DR_1, DR_2, \ldots, DR_n)\} \qquad (7)$$

Figure 1 illustrates an abstract model of the trust decision strategy comprising of opinions $(O_1, \ldots, O_n)$ and decision rules $(DR_1, \ldots, DR_n)$ respectively representing the evaluation and decision aspects of the model. The novelty of this model is derived from it's competency to define ontologies representing subjective trust opinions as well as decision rules reflecting opportunistic courses of action once the resource evaluation criteria has been completed.

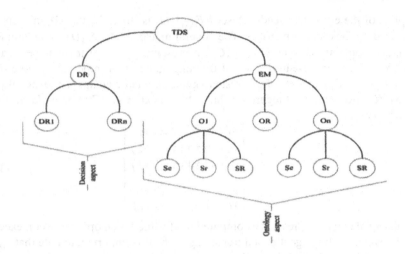

Fig. 1 Trust Decision Strategy Model

4.2 Opinion Matrices (OM)

Opinion matrices are tabular data structures which store the historical evaluation feedback values reported by trusting agents. They are based on the reputation definitions made by [2]. For each opinion defined in the MP universe there is one and only one correspondent matrix, storing evaluation feedback data regarding that opinion. Let MP denote a set of existing opinions in the metrics pool and let MS denote a set of matrices. The symmetric difference condition $MP \triangle MS = \{\oslash\}$ must always be kept in order to ensure validity of the data model. This is of particular importance during the correlation process, where each opinion defined by the trusting agent is matched with its matrix counterpart. When an execution is completed, a trusting agent is required to rate the quality of the transaction using an evaluation feedback mechanism. This mechanism gathers a score value for each opinion originally defined by the trusting agent using the trust decision strategy. Let $EF_\alpha(\beta, O)$ denote an evaluation feedback EF made by trusting agent α on trusted agent β regarding opinion factor O. The following data set is contained within each feedback:

$$EF_\alpha(\beta, O) = \{TS, V\} \tag{8}$$

The set contains TS, which denotes a UTC time stamp and V, which denotes a fuzzy value in the interval of $[0, 1]$. The complete evaluation feedback set $EFS_\alpha(\beta)$ is described in the following way:

$$EFS_\alpha(\beta) = \{EF_\alpha(\beta, O_1), EF_\alpha(\beta, O_2), \ldots, EF_\alpha(\beta, O_n)\} \tag{9}$$

A replica of the evaluation feedback set $EF_\alpha(\beta, O)$ is stored by the MP in order to be utilized by the opinion matrices. The general matrix model $M(O)$ for an opinion O context, contains columns $\{C_1, \ldots, C_j\}$ representing a set of trusted agents and rows $\{R_1, \ldots, R_i\}$ representing a set of trusting agents. It is important to note that the set $\{C_1, \ldots, C_j\}$ is a set of all trusted agents evaluated against an identical job context JC and opinion O regarding that job context (e.g. $JC := storedata, O := availability$)

$$M(O) = \begin{bmatrix} v_{1,1} & v_{1,2} & v_{1,3} & \cdots & v_{1,j} \\ v_{2,1} & v_{2,2} & v_{2,3} & \cdots & v_{2,j} \\ v_{3,1} & v_{3,2} & v_{3,3} & \cdots & v_{3,j} \\ \vdots & \vdots & \vdots & \ddots & \vdots \\ v_{i,1} & v_{i,2} & v_{i,3} & \cdots & v_{i,j} \end{bmatrix} \tag{10}$$

The fuzzy value $v_{(i,j)}$ represents a computed trust value for an opinion over n executions between trusting agent α and trusted agent β. It is important to note that $v_{(i,j)}$ can be x (null). Normally, $v_{(i,j)}$ will be computed using standard mean:

$$v_{(i,j)} = \frac{1}{n} \sum_{a=1}^{n} V_a(\alpha, \beta, O) \tag{11}$$

However, the computation of $v_{(i,j)}$ can be controlled by the trusting agent using a decision rule DR. For example, a trusting agent can decide that the preferable way to compute the trust value is to weight each individual value against a time performance analytics resulting in a time weighted average value. This allows the trusting agent not only to rely on values supplied by other trusting agents but also use sophisticated statistical measures to correct potential biased ratings. The opinion matrices set MS containing all the matrices in the matrix pool (one per opinion), defines the complete structure:

$$MS = \{M(O_1), M(O_2), \ldots, M(O_n)\} \tag{12}$$

The Correlation Process (CP) involves matching each opinion defined in TDS with its historical references in the OMs and calculating the trust value for that opinion. Each TDS opinion type O is routed via the MP in order to return a correspondent OM. The CP examines the opinion's source nodes $(O(S_e), O(S_r))$ and their weight factors $(W(S_e), W(S_r))$. For each trusted agent β, the CP generates two vectors $(V_\beta(S_e), V_\beta(S_r))$ one for holding trust values by other trusting agents and the other for the current trusting agent. The trust value formula for an opinion is done in the following way:

$$OV_\beta = \frac{WV_\beta(S_e) + W \sum_{i=0}^{n-1} V_\beta(S_r)}{\sum_{i=0}^{n} W(S)} \tag{13}$$

An identical calculation is performed on a set of opinions yielding overall trust value for a trusted agent. This is repeated for all other trusted agents in the OMs which are matched DRs to return a subset of potential trustful resources for selection. The following subsection describes the CP in greater depth.

4.3 Correlation Process (CP)

Algorithm 1: Correlation Process Algorithm(O, R, P)

---

1   SzO: size of O
2   SzR: size of R
3   Weight: opinion weight
4   OT[SzR]: opinion tuple
5   OSM[SzO][SzR]: opinion summary matrix
6   RTV[SzR]: resource trust vector
7   RVM: resource value mapping

8   **foreach** *opinion in O* **do**
9 | $OT \leftarrow$ fork child process(*opinion*, R, P)
10 | **for** $i \leftarrow 0$ **to** $SzR - 1$ **do**
11 | | $OT[i] \leftarrow Multiply(OT[i], weight)$
12 | **end**
13 | $OSM \leftarrow Put(OT)$
14   **end**

15   **if** *all child processes returned* **then**
16 | **for** $row \leftarrow 1$ **to** $SzO - 1$ **do**
17 | | $pre \leftarrow OSM[row - 1]$
18 | | $cur \leftarrow OSM[row]$
19 | | **for** $col \leftarrow 0$ **to** $SzR - 1$ **do**
20 | | | $cur[col] \leftarrow Sum(cur[col], pre[col])$
21 | | **end**
22 | | $OSM[row] \leftarrow cur$
23 | **end**

24 | $RTV \leftarrow OSM[SzO - 1]$
25 | **for** $i \leftarrow 0$ **to** $SzR - 1$ **do**
26 | | $RVM \leftarrow Put(R[i], RTV[i])$
27 | **end**
28   **end**

29   **return** RVM

The CP is modeled as a multithreaded algorithm. It is supplied with three arguments: O, R and P. O represents a set of opinion nodes $\{O_1, \ldots, O_n\}$ extracted from the TDS, R represents a set of resources $\{R_1, \ldots, R_n\}$ denoted by resource identifiers and P represents arbitrary processing instructions extracted from the reputation query. Processing instructions dictate context factors (e.g. time fragment, trust decay function, etc.) which influence the values contained by an opinion matrix.

During the first step (Algorithm 1, lines 8-14), the CP iterates through the opinion set. For each opinion O, the CP forks a child process, passing the opinion and a reference to R and P into its address space (Algorithm 1, line 9). Each child process operates on a single opinion by contacting the metrics pool MP to return a correspondent opinion matrix OM (Algorithm 2, line 10).

Algorithm 2: Child Process Algorithm(opinion, R, P)

---

1 Type: opinion type
2 ExV: experience value
3 ExW: experience weight
4 ReV: reputation value
5 ReW: reputation weight
6 SzR: row count of OM
7 SzC: column count of OM
8 OM[SzR][SzC]: opinion matrix
9 OT[SzC]: opinion tuple

10 $OM[SzR][SzC] \leftarrow MetricsPool(GetOpinionMatrix(Type,R,P))$

11 **for** $col \leftarrow 0$ **to** $SzC - 1$ **do**
12     $row \leftarrow 0$
13     $ExV \leftarrow OM[row][col]$
14     $ReV \leftarrow 0$

15   **for** $row \leftarrow 1$ **to** $SzR - 1$ **do**
16         $ReV \leftarrow Sum(Rev, OM[row][col])$
17   **end**

18     $OT[col] \leftarrow Sum(Multiply(ExV,ExW), Multiply(ReV,ReW))$

19 **end**

20 **return** OT

The opinion matrix OM consists of rows and columns representing trusting agents and resources respectively. The computation of the accumulated value $OM_{(i,j)}$ is dictated by the opinion type routed to the metrics pool, the volume of historical rating data and the processing instructions P. The first row of $OM[0]$ contains experience values supplied by the current trusting agent while the rows $OM[1 \rightarrow SzR - 1]$ contain reputation values supplied by peer trusting agents. For each column col in OM, the experience and reputation values are extracted. The experience value ExV is extracted by referencing to the first row of each col (Algorithm 2 line 13) while the reputation value is extracted by summarizing the values at row to $SzR - 1$ (Algorithm 2 lines 15-17). Finally, each value (ExV, ReV) is multiplied with its correspondent weight factor (ExW, ReW) and the products of these multiplications are summarized and stored in $OT[col]$ (Algorithm 2 line 18).

For each tuple returned by a child process, the correlation process multiplies each opinion trust value with its weight (Algorithm 1 lines 10-12) and inserts the updated tuple into the opinions summary matrix *OSM* (Algorithm 1 line 13). The opinion summary matrix *OSM* consists of rows and columns representing opinions and resources respectively. The accumulated value $OSM_{(i,j)}$ represents a distinct opinion referencing a particular trusted agent. The second step commences once all child processes have returned to the parent process. During this step, each *row* value in the *OSM* is iteratively summarized with its previous row *row* − 1 and restored in *OSM*[*row*](Algorithm 1 lines 15-23). As a result of the calculation, the overall trust value for each resource is contained in the last row of *OSM* (*SzO* − 1). This row is copied into the resource trust vector *RTV* (Algorithm 1 line 24). The third step involves populating the *RVM* by iterating through each resource, inputting the resource id as a key and the resource value from *RTV* as value. The CP algorithm returns a hash table structure containing resource identifiers as table keys and overall trust values as table values (Algorithm 1 lines 25-17). It is important to note that the CP is not involved in applying decision rules to each resource. It is merely concerned with calculating a trust value for each given resource identifiers. Once the CP is returned to the reputation algorithm, decision rules can be set based on the calculated values and return a complete trust report to the calling trusting agent.

5 Conclusions

This paper presented a novel approach for managing trust in Grid computing. While current Grid reputation-based models offer a single, community-based deterministic algorithm for computing trust, the reputation-policy trust model allows heuristic fine-grained resource selection based on a trust decision strategy defined by a trusting agent as opposed to the reputation algorithm. This grants a trusting agent to subjectively define trust decision strategy using opinions, sources and rules. The internal artifacts of the model TDS, OM and CP were proposed in order to support trust data management and cooperation between entities on the Grid. Future work should concentrate on deriving a reputation-policy service architecture based on the presented reputation-policy model. Substantial considerations will be made in order to apply the architecture and evaluate it using a rich execution environment, such as the NGS P-GRADE portal [10].

References

1. Diego Gambetta. *Trust: Making and Breaking Cooperative Relations*, Chapter Can We Trust Trust?, pages 213-237. Department of Sociology, University of Oxford, 1988. http://www.sociology.ox.ac.uk/papers/gambetta213-237.pdf
2. A.Abdul-Rahman and S.Hailes. Supporting trust in virtual communities. In *Proceedings of the Hawaii International Conference on Systems Sciences* 33, 2000.

3. K.Aberer and Z.Despotovic,Managing trust in a peer-2-peer information system. In *Proceedings of 10th International Conference on Information and Knowledge Management*, 2001.
4. I. Foster, C. Kesselman, and S. Tuecke. The Anatomy of the Grid: Enabling Scalable Virtual Organizations. *International Journal of High Performance Computing Applications*, 15(3):200-222, 2001.
5. CoreGrid. D.ia.03 survey material on trust and security. Technical Report D.IA.03, CoreGrid, October 2005.
6. Reputation-based trust. management systems and their applicability to grids. CoreGRID. Technical Report TR-0064, 2006.
7. V. Welch, F. Siebenlist, I. Foster, J. Bresnahan, K. Czajkowski et al. Security for Grid Services. In *Proceedings of 12th IEEE International Symposium on High Performace Distributed Computing*. IEEE Computer Society Press, 2003.
8. B. Alunkal, I. Veljkovic, G. von Laszewski, and K. Amin. Reputation-Based Grid Resource Selection. In *Workshop on Adaptive Grid Middleware*, 2003.
9. F. Kerschbaum, J. Haller, Y. Karabulut, and P. Robinson. Pathtrust: A trust-based reputation service for virtual organization formation. In *iTrust2006, 4th International Conference on Trust Management*, Vol.3986, Lecture Notes in Computer Science, pp. 193-205. Springer, 2006.
10. NGS P-GRADE portal, Web page. Available: http://www.cpc.wmin.ac.uk/cpcsite/index.php

Author Index